THE STOTTERS' STORY – 50 YEARS OF GOLF IN MINUTES

IN MEMORY OF THOSE WHO
CAME AND PLAYED BEFORE US

HAMISH ROBERTSON

The Stotters' Story – 50 Years of Golf in Minutes, Published in Great Britain by Hamish Robertson Publications, Liberton, Scotland

First edition published 2017

Set in Garamond by Ebooks by Design

ISBN 978-0-9555555-2-7

Stotter: Verb: stagger, totter, and stumble.

      Noun: 1. the act of stottering, a stumble, stagger, unsteady gait.
                 2. a large whisky – often causing the above effects.
                 3. term of admiration for (chiefly) women – a smasher.

Dr. John Jamieson's 1808 4 Volume Etymological Dictionary of the Scottish Language defines "to stot" as "to strike any elastic body on the ground, to cause it to rebound; as, *to stot a ball*".

The Stotters' Story is true though some of the dates may be deliciously approximate, as indeed are some of the characters and their own stories (!).

Every effort has been made by the author to confirm and validate dates and events. The author has also received permission from all those he has been able to contact, including any known surviving relatives, to publish their biographies and anecdotes.

Any mistakes or misrepresentations in this respect are those of the author, and entirely accidental. Every aspect of the Stotters' Story is intended to be sympathetic to The Stotters, their families and friends.

CONTENTS

INTRODUCTION

The Royal Burgh of Tain was granted its first royal charter in 1066, making it Scotland's oldest Royal Burgh. The charter confirmed Tain as a sanctuary, where people could claim the protection of the church, and an immunity, in which resident merchants and traders were exempt from certain taxes. This encouraged the development of the town.

The relative flatness of the surrounding land of Easter Ross gave the area's inhabitants the name "The Lowland Highlanders".

Golf was played in Tain many years before the present golf club was established, though there is little firm evidence before the mid-19th century.

In 1889, a few local players invited Old Tom Morris, the founder of golf architecture, and designer of dozens of golf courses world-wide, to look at a piece of land they proposed to lease from a local land owner.

As a result, Tom instituted a fifteen-hole course which opened in 1890.

Tain Golf Club member W. Cromb described it in the magazine "Golf" in 1892.

"Due south across the Firth from Dornoch Links, and a mile or so to the east of Tain stretches an extensive tract of ground, liberally besprinkled with whins, bents and bunkers and locally known as the "Morich More", at present the home green of the St Duthus Golf Club, Tain. Affording ample space for a course of 18 holes, it, as originally laid out by Tom Morris in 1890, extended to 15 only".

In1894 alterations and improvements to the original holes were made and some extra land secured, enabling the course to become a good eighteen-hole course.

The St. Duthus Golf Club, named after the patron saint of the town, was then born.

A few holes still remain as they were originally designed.

These are the ninth (playing to the original green), tenth, fourteenth and fifteenth, although these were not their original hole numbers. Several others retain parts of the original Tom Morris design.

In 1895, a club player wrote an article on the club in a golf magazine, concluding by saying: "The Hon. Secretary will be pleased to give any further information, and the stranger may rest assured that the members of St. Duthus Club will be always ready to extend to him a hearty Highland welcome".

The club and its present members, over 125 years later, continue to live up to these ideals.

The course is one of the most highly rated and enjoyable links courses in the country, and it is this golfing paradise that for the past 50 years has been attracting an eclectic mix of families and friends from around Scotland, England and Ireland, who form the extended family of The Stotters.

The heart of this story lies in the Minutes of their AGM which have been assiduously kept in almost every year from 1966 to 2015.

Unique, unexpurgated, and often uncomfortably uncouth.

The Minutes have been typed (with some necessary editing) by Bridget Ross, directly from The Book of Stotters' Minutes which was presented by the First Captain of the Stotters, Dr John Houston, in 1966.

From 1966 till 1970, The Stotters' Captains penned a brief resume, rather than a Minute, of the AGMs and when Walter Kerr became Secretary and wrote the first full Minutes in 1971, the present day format appeared in rough form.

In the years following, the content of discussion for the purpose of this book has not been diluted, but some of the repetitive matters have been précised to reduce the lengthy content.

The change to electronic format for the Minutes superseded the hand-written word in 2012, and during the 50 years there have only been 3 Secretaries – until 2016, when Hugh Walkington was elected as the 4th.

Walter Kerr, Wilson Kemp and Simon Houston, all gifted with a great sense of humour and a wicked turn of the pen, have filled the Minutes Book.

The first AGM in 1966 was held at the 'Summer Residence' i.e. The Royal Hotel, Tain.

The original Stotters were: Messrs John Houston, Walter Kerr, Roddy J. Mackenzie, Willie W. Mackenzie, Hamilton (Hammie) Mitchell, J. L. (Ian) MacPherson, Ian McColl, J.G. (Hamish) Robertson, W. Raeburn

Robertson, Gilbert Tocher, Ian Walkington, and Tommy S. Young with Mrs. Ann Chalk as Most Hon. President.

This is their story.

SUNDAY 31ST JULY 2016

It's 7.20am, and a very pleasant morning in Tain.

The sky has that faint blue-grey tinge that characterises days not quite sure what weather to bring, but at least promising some golf to be played.

The Tain Golf Club car park is almost deserted, with only four cars in it, two of them parked beside the Clubhouse and two left the previous night by golfers persuaded to abandon them in the interests of licence preservation.

Into the still silence comes the throaty roar of a heavy-duty vehicle, the noise echoing against the walls of the adjoining St. Duthus Cemetery.

Into the driveway of the Club, and under the watchful gaze of Old Tom Morris, beautifully carved from one of four cut-down fir trees bordering the first tee, comes a minibus which carefully circles the car park and disgorges the first of the Stotters and their supporters to arrive.

Hamish Robertson, this year's Vice-Captain and his niece's husband, Chris Rafferty appear, both still slightly alcoholically challenged from the successful Duthac Centre Dinner the night before.

With them the travelling support consists of Hamish's wife Shirley, his eldest son Dale, wife Julie, and two sons Chris and Adam, whilst Chris is supported by mother-in-law Alice.

The car which follows unloads Hamish's second son, Scott, wife Jenny, and two sons, Corey and Nathan, with that teenage dragged-from-bed look.

They are greeted by Honorary Stotter and Tain team organiser Donald Sutherland, his bearded face cheerfully lit up by an insanely large grin.

Hugs and handshakes are exchanged and the car park begins quickly to fill up with an assortment of cars, four-wheel drives and a large McLeod's bus from Portmahomack which carries the bulk of the Stotters' team and families – 14 Stotters and 22 family and friends, led by this year's lean and slightly lopsided Captain, Johnny Houston, son of the 1966 Stotters' Captain, Dr John.

The cars spill out more and more people, including the Tain team, clad in specially designed green polo tops with the Tain emblem picked out in Stotters' yellow and a left arm motif proudly boasting the Stotters' logo of an upturned glass encasing the letter S. Underneath is the simple legend:

"STOTTERS 1966-2016".

The Stotters' team wear mirror image tops, in their trademark bright yellow with the Stotters' logo on the left breast and the Tain GC logo on the left arm. They are also sporting specially designed stone coloured caps with the1966-2016 logo.

Hugh Walkington, son of founder member Ian/Sport, at 6ft8, has the best view of proceedings as the crowd mass round the Professional's Shop and the first tee – a complete riot of green and yellow, with most of the Stotters' support wearing yellow hoodies, tops and caps.

There are now close to 100 people joking, laughing, chatting, and reuniting friendships and relationships formed over the many years the two teams have played against each other.

Golf bags, backpacks and cool bags bulge with an amazing array of whisky and Drambuie bottles, rusty nail hip flasks, cans and bottles of lager and beer, and an odd soft drink or bottle of water for the youngsters and those who will need rehydration later in the round to come.

Donald sets the tone by beginning the annual and rather pleasant ritual of Roddy's Round, which consists of a nip of whisky served to everyone in glasses carried on a silver salver engraved "Roddy's Round" in memory of Hamish's young brother who died 10 years previously.

Like all those Stotters no longer with us, Roddy's name and the years of Stotter-ship are engraved on a rectangular plaque on the Stotters' bench which sits outside the pro shop. This bench is now surrounded by the press of whisky- drinking golfers and supporters.

Captain Johnny proposes the toast to absent friends and Tain Captain Ewan Forrest welcomes the visitors in his inimitably whimsical way hoping for a resounding victory for his Team.

They promptly pose for photographs and form a rugby-team-like huddle on the first tee muttering victory mantras and erupting in a victory cheer.

More sedately, the Stotters assemble on the tee for photos and recreate the pose of the early Stotters which features in their Facebook Photos Section, front row kneeling and back row standing, with their Honorary President Frank Cougan in the centre.

The summer smell of freshly cut grass permeates the air as Frank appears with one of his hickory clubs to perform the ceremonial Presidential tee-off.

Unfortunately, he narrowly misses the ball with a majestically supple swing.

At the second time of asking the ball soars down the fairway and the stage is set.

Since 1966, the Stotters have won the Stotters' Trophy 25 times and Tain have won it 24 times.

Ewan wants to tie the contest up at 25 all, and his tee shot displays his determination – 220 yards straight up the middle to gasps of amazement all round, not least from himself. Vice-Captain Graeme Ross hits his drive nearly as far as Ewan but off centre.

To a massive cheer up steps Johnny Houston playing off 8, and his drive bounces 10 yards past Ewan's and rests at the top of the slope a hundred yards from the 365-yard first hole's green.

Hamish's drive is not one of his best, landing in the left rough, but it doesn't matter as the format is Greensomes, with each duo playing alternate shots.

Hamish's and Graeme's balls are picked up and the match is off!

THE STOTTERS' TAIN CONNECTIONS

The Robertsons, Tochers and Rosses

The Stotters are a group of families and their friends, who every year come to Tain to holiday and play golf.

Their family connections go back to the mid-19th century, beginning with George Ross – born in 1846, one of 6 children, the eldest of whom – Isabelle – was born in 1840, in Reiskmore, a Hamlet near Tain. George married Mary Aird of Montreal in Canada.

They had 10 children, amongst them Annie, Kenneth and Christina.

Annie married William Miller Robertson whose children were Raeburn, Alan and Hamish Robertson; Kenneth married Constance Knapp in New Zealand and their 4 children included Kenneth Aird Ross; and Christina married James Williamson Tocher, one of whose children was James Ross Tocher (known as Gilbert).

Hence, Raeburn, Alan and Hamish (Senior) Robertson; Ken Ross (Senior); and Gilbert Tocher – some of the Tain stalwarts who laid the foundations for the Stotters – were cousins.

The three Robertson brothers – Raeburn, Alan and Hamish, were all brought up in Tain, but ironically only the youngest – Hamish – was born there.

Their father William became an architect with the practice of A. Maitland and Sons.

Andrew Maitland of Keith, in Banffshire was the first architect of note to work in and around Tain and the man responsible for a number of fine buildings there, including the 3 main hotels – the Royal, Morangie House and Mansfield House Hotels, and also the Town Hall, the Parish (former Free) Church, and the Tudor-gabled shops along the High Street.

William's second son Alan lived longest in Tain after a few years in Glasgow and two in Nairobi in Kenya, coming to Tain at the age of 6.

After qualifying as a pharmaceutical chemist in 1928, he joined his uncle in the well-established Tain business of David A. Ross and Co.

Whilst a golfer, Alan did not have the same skill as the other brothers, and confirmed this in the early years of the Stotters by throwing all his clubs and equipment into the river off the then Black Bridge at the 17th hole!

He was playing once with Cecil Phillip, who at the time was proprietor of the Royal Hotel. Both were in "good spirits" and arrived at the last green all square.

Alan managed to get down in 5 which left Cecil a long putt for a 4 to win the match.

It is said with a smile that Alan surreptitiously removed the flag and held it at least two yards from the actual hole to misguide Cecil, who, aiming for the flag, proceeded to put it in the hole to win the match!

Alan was Captain of Tain Golf Club from 1946-48, played a large part in the civic and social life of Tain, and was acknowledged as the local historian, maintaining a well-stocked literary library.

In 1968, he published a fascinating account of the history and the people of Tain and District called The Lowland Highlanders.

He often would drive to nearby Pitcalzean House to exchange views and whiskies with fellow author, Eric Linklater.

Alan had that lovely Highland sense of time summed up on one occasion when out walking.

A neighbour drew up and offered him a lift.

The reply from Alan came back: "No thanks, I'm in a bit of a hurry myself!"

Raeburn and Hamish both joined the banking profession - Raeburn originally with the North of Scotland Bank which ultimately morphed into the Clydesdale Bank.

In his early days, he was sent to various branches around Scotland and was then posted to London.

Hamish started work with the National Commercial Bank which ultimately became the Royal Bank, moved to Edinburgh and subsequently to Glasgow, where he reached the position of General Manager for West of Scotland.

Both Hamish and Raeburn invariably made the pilgrimage to Tain for the annual Tain Golf Tournament over many years, Raeburn travelling from London.

In the 1930s, he acquired an open old bull-nosed Morris, the gears for which he hadn't fully mastered.

In late July, after a very slow journey north in clammy hot weather, he and his wife Chryss (affectionately known as Tommy) eventually got to Derby and stopped at a coaching inn for the night. As Raeburn couldn't reverse the car, parking took a while.

They did however safely make it to Tain the next day and subsequent journeys were made in their beautifully stylish Singer – a two-seater open Le Mans model sports car, nicknamed "The Divine Wind", which they drove to Brooklands to watch motor racing.

Raeburn's son, Ross, remembers being taken up for Golf Week from the south and driving through the night to stop in the morning near Scotch Corner (on the A66) on the old A1 and having breakfast either at the hotel there, or at the Morrit Arms Old Coaching Inn (famed in Dickens' Nicholas Nickleby for where the brutal Wackford Squeers stopped with Nicholas and the boys en route to Dotheboys Hall School).

After breakfast the race resumed to get to Tain by nightfall.

In the late 1940s driving north in the pass of Killiecrankie, Raeburn's car crashed into the back of a Rolls-Royce.

Fortunately there was no real damage done, but being a public spirited character, he reported the accident to the police in London (on his return from Tain!).

The desk sergeant told him there were over 3000 police stations between London and Killiecrankie where he could have reported the accident, so he could quietly forget it.

Raeburn had a low single figure handicap, and his wife Chryss was Tain's Ladies' Captain in 1978/9.

His brother Hamish was a scratch golfer for over 10 years, playing at one stage off the dizzy heights of plus 2.

Christened James, Hamish served during the 2nd World War in the Argyll and Sutherland Highlanders, reaching the rank of major, and was affectionately nicknamed as such by the Stotters. His trademark top lip bristle moustache enhanced this image.

A talented club bridge player, Hamish also used to play bowls and curl, and enjoyed most sports, but golf was his real talent.

He played variously at Newbattle, where he was Club Champion pre-war, Luffness, East Renfrewshire, Western Gailes (where he was Captain in 1970), and latterly at Pollok.

He was a three-times winner of Tain Golf Week's McVitie and Price Cup (the Scratch Tournament Trophy) – in 1939, 1947 and 1949, in that year beating title holder and fellow Stotter-to-become Willy Mackenzie 5 and 4.

Quietly spoken, and with an easy smile and a ready quip, he never lost his Highland lilt, and relished his trips back to Tain. Latterly he was chauffeured to Tain, firstly by son Roddy and his wife Alice, and then by Hamish Junior and his wife Shirley and he would typically break into song as they reached Inverness.

Over the years, he introduced some of his friends to Tain and Golf Week. These notables included Walter Kerr, Willie Mackenzie and the unrelated Roddy Mackenzie

Two of Hamish and wife Helen's three sons, Hamish (Junior) and Roderick (Roddy) were to follow Hamish into the Stotters, whilst his eldest son, Rae, the best golfer of the three, remains an occasional Golf Week player.

Dr J.R. Tocher (Gilbert), cousin to Raeburn, Alan, Hamish and Ken, was a GP who lived in Arbroath and he also loved his golf, being a low handicapper, joining the others each year for Golf Week with his wife, Mary.

During the 2nd World war, Hamish Senior was wounded in the North African campaign and was lying in a tented forward hospital bed prior to evacuation.

He heard a familiar voice approaching, saying: "Oh my God, I'd know those bloody feet anywhere!"

Dr. Tocher, RAMC, was tending the wounded.

Gilbert and Hamish then got rather "well oiled" in the Officers' Mess, but while returning to his quarters, Gilbert stumbled into some cactus. Next day he had rather more of a hangover than normal and a very painful head, but carried on his duties.

Apparently, nobody had the nerve to tell the good Doctor that his scalp prickled with cactus spines!

Gilbert's grandfather – Dr James F. Tocher – was a brilliant and versatile scientist, consulting chemist, author and humourist, with few equals as a storyteller, and this skill was passed on through his son, Dr. J. W. Tocher to Gilbert.

A first-class cricketer, his swing was a low-slung cricket bat effort ("as flat as a pancake" as long term Tain and Stotters' stalwart, David Rutherford remembers) which nevertheless produced prodigious results, amongst them winning the Stirling Challenge Cup (originally the only Handicap Tournament Trophy awarded during Golf Week) in 1937 and 1954.

On one occasion at the river at the 17th, Gilbert tried to pick his ball out of the water – and ended up in it himself, an event not unrepeated in the annual Tain v Stotters' match.

He was often true to his maxim: "I'll stay up drinking until I fall over".

Kenneth Ross, was, like Hamish, born and bred in Tain, and having achieved distinction at its Royal Academy, went on to study medicine at Aberdeen University where he set a sporting record which still survives, receiving a Blue for five sports and representing Scotland in three of them.

He then emigrated to the South Island of New Zealand where he practised as an Ear Nose and Throat Surgeon. He continued playing golf at a high level representing New Zealand over three decades.

His elder son Kenneth Ross, current Stotter Ken Junior's father, returned to Aberdeen where he also qualified in medicine. During this time, he got to know his cousins whilst visiting Tain.

After marrying Mary Long, also a doctor, he took up General Practice in Tunbridge Wells.

Unsurprisingly, and with what "young" Ken calls a distinct lack of imagination, he also qualified in medicine, albeit in London, eventually becoming a Consultant Orthopaedic Surgeon in Eastbourne on the South Coast of Sussex.

Ken (Junior) was to become a Stotter, and subsequently also his two sons, George and Simon.

Ken Junior's first visit to Tain was in about 1958 at the age of 11, and over the next few years he was introduced to his Scottish cousins who either still lived in Tain or made the annual pilgrimage for Golf Week.

Initially the family stayed at the Royal Hotel, at that time owned by Cecil Phillips who only closed the bar when the last customer passed out or went to bed!

The Stotters were yet to be founded, but the Royal was the focus for these visiting golfers.

As a young boy Ken met Big Willy Mackenzie, Roddy Mackenzie, Ian MacPherson, Ian McColl, Ian Walkington, Hammy Mitchell, and his uncles Raeburn, Alan and Hamish Robertson and Gilbert Tocher, all supporting the bar and downing large stotters.

Ann Chalk subsequently became the proprietrix of the Royal and under her roof the Stotters was formed in 1966.

Each year the Ross's Bentley was put on the car train north and Ken Senior and Junior, and sometimes Ken's mother, Mary, travelled north to Glasgow often having early breakfast with Hamish Senior before driving on to Tain.

Ken Senior loved stopping at the wayside and cooking steaks on his rusty portable gas stove – a rather incongruous sight.

The Walkingtons

Born in Fawley, Hampshire, Ian Walkington joined the Army on leaving school in 1945 and served in India in the Artillery Regiment and the Paras.

He was stationed at the Woolwich Arsenal in the early fifties, and was ordered along with other young adjutants by the commanding officer to "go out and find women" for an upcoming dance!

One of these young women was Shelagh Munro, a native of Tain, who was teaching at the appropriately-named Culloden Street primary school in a very deprived and war-torn part of the East End of London. The dance must have gone well, as he persuaded her to join the Army Education Service and follow him out to Hong Kong, where they subsequently married.

He returned to the UK, seconded to GCHQ, and then joined GCHQ on leaving the Army, relocating to Cheltenham.

When he left the Army, Ian met his in-laws for the very first time – a scary prospect. Introduced to Shelagh's golf-playing family friends, he fell in love with the game, and even helped to mow the fairways during the months he spent in Tain at that time.

Thereafter, he always holidayed in Tain, and met many of the early Stotters at the Golf Club and socially in the Royal Hotel.

He often addressed people as "Sport", partly because it avoided embarrassment when he had forgotten their name, and this soon became his nickname – forever called "Sport" by the Stotters.

Though not an all- year-round golfer, he was steady, and had a fine putting stroke – often accompanied by the cry to the ball: "Get in there Norbert, it's your birthday!"

He was a tall dashing character, the archetypal Received Pronunciation Englishman, complete with a fine handlebar moustache (self-described as Pilot Officer Prune). A real fun-loving man with a great sense of humour and very intelligent, at one point having the nerve to sign on at the Tain Labour Exchange as a Turkish Interpreter.

His secret work with GCHQ caused him no end of teasing from the Stotters with their merciless sense of humour.

He played golf in Tain, and at Cotswold Hills, Gloucestershire in early retirement, normally playing off 18.

When he later became President of the Stotters, he initiated the "drive-in" at the first hole preceding every Stotters' match.

He never qualified for the knock out stages of Golf Week, but one year was involved in a play-off for the final qualifying place against the local minister. Unfortunately, he had "socialised" fairly heavily with Roddy Mackenzie in the club house on completion of his round and found standing in an upright position a significant challenge, let alone swinging a golf club in the vague direction of a small spherical object.

The minister unsurprisingly suffered no such disadvantage and duly dispatched him at the first play-off hole.

Sport's sister-in-law Rosemary was Captain and Club Champion on four occasions, and played golf for the North of Scotland; and father-in-law – W.J. Munro – was Captain of Tain GC from 1912-1922, helping redesign the course and relocating the clubhouse to its current site from where it originally stood beside what is now the 17th green.

Amusingly, W.J.'s wife Winnie, Art teacher at Tain Royal Academy and renowned local watercolourist, was Ladies' Captain, although to the best of anyone's knowledge she never once took a swing with a golf club!

Sport was father to William, Fiona, and Sandy; and third son Hugh was himself to become a Stotter, with Minister Fiona often his trusted caddy and motivator.

The Houstons

The first Stotters' Captain, Doctor John Houston, began his medical career as a young graduate in 1954, and started his own medical practice in the Renfrewshire town of Johnstone, a practice which he ran for the rest of his life. A man of great charisma and warmth, he was liked and respected by all who knew him, and he loved his golf.

He originally came up to Tain in 1960, having heard about the town in unusual circumstances.

Mr Mackenzie, the Headmaster of Edderton School near Tain had two sons called up in World War 2.

The elder, Alistair, an RAF pilot, died when shot down over Germany, and the younger, Lewis, a naval medical officer served in the Far East.

He survived and on completion of his medical degree went on to be a GP in the Tain practice. While studying in his final year, scrubbing-up before an operation, he met John who had also served in the Far East as an RAF Navigator.

John was awarded the Burma Star for his contribution to the Burma campaign.

The two got talking, and John asked Lewis where he came from, and whether there was a golf course in Tain. Lewis told him there was a fine links course – a test for the best players.

He said that the 3 finishing holes, depending on the wind, could make or break your score. The 16th 147-yard par 3 had a river and bunkers on both sides of the green. The 17th 215-yard par 3, with the tee cut into the side of the hill and the tidal river in front of it, played anything from a 5 iron to a driver, depending on conditions.

Lewis sketched the course of the river, twisting to 20 yards short of the green and flowing back again round the right edge of the green.

To complete the picture, two green side bunkers with a stretch of rough on either side further protected the green.

Lewis invited John to Tain.

He camped in Fortrose with wife Pat and baby Anne in 1960, and seeing a poster for the 4 Day Open Tournament, asked Pat if she would mind if he entered.

He was drawn to play with Hamish Senior in the qualifying rounds (and, as Stotters' stalwart Forbie Urquhart, remembers: "with some other poor sucker!").

John was a fine 3 handicap player, and Hamish was playing off scratch.

John played a good first round, and all was going well in the second round until the difficult par 3 17th which Lewis had described.

He pushed his drive, couldn't find his ball, and hadn't played a provisional. Not keen to go back to the tee, he was going to tear up his card, but Hamish pointed out he had two good scores, and should go back and play 3 off the tee.

John did so, qualified, and went on to win the McVitie & Price Trophy.

He said to Pat: "We'll have to come back to Tain next year. I need to defend my trophy".

Stefan Pater, born in Tain but now living in Wilmslow remembers, as a youngster, caddying for John over 50 years ago: "He gave me a very generous 10 bob!"

When John met Hamish during Golf Week, he was smitten, and a lifelong friendship developed which has continued through both families to this day.

John's two sons, Johnny and Simon were to become Stotters as have three sons-in-law – Chris Fraser (marrying Anne Houston), Robert Towart (Anne's first husband) and Liam Hughes (marrying Geraldine Houston).

In 1966, Hamish (Senior), Raeburn, Alan, Gilbert, Ian Walkington and Dr John Houston formed half of the Stotters' 12 members.

In 2016, 10 of the 20 Stotters are related to these stalwarts.

THE EARLY YEARS AND THE TWO PRESIDENTS

Two of the stalwarts who have been an integral part of the Stotters' story from the very early days were Forbie Urquhart and Frank Cougan, and it is extremely fitting that 2016 saw them occupying equivalent positions, Forbie as President of Tain GC and Frank as Honorary President of the Stotters.

The first Stotter to become President of Tain GC was Hamish Robertson (Senior) who held the position for 17 years from 1987 till his death in 2004. Forbie succeeded him.

Hamish was also the 2nd Honorary President of the Stotters, elected in 1999 till his death in 2004. The first was Ann Chalk.

Ian Walkington (Sport) held the position of Stotters' Honorary President from 2005 till his death in 2012. Frank succeeded him.

William Forbes Urquhart (Forbie) was born in Gower Street in Tain in October 1927. He became a retailer (he would have said Shopkeeper) owning his High Street shop with drapery, ladies, children's and nursery, and shoe departments.

Forbie was a great character, always with his slightly lopsided smile brushing his lips. He had a fund of memories and stories of people and places throughout the years and was a great source of information about Tain and events that took place there during his lifetime, committing many of his memories in various pieces of writing over the years.

One of the first major events he recorded involved the 311 Czech Squadron which operated out of the then airfield close to the village of Inver near Tain in 1945.

He witnessed the crash of a 311 Sq. Liberator, captained by Warrant Officer Jan Matejka. He recalls he was coming home from the ATC at 10pm one evening when he saw a glow in the sky and an aircraft overhead losing height. It came down by Kirksheaf Farm and the pilot was later praised for avoiding the town. Forbie was the first on the scene but there was nothing anyone could do for the crew.

He subsequently discovered that the Liberator, fully laden with fuel and depth charges for the trip that could last as long as 16 hours, had lost its starboard inner engine on take-off.

During the 2nd World War, Civil Defence exercises were held to allow groups to co-ordinate their efforts. Forbie recalls volunteering to be a patient during one exercise.

The scenario had him as a victim of a bomb blast on Tarlogie Farm steading. He had to climb on to a ledge via extension ladders where he was then strapped to a stretcher, dangled over the ledge and lowered to the ground by a block and tackle rigged by the participants. It was an experience he found "quite exciting".

Forbie was to become a key figure in Tain, and was closely involved in many local initiatives.

He was Chieftain of the Tain Highland Gathering in 2006, and thereafter always part of the colourful annual parade through the streets of the town with other local dignitaries and former Chieftains marching behind the pipers, Forbie in his tartan trews and Balmoral Bonnet.

Passionate about his golf at Tain, he won several internal club trophies, before winning the Stirling Cup in 1955, and was Captain of the Club in 1976/7.

He played off a Handicap of 4 at his peak.

In the early years, Forbie always played host to the Stotters for Monday evening drinks and the Stotters' prizegivings.

Living close by the Royal Hotel as he did was an added bonus for The Stotters, ensuring that there was little distance to walk between the two residences.

Forbie grinned as he recalled:

"One year when we had relatives staying over the weekend, the occasion was switched to the Tuesday instead of Monday. Somehow (I can't think why!) the message did not get across at the Stotters' AGM on the Sunday afternoon.

On Monday evening, Margaret (Forbie's wife) observed, from the sitting room window, a group of Stotters out for what she thought was a pre-dinner stroll.

Imagine her consternation when they turned in at the front gate and, as they advanced up the path, it suddenly dawned on her that this was no casual social call. No food or drink had been bought in, never mind prepared.

Frantic messages were relayed to the Royal and elsewhere that this was not the Stotters' night.

Meanwhile the "advance party" were not turned away without an "aperitif" or two and were happy to return the following evening to resume where they had left off".

Forbie played for the first time in the Stotters' match in 1968 and continued to play every year until 2008.

He sadly lost his battle with cancer in March 2017, aged 89, and is fondly remembered in Appendix 5.

Francis E. Cougan (Frank) was born in Carnoustie in Angus on 6th May 1934.

A son of the manse, Frank was a Dental mechanic, and did 3 years regular service in the R.A.F. Dental branch.

He was then a commercial traveller with McVitie & Price, and later the S&G shirt company from Taunton.

For 18 years, he ran his own clothing manufacturing company in Belfast hence his subsequent appointment as Honorary Shirt Maker to the Stotters.

When he returned to St. Andrews, Frank extended his business interests to hotel management, property management and a vintage car hire company. Ill health forced him to retire at 60 from most of those activities.

Very much a family man, his two daughters, Claire and Catherine are regular visitors to Tain Golf Week.

A good golfer in his prime, Frank got his Handicap down to 7, and was proud to play off 5 for two weeks.

Whilst he didn't actually play in the first Stotters' match, he remembers meeting the Stotters:

"Walter Kerr, Tommy Young and Ian McColl – all Kilmacolm Golf Club members – were my introduction to Tain and the Stotters.

In the early 1960s and for 2 or 3 years they all tried to persuade me to come and play in the Tain Golf Week Competition".

After a tri-am at Haggs Castle in Glasgow, the team came back to Kilmacolm, where Frank bumped into an old school chum – Bob Beveridge.

Bob convinced Frank he should come to Golf Week, so he and his best man took a caravan and parked up for the week in the Golf Club car park.

Bob then invited Frank to stay with him and his wife Nan, and by this time Frank had already met a few of the Stotters.

He became one of the regular Royal Hotel visitors, together with Kilmacolm friends and Stotters.

"Though a number of wives, some of whom played golf, came to Tain with their husbands, it was more of a boys' week and main family holidays were taken elsewhere after Golf Week".

In the first year that Frank played in the Tain Tournament, he was drawn to play with Forbie.

There was a hold up at the 4th tee, but fortunately, Forbie had a flask in his bag left over from the Stotters' Match, so they shared a dram which Frank rather appreciated.

They then played against each other in the match play stages of the Stirling Cup – Forbie playing off 7 and Frank off 8. They played the 1st 16 holes in 1 over par with Forbie one up reaching the 17th.

They both drove the green, and Forbie putted close so Frank gave him the putt for a 3. Frank had a 2-foot putt over the Hogs Back for the hole but hit it hard 6ft past and then missed the return, so lost 2 and 1.

They became great friends.

In the early days, they always tried to play together, laughed a lot and "sometimes the golf was good" (!)

Forbie always turned up with a funny hat for Frank – most of them are in a bag which Margaret Urquhart still has. They include a 'Viking' horned helmet, an M-K Shand hard hat, a Tyrolean soft hat complete with side 'brush' decoration, a 'Formula 1' helmet, a Cossack style fur hat and an outsize tartan St Andrew's Old Course bunnet.

However, as Frank said: "I did him once, by switching his ball on the first tee – for an exploding one!"

Frank claims little success in Golf Week – however: "I did win the mixed foursomes with Jean Duncan sometime in the early 80s. I also won the Wednesday Bogie competition playing with Gilbert Tocher, in the 70s".

Frank, living in St Andrews, is a devotee of Old Tom Morris.

Two of the cabinets in the Clubhouse were donated by him, one featuring memorabilia including small statues of Tom Morris and his equally famous son, Tom, and another which features a book about his life and a set of hickory clubs.

Forbie was a joint contributor to this magnificent display case.

Forbie was also a benefactor to the club and when you clean your golf shoes and caddy car from muck, grime and grass after a round on the links, it's the machine donated by Forbie doing all the work!

He was also responsible for providing and digging in the plants in the large flower bed on the right-hand side entry to the Golf Club car park, which he maintained for several years.

Forbie and Frank

MINUTES FROM THE FIRST MEETING OF THE STOTTERS HELD DURING GOLF WEEK IN THE ROYAL HOTEL IN AUGUST 1966

In 1966 a group of golfers who had been attending the Tain Tournament for a varying number of years, got together and decided, if the Tain Golf Club were willing, to play an annual match against their Captain's select for a cup to be purchased by the group.

The objective was to further social contact with the Tain members, whose welcome to their Club was always most warm and generous, and the group felt that the proposed Match would go some way towards demonstrating the warmth and affection felt for Tain, the Golf Club and its members.

For better or worse the group decided to call themselves 'The Stotters' and the following are the fully paid up members:

Messrs John Houston, Walter Kerr, Roddy J. Mackenzie, Willie W. Mackenzie, Hamilton (Hammie) Mitchell, J. L. (Ian) MacPherson, Ian McColl, J.G. (Hamish) Robertson, W. Raeburn Robertson, Gilbert Tocher, Ian Walkington, and Tommy S. Young with Mrs. Ann Chalk as Most Hon. President.

Messrs. MacPherson and Mitchell undertook to purchase a cup on behalf of the Stotters with one condition – that it held a bottle of whisky (for the record when purchased it held two bottles).

Contact was made with Tain Golf Club, through their Captain Robin Graham asking if they were agreeable to playing this annual match, and the challenge was accepted.

It was decided that the first match would take place on the Sunday prior to the start of Tournament Week in August 1967 at 9.30 a.m.

By a unanimous decision John Houston was elected first Captain of the Stotters and he in turn proposed Roddy Mackenzie as Vice-Captain and this was agreed unanimously.

The newly formed Club had no Constitution – neither had the founders, and there were no Rules, as the founders would never have kept them.

1966 was a big year for Tain and The Stotters.

It was obviously the year in which The Stotters were founded as the foregoing Minutes describe, and in the same year The Royal Burgh of Tain celebrated its 9th Centenary.

As the oldest Royal Burgh in Scotland, recognised by King Malcolm Canmore in the momentous year of 1066, the Celebrations officially ran from the 5th till the 12th of June – the Souvenir Programme cost 2 shillings and sixpence.

Bob Beveridge, one of the original Tain team players, and a Tain legend, remembers: "In the early 1960s, the Tain Golf Club Golf Week consisted of a one-day two round competition on the first Saturday; a men's pairs competition on the Monday; a three-day competition on Tuesday, Wednesday and Thursday; a mixed foursomes on the Friday; and a Ladies' competition on the second Saturday. This left the opening Sunday with no official competition.

A number of golfers, many with Tain connections, stayed at the Royal Hotel for the duration of Golf Week and in 1966 they made a suggestion that perhaps a match could be arranged for that day between the visitors and members of the golf club. As a result, a meeting was arranged on that Sunday in 1966, to discuss this. The golf club was represented by Dr. Robin Graham, Captain; Hugh Munro, Vice-captain; Andrew Gardiner, Treasurer; and myself as Secretary.

The visitors were represented by Hamish Robertson, Raeburn Robertson, Willie Mackenzie and Roddy Mackenzie. The outcome was that a match was arranged for the following year, 1967. The origin of the name "The Stotters" which was adopted by the visitors, came from an expression used by "Big Willie" Mackenzie, a Chartered Accountant from Glasgow, but whose family came from Tain. When ordering a whisky at the bar (invariably a large one) he would say, "Gie's a stotter", hence the name".

Forbie Urquhart remembers the same events:

"In 1966 there was no competition played on the Sunday of Golf Week and Ann Chalk, behind the bar after dinner one evening, asked: "Why don't you arrange a friendly game against a group of Tain members?"

Hugh Munro, solicitor, and his wife, Margaret, were having an after dinner drink and agreed with her, and after a few phone calls, got together a good Tain team, amongst them Dods Mackay, Dr Robin Graham, Sandy Gordon, Davie Buchanan, Hugh Mackenzie, and Hugh Munro himself. After the enjoyable game, Ann suggested they should do it again next year but involve more golfers and she would put up a cup to be played for.

After much alcohol fuelled discussion, the question of what the cup should be called was posed.

At that point, Ian MacPherson, or perhaps Roddy Mackenzie, asked the barman for 4 "stotters" and immediately it was agreed that it should be called 'The Stotters' Trophy'"

The name came as no big surprise to the Tain golfers as Davie Buchanan, a Tain worthy who came originally from Greenock, also used to ask for a "stotter" at the bar.

And thus the annual match emerged.

Tain Golf Club with Old Tom Morris presiding.

The Stotters' Trophy

MINUTES OF THE 2ND MEETING OF THE STOTTERS HELD DURING GOLF WEEK IN AUGUST 1967

Held at the Royal Hotel, Tain.

The First Match – The Stotters v Tain Golf Club – The Stotters lost by an unrecorded margin to Tain.

Mrs Ann Chalk presented the cup to Robin Graham.

Present: J. Houston, W. Kerr, R.T. Mackenzie, W.W. Mackenzie, I. McColl, I. MacPherson, H. Mitchell, J.G. Robertson, W.R. Robertson, G. Tocher, I. Walkington and T.S. Young.

MINUTES

None.

CAPTAIN'S REMARKS

Not heard above the uproar.

ELECTION OF OFFICE BEARERS

J. Houston proposed R.F. Mackenzie as Captain for 1968. This was agreed unanimously, with a call for a round of drinks. After ordering the drink R.F. Mackenzie proposed I. McColl as Vice-Captain. This was agreed unanimously.

ANY OTHER COMPETENT BUSINESS

The day was voted a great success by all.

Bob Beveridge remembers:
"The Match duly took place in 1967 and the Stotters' team consisted of Hamish and Raeburn Robertson, Big Willie Mackenzie, Roddy Mackenzie, Ian McColl, Ian

Walkington, Dr. John Houston, Dr Ken Ross, Tommy Young, Gilbert Tocher, Hammy Mitchell, Ian MacPherson and Wattie (Walter) Kerr.

The Tain team consisted of, among others, Dr. Robin Graham, Hugh Munro, Andrew Gardiner, myself, John Urquhart, Forbie Urquhart (he says not), David Buchanan, Bob Lindsay, Hugh Mackenzie, Ian MacGregor, Neil Robertson, Ronnie Duncan and Ian Anderson".

The irony of Bob's recollection is that this would have made the 12 a side match 13 a side.

Anything is clearly possible.

Frank Cougan remembers the Tain Team "wiping us out!"

Bob continues: "The match was won by the Tain Golf Club Captain's Select, although after the amount of drink consumed on the course (including a mobile bar run by Florrie Duncan behind the 10th Green), I am surprised that anyone remembered!"

The provision of the bar was a regular feature of the opening years of the Stotters v Tain matches, and Florrie was the expansive and charming Royal Hotel Housekeeper. The otherwise named "Alps Bar" was where further discussion, condolences and stories about the front 9 holes were recounted over a dram or two.

There was a tap of sorts at the 10th green for the greenkeeper (this was before Willie Russell's memorial water fountain was set up), and after downing their drinks, the Stotters went off to the 15th tee, thus playing 14 holes.

Unfortunately getting the car there – with drinks – became more and more of a hazard and because everyone started to turn up with enough drink to stock the Royal Hotel never mind the match (!), the Alps Bar fizzled out over time.

Sport's son, Hugh, remembers Chryss/Tommy Robertson, driving the car loaded with fresh supplies of alcohol, arriving at the 11th tee, and recalls stories of at least one Stotter falling off a tee – probably the 15th!

Florrie, wife of Ronnie Duncan, who played in 1967's match, always kept an empty gantry-sized Highland Queen bottle (2½ size) for Frank Cougan, into which he put a normal-sized bottle of Highland Queen and a bottle of water. The other three members of the foursome each put in ½ bottle more of the whisky and ½ bottle of water as the level dropped. The bottle had to be empty by the bridge over the burn at the 17th though in fairness to the foursome, they did not drink the lot by themselves, sharing it with others at any hold-up in play – often at the short 5th hole tee.

At the 17th a short ceremony was held to mark the "bottle farewell" as it was cast into the river accompanied by the "dead men's" chant and hankies to wipe away the tears!

Hamish (Junior) remembers caddying for his dad and meeting Dr John at the corner of the clubhouse early on the Sunday morning before the match. Attached to his golf trolley, Dr John had a cleverly constructed medical drip topped with an upside-down bottle of whisky, and fuelled by a tap which allowed a dram to be poured into a waiting tumbler atop a small platform.

All the players carried a stock of drink – mainly whisky, whisky derivatives like Rusty Nails, Drambuie and an occasional bottle or three of lager. The end result was – and still is – an extremely happy group of golfers merrily and gently swaying up the 18th Fairway on a Sunday morning.

One aspect which bound the original Stotters was the fact that they were, in the main, good low handicap golfers – sociable characters – and big but usually well behaved drinkers.

The format of the match, in the beginning, was foursomes, with players hitting alternate shots. It was match play, decided by the most holes won by either team.

To decide the match overall, the team with the most matches won took the trophy. In the event of a tie, the match was decided by the most holes won, an important fact very often forgotten by the players who allow drink to get in the way of memory and logic.

David Rutherford was closely involved with the origins of the Stotters – an accountant by profession, he was a keen golfer and, through his connection to Ann Chalk, got to know all the Stotters.

He is something of an anomaly in having played for both Tain and the Stotters (no bad thing!), a position subsequently shared by Forbie Urquhart and later by Andrew Urquhart.

David's connection to the Royal Hotel made him a natural for the Stotters' team.

He remembers: "I first played for the Stotters, aged 31, in 1968 when I was courting Ann Chalk and she asked if I would play in her place. I was the Company Secretary and Chief Accountant of the Invergordon Distillers, having joined them in 1964 as a newly qualified CA.

I felt very proud and privileged to wear the distinctive yellow sweater, orange check shirt, and the formal blue shirt and tie". (Though some of this apparel came later).

After Ann passed away in May 1971, he was designated "Mine Host" on the Stotters' letter heading and played regularly in the Stotters' match until 1978 when the Royal Hotel was sold and he moved to Campbeltown.

Returning to Tain in 1983, he again played for the Stotters until 1990 when he became Vice-Captain of Tain GC and had to change his allegiance. He captained Tain GC in 1991/2, and again in 2001/2.

A man of gentle bearing, with a boutique walrus moustache, his sense of fun and twinkling eyes were, and are, a fixture around the Clubhouse during Golf Week. David is a big supporter of the allegiance between the Club and the Stotters.

Drives from the first tee are always quite difficult for some and scary for others as the pressure builds with admiring viewers around the tee.

David has probably the unenviable record of hitting the shortest tee shot on the first when his drive went some 2 yards and didn't leave the tee area. Silence prevailed until a loud voice boomed: "I see your lessons with Mike Sangster are paying off David!"

Having said this, there have been a number of fresh air shots, not the least of which came from the late Derek Mackenzie. This time the comment was: "take your time with your second shot Derek!"

Bob Beveridge (Bev) was another of the characters from Tain who helped make the annual match between Tain and The Stotters such a special fixture in the golfing calendar.

He came to Tain initially in 1959 and won the Tarlogie Cup and the Cazenove Shield in that year.

An accountant with a penchant for whisky and red wine (though not often together) he is remembered by one of his early trainees who met him on a project in Inverness.

Robbie Robertson had been warned in advance that Bob was extremely sociable and after a long day's work, he suggested to Robbie going out for a "bite to eat".

Somehow the "bite to eat" became a bit more for Robbie to bite off and chew than he'd expected, and the next morning he arrived white as a sheet and late for work.

Bob, his florid face lit up with amusement, had been in since 9am.

"Put it down to experience," he told Robbie – and he did from then on!

Bob was a regular for the Tain team for many years, his trademark clubhouse tipple being a large glass of red wine.

He was Captain of Tain in 1971/2, and won the Teddy Brookes Handicap Trophy in 1976.

Roderick F. (Roddy) Mackenzie, elected as Captain for 1968, hailed from the Isle of Lewis, and he and his wife Helen were good friends with the McColls – it was Ian who brought them to Tain.

Forbie remembers a Wednesday entertainment night at the clubhouse when the Tain Pipe Band were marching back and forth in front of the clubhouse – "led by 'Drum

Major' Roddy with his trademark white floppy cotton hat, carrying a mop and that lovely smile of his".

Roddy had simply stepped in to lead the band!

He had some stomach problems and used to have a pint of milk behind the bar at the Royal. His tipple was half milk and half whisky in a ½ pint tumbler. Working as a stenographer with the Scottish Daily Express in Glasgow, years of typesetting caused him to suffer from Dupuytren's contracture, a condition that affects the hands and fingers which causes one or more fingers to bend into the palm of the hand.

One of his hands was so crippled he had to thread the shaft of his club through his fingers; and his putter, before the days of broom putters, was a foot longer than normal so he could putt with an upright stance.

His great theory was that you just picked up the club and dropped it down – it was all about rhythm, swing and timing.

He used to cry: "look at that thing of beauty," as his ball flew straight and far.

Despite his hand problems he was always cheerful and played to a 3 handicap.

His home club was Cowglen in Glasgow, and he once reached the final of the Scottish Amateur Championships.

Sometimes, after Golf Week, Roddy and Helen would go to Lewis to see his mother, but one Golf Week, after the qualifying round, the Stotters were in the bar of the Royal when Roddy announced in his familiar lilting Highland accent that he had heard that morning his mother had died, and he was just going upstairs to have " a good old fashioned greet to myself".

He was a gentle giant and a lovely man.

His Vice-Captain for 1968 was Ian McColl, who had been introduced to Tain by Hamish Robertson. He worked in sales for Goray Skirts – a clothing firm in Glasgow – and was a low handicap player at Pollok Golf Club, where Hamish was also a member.

When he came to Tain, with his wife Christine, an air hostess, he always visited Hugh Mackenzie, a Gents Outfitters in Tain, presumably to lend a business aspect to his holiday.

Frank recalls him: "As a character – a smoothie who could have bought and sold ice cream to the Eskimos. He fancied himself as a crooner and he entertained us to everything from George Formby to Bing Crosby".

Roddy Mackenzie with a young Hugh Walkington

MINUTES FROM THE 3RD MEETING OF THE STOTTERS HELD DURING GOLF WEEK AUGUST 1968

Held at the Royal Hotel, Tain

The Second Match – the Stotters v Tain Golf Club – the Stotters lost to Tain.

Mrs A. Chalk presented the cup to Hugh Munro.

Present: J. Houston, W. Kerr, R.F Mackenzie, I. McColl, I. MacPherson, H. Mitchell, J.G. Robertson, W.R. Robertson, G. Tocher, I. Walkington, T.S. Young.

APOLOGIES
W.W. Mackenzie.

MINUTES
None.

CAPTAIN'S REMARKS
Not heard above the uproar.

ELECTION OF OFFICE BEARERS
R.F. Mackenzie proposed I. McColl as Captain for 1969. This was agreed unanimously with the usual call for drinks all round. Having ordered drink, I. McColl proposed I. MacPherson as Vice-Captain. This was agreed unanimously.

ANY OTHER COMPETENT BUSINESS

I. MacPherson presented members with club ties which he had designed specially for the Stotters. The tie to be worn at all times they met. To show their appreciation for I. MacPherson's kindness they allowed him to stand a round of drinks.

The day was voted a great success.

R.F. Mackenzie felt there was a terrible strain being put on the two Doctor members of the Stotters, namely J. Houston and G. Tocher, looking after the health of their fellow members and he proposed A.G.R. Robertson M.P.S. as Hon. Pharmaceutical Advisor to the Stotters to give aid and succour and help out the over-worked Doctors.

This was agreed unanimously and for being elevated to this high office A.G.R. Robertson would be entitled to wear the club tie.

The meeting was duly brought to a close after this excitement.

The match was beautifully portrayed in the People's Press and Journal of Saturday August 10th 1968.

Under the Headline:

"THE STOTTERS ENJOY A FEW ROUNDS"

The article read:

"For many years and from many airts, the same well kent faces have, without fail, arrived in Tain for Golf Week.

Last year a number of the regulars clubbed together and bought a beautiful silver trophy and decided to put it up for annual competition, to be played for on the Sunday morning – the day after the One Day Open Competition.

It was to be a team competition with Tain Golf Club as one of the teams but what about a name for their own team?

They held a meeting, and it did not take the bold lads long to decide that, since Sunday morning was "the morning after the night before" what could be more appropriate than "The Stotters" and the cup was duly inscribed as the Stotters' Trophy.

Last Sunday "Big Roddy" Mackenzie, of Cowglen, Captain of The Stotters, led his team on to the first tee punctually at 9.15am.

A motley throng they were, arrayed in various types of headgear and with mysterious bulges in the pockets of their golf bags.

Wisecracks flew fast and furious between both teams, though one or two could be seen holding their heads and desperately trying to get their eyes open, and who is to say that it wasn't the brilliant sun that was bothering them?

Immaculate Ian Walkington, with his "Pilot Officer Prune" moustache, said, on seeing the huge figure of Watty Kerr (Kilmacolm) moving off: "I've never seen anything more like the north end of a bus going south".

Royal Aberdeen and Balgownie were represented by the two Robertson brothers and young Ross Robertson, all the way from Bengal, India.

Ian MacPherson came from Kilmacolm, McColl from Pollok, others from Turnberry, Old Ranfurly, Stranraer – indeed, all parts of Scotland.

For three hours after the teams moved off the Tain golf course rang with laughter, and a stranger taking a morning stroll would have heard some very strange remarks, like: "Don't take the flag out, it helps to keep the hole steady!"

On such a glorious morning no one would grudge the players refreshment on the way round, but alas, there wasn't a bar in sight, yet strangely enough mysterious empty containers began appearing in different places on the course.

When the last weary but happy competitors had arrived back at the clubhouse many's a tale was told, but no doubt they were greatly exaggerated.

For instance, who would believe that the Captain of the Tain team had to walk slowly up the twelfth fairway for fear he might spill a drop out of his glass.

The game over, the Stotters narrowly defeated, Mrs Chalk, proprietrix of the Royal Hotel, "home" of the majority of the Stotters, graciously presented the trophy to Hugh Munro, the Tain captain.

It was duly filled and truly emptied, and another glorious competition ended".

This amusing article highlighted the fact that the 1968 match was much more of a jovial occasion than 1967's –one or two turned up in fancy dress and the local barber appeared dressed in an undertaker's outfit!

The appearance of Raeburn's son, Ross, was unique in that he was home on leave from managing a tea plantation in India. At the time, he proudly claimed membership of the Toorsa Gymkhana and Polo Club.

Walter Kerr ("Wattie" in the article), played his golf at Kilmacolm, in common with a number of other Stotters.

He was a gentle giant of a man, quiet by nature but with a good sense of humour.

Well over 6 feet tall with what he would have described as a modest beer belly (!), he was Company Secretary of the retailer Goldberg's, and a great friend of the Robertson brothers, but especially Hamish and his wife, Helen.

After Walter's wife, Nessie, died suddenly, Hamish and Helen (or Hellish and Hamen as Pat Houston – Dr John's wife – called them), took Walter under their wing, going on holiday together on a number of occasions.

Forbie remembers an incident involving Walter and John Houston: "They were about to set off to attend a dinner together – a black tie affair – when Dr John got a phone call from a woman saying she wasn't well. John decided they would call on her on the way to the dinner. The woman was a bit of a hypochondriac. When they got there, John asked Walter to go in with him to be a "Specialist". Somewhat reluctantly, Walter complied.

"How are you, hen?" said John and took off his coat. After examining her, he turned to Walter and said: "Would you examine this lady Mr Kerr? I would like a second opinion".

Walter had to go through the motions of an examination as best he could and John asked him: "Would you agree this is ………?"

The "Specialist" readily agreed and they proceeded to their dinner leaving a satisfied patient".

Walter's favourite song was "Raindrops Keep Fallin' on My Head", written by Hal David and Burt Bacharach for the 1969 film Butch Cassidy and the Sundance Kid. It won an Academy Award for Best Original Song, and was recorded by B. J. Thomas in seven takes, after Bacharach expressed dissatisfaction with the first six. In the film version of the song, Thomas had been recovering from laryngitis, which made his voice sound hoarser than in the 7 inch single version.

Walter didn't perhaps match B.J Thomas, but this didn't stop him singing.

Frank recalls: "He could never remember anyone's name but always nodded and smiled, saying: "Hello doll," or "Hello there, how are you?" He was one of nature's gentlemen".

Walter was the unwilling Stotters' Secretary from 1970 until 1985, the Captains from 1966 until 1969 having taken the Minutes.

It was a feature of each year's AGM that he resigned, was ignored and often fined for resigning, and of course carried on regardless.

Ian MacPherson was affectionately known as MacPhearson and the Stotters' soft toy mascot was named after him – possibly because of their similar red and bulbous noses! Pat Houston and Rita Kemp bought the wee doll, which lives in the Stotters' Trophy, originally in the Royal Hotel but subsequently in the club trophy cabinet.

Ian himself was from Kilmacolm and married to Nan – although he always brought Elspeth his PA with him to Golf Week.

As a director and ultimately Chairman of Morton Football Club, he was to become instrumental in carrying out major improvements at Cappielow Park, their home ground. He was also a life member of the Scottish Football League Management Committee.

He spent most of his working life with civil engineering firm Baird Brothers of Port Glasgow. His time there was interrupted only by World War 2 when he served as an officer with the Royal Engineers.

A director of Bairds for many years, he set up construction firm Inverclyde Land and Marine in 1987.

Golf was his other great love and he was to become Captain of Kilmacolm Golf Club as well as holding a dear love for Tain.

He had an acerbic sense of humour, took time to listen and offer practical advice, and had an eye for the ladies. He also had a tendency to fall fast asleep and snore heavily in whatever position he was in after a few drams (though not alone in that, he was one of the worst offenders).

Ian and Walter Kerr were good friends.

He is fondly remembered for his generosity to Tain GC when he donated defences against coastal erosion. He provided the gabions – the rock-filled cages – that although now much battered and depleted, still give protection from erosion to the Alps (11th green, and the 12th fairway.

Frank speaks affectionately of Ian: "He was the gregarious Stotter, always game for anything that might involve a bit of mischief and he would be at the heart of it!

One night in Kilmacolm, it was too late to order food, but Ian knew the butcher, who reopened his shop and took out enough steaks for us all. I grilled them for an impromptu supper at Ian's house, washed down of course with whisky.

When Ian came to Belfast for a football meeting, I drove him in his new Toyota Supra and got him from the hotel to the Airport in 5 minutes —3½ miles. For once, Ian was silenced!

Dr. John used to wind Ian MacPherson up and he always took the bait. They had some epic arguments but none of it carried on for long and they were great friends

He lived life to the full – a great character and very generous to the Golf Club.

Thanks to his benevolence a lot of work at the Alps was done on coastal erosion – all done by Ian when he had a team up working nearby in Dingwall. He was very much an enthusiast who loved Tain like nobody else".

(c. 1968)

FROM THE CAPTAIN OF THE STOTTERS

SUMMER RESIDENCE :
THE ROYAL HOTEL,
TAIN,
ROSS-SHIRE.
TEL: TAIN 13
(Mine Host: David Rutherford, Esq.)

THE BOARD

John Houston, Esq; Walter Kerr, Esq; R.F.Mackenzie, Esq;
W.W.Mackenzie, Esq; Ian Macpherson, Esq; Ian McCall, Esq;
Hamilton Mitchell, Esq; Hamish Robertson, Esq; Raeburn Robertson, Esq;
Gilbert Tocher, Esq; Ian Walkington, Esq; Thomas Young, Esq.

Hon. Pharmaceutical Adviser:
A.G.R.Robertson, Esq., M.P.S.

MACWALKINGTON STANDING ON "THE ALPS"

MERRY XMAS.

TO THEE AND THINE.

FROM SHANE Mrs. & FAMILY

36

THE OPENING OF THE SAFE

Forbie Urquhart, in his High Street shop, inaugurated a tradition which was to last for a good number of years – The Opening of the Safe.

He recalls: "The first I saw of the Royal invaders, was about 4 pm on the Friday, when Dr John Houston, Hammy Mitchell, Ian MacPherson, "Big Walter" Kerr, "Gentleman" Tommy Young, Hamish and Raeburn Robertson would all troop into the shop. I can still picture all these big men in amongst the female customers.

Thankfully, the Ladies Underwear Department was in a secluded part of the shop!

However, after exchanging hellos and general greetings with my all-female staff, they advanced to the back shop for the "opening of the safe," which had been suitably stocked up with the local beverage for the occasion. It was a bit of a squash but they all found a chair or a box to sit on and the crack was great.

Dr John was the "water man", filling the jug in the staff toilet in the corner.

On very warm days we would take our chairs and boxes into the garden at the back of the shop".

Frank Cougan remembers one particular occasion when a team from Belfast was en route to play at Dornoch – across the Dornoch Firth from Tain, but before the Dornoch Bridge was built in 1991, a fair distance to drive via Bonar Bridge.

"On the Monday morning Forbie invited all the Belfast boys to help him open the safe in his shop at 9am before heading to Dornoch. One or two of the Belfast boys were Irish International level and keen to get to Dornoch to play.

So, it was a case of "what the hell are we doing", but they visited the drapery shop, and upstairs and next to the toilet was this massive safe. On the stroke of 9, Forbie asked for silence while he opened the safe which he did silently and reverently. Whenever the safe was open, all you could see inside were bottles and cases of whisky.

Forbie asked me to fill a jug in case anyone wanted water with their whisky.

I went to the toilet and flushed it, but unbeknown to the others I did actually fill the jug quietly from the tap. Everyone thought I'd used the loo to fill the water so folk weren't sure whether to drink it or not.

Suffice to say they didn't leave Tain till mid-day and only the drivers were sober enough to drive and get there but they did and played Dornoch too".

The opening of the safe always marked a successful start to Golf Week, and made a good springboard for the Stotters as they awaited the bars to open given the parsimonious opening hours of old.

Unbeknown to most of the current Stotters, Margaret Urquhart lovingly kept a miniature replica of "the safe", and the accompanying photographs reproduce the atmosphere of the occasions.

4B's Safe

The Opening of the Safe

THE ROYAL HOTEL

The Royal Hotel occupies the most imposing position in Tain town centre, standing at its end, its impressive façade presiding over the High Street.

Advertised as "The Scottish Victorian Hotel", it was the Stotters' main "residence" during Golf Week and acted as a vital pivot point for their activities – and for the chaotic AGMs.

Johnny Houston, elder son of Dr. John, remembers these times: "As kids we used to sneak up to the door of the Residents Lounge to try to listen to the chaos inside before being chased away by the women, who wanted to listen themselves!"

The Manageress in the early years of the Stotters was the amazing Mrs Ann Chalk (also called Nan) – or Mrs Chalk – who ran the Hotel with an incredible degree of hospitality and warmth.

At that time, she was being "courted" by David Rutherford, "Mine Host" on the Stotters' letter heading with The Royal Hotel proudly displayed as the home of The Stotters.

Frank Cougan remembers the atmosphere in the Hotel as being very free and easy: "You could come in at 2 or 3 in the morning and help yourself to something from the fridge. Everybody made themselves a plate of sandwiches".

Forbie fondly remembers: "During Golf Week (then called 'The Tournament'), the Royal Hotel was full of golfers and their families who on leaving usually booked in for the same week for the following year. They nearly all arrived in time for lunch on the Friday. The Houstons used to arrive in two cars, Pat driving one and John the other, and normally rolled up no later than mid-afternoon.

One time John's car broke down and he did not reach Tain till 8 pm. I was on my way down St. Duthus Street, heading for the Royal, when John's car passed and pulled up by the front door of the hotel. Mrs Chalk came out to greet him and I lent a hand to unpack the car. As I was about to shut the boot, John shouted, "Hold it!" then proceeded to unload four building bricks.

Mrs Chalk's words were, "Is there something wrong with your brakes?"

40

"No", came the reply: "The bricks are to prop up the bed. Pat's pregnant!"

Sunday evening dinners in the Royal were followed by a Hooley, and my wife and I were always invited to take part in the Sunday proceedings. On Wednesdays round about 4-5 pm before dinner, the children of the Stotter families staying at the hotel would put on a show – a children's concert – song, dance, poetry and piano playing – which was always one of the highlights of the week.

These occasions ended with "Uncle" Frank's auction of shirts, all the way from his factory in Northern Ireland. This was also great fun.

On one occasion, Frank had a late tee-off time and I had to do the auction. The money raised went to a local charity – the cubs, brownies, or scouts often. One year, Frank asked me who to give the money to. I suggested the British Legion as they did a good job at Christmas.

The British Legion Secretary, Bobby Sellar, came along with his camera, took a nice photo and put a lovely write-up in the Ross-shire Journal".

David Rutherford recalls: "My earliest (hazy) recollections of the characters who made up the Stotters are mainly of those who stayed in the Royal which was like a family house party with the Houstons, the Robertsons and the Cougans, their children and several Stotters' wives. After the match on Sunday, the AGM was held in the afternoon, with the always very amusing children's concert on a Wednesday evening. I used to attend the pre-match dinner when everybody toasted each other, and by the end of the meal nobody could remember who had toasted who, so the toasts started all over again.

John and Pat Houston always stayed in Room 14, a large room, in which their five children slept as they were born over the years".

Anne was born in 1959, Patricia (Trish) in 1962, Geraldine (Deen) in 1964, Johnny in 1966 and Simon in 1968.

David also remembers Frank's daughter Claire "aged about four or five limping into breakfast one morning saying: "I fell off a swing and hurt my bum," in her lovely Irish accent".

Simon, who was to become Secretary to the Stotters, slept in a drawer in the chest of drawers when he was a baby!

One evening in the small cocktail bar before dinner a middle-aged lady resident was heard asking John: "Doctor, may I have a word with you?" to which John replied in a loud voice: "Certainly – is it about the pill, hen?"

In the same vein, Hamish (Junior) remembers, when getting engaged, being asked by John. "Is she on the pill?"

Forbie continues his memories: "After dinner drinks in the Royal bar one year in the late 60s, Ann Chalk announced, "It's about time one of you came back with a cup for me to fill".

Someone shouted, "They're not fit enough!"

This gave me an idea. I was Tain Royal Academy's supplier for school uniforms, including gym outfits. They wanted a change in style and pattern, leaving me with a number of the old ones. So, without telling anyone where I was going, I went along to the shop and returned with a carton of shorts and tops, and suggested there should be jogging at 7am next day before breakfast to get fit.

Can you picture the trying on for size in the bar?!

Dr. John, Pat and the kids were first on parade at 6.45 am, followed by half-awake Scott Ferguson, Ian MacPherson and I can't remember who all else. Just imagine 20 assorted Stotters and family, each with their own unique jogging style going along the High Street, to the amusement of about 50 workmen at the Post Office bus stop waiting for the Nigg oilrig yard buses – all whistling and calling as we passed at not a great speed.

The run was to be down the Woody Braes then to the Railway Bridge and back. As you can guess, the young ones were way ahead. By the time we (the oldies) reached the Public (Knockbreck) School, sensing a weakness in some legs, I suggested refreshment. This suggestion was greeted with great relief and received overwhelming support. On my command, "About turn!" the manoeuvre was performed beautifully and the next stop was the shop – yes, you've guessed it – to open the safe".

Johnny Houston remembers it, albeit slightly differently: "The Stotters went jogging en masse during Golf Week (I kid you not). It came about because our Anne got into running and persuaded them all out for a run round the town and golf course. I think there may even have been yellow running vests involved but might just be imagining that one.

Back in those days before jogging became popular it was rare to see anyone out running in public let alone a group of men of a certain vintage, some of whose legs had not seen the light of day for decades! Predictably there were mixed results with a couple of the guys getting as far as The Railway Inn before thinking "I'm out of it" and ducking in there for a few drams.

I do remember Scott Ferguson and Anne having a sprint finish so there must have been some kind of race involved too. It was just a relief that no ambulances were required.

I don't think the venture improved their fitness, but they enjoyed a full breakfast – in the Royal of course!"

Johnny also remembers: "My Dad's party piece, or one of them, was to sit on the bonnet of the car and my Mum would drive it up from the club to The Royal for the AGM. He would be waving to astonished pedestrians, and we kids in the back loved it – not sure he'd get away with it these days!"

Frank remembers Dr. John's infallible remedy for a hangover: "I was very much under the weather one morning and John suggested we walk over the road from the Royal to the St. Duthus.

The owner greeted us heartily and John ordered two stotters and milk, which he stirred in with his faithful behind-the-ear pen. "Force that over" he urged, and the stotters were duly dispatched".

The owner then presented the duo with a half bottle of whisky and off they went to the Railway Inn where the stotters and milk tonic was duly repeated.

The Golf Club then did similar honours and the Star Bar finished the cure.

Frank remembers that he felt absolutely fine after a morning of hairs of the dog!

MINUTES FROM THE 4ᵀᴴ MEETING OF THE STOTTERS HELD DURING GOLF WEEK AUGUST 1969

Held at the Royal Hotel, Tain.

The Third Match – the Stotters v Tain Golf Club – victory for the Stotters. Mrs A. Chalk presented the cup to I. McColl.

Present: J. Houston, W. Kerr, R.F. Mackenzie, W.W. Mackenzie, I. McColl, I. MacPherson, H. Mitchell, J.G. Robertson, W. R. Robertson, G. Tocher, I. Walkington and T.S. Young.

MINUTES

None.

CAPTAIN'S REMARKS

Drowned in the uproar.

ELECTION OF OFFICE BEARERS

I. McColl proposed I. MacPherson as Captain for 1970 and this was agreed unanimously with a call for stotters all round. Having ordered stotters, I. MacPherson proposed W.R. Robertson as Vice-Captain. This was agreed unanimously.

ANY OTHER COMPETENT BUSINESS

The day was voted a huge success.

To celebrate Raeburn Robertson's 64ᵗʰ birthday, on Thursday 7ᵗʰ August, Ann Chalk had a table set up on the road out in front of the Royal Hotel, just before midnight, complete with a bottle of champagne, glasses and an iced tea-cake with one lit candle.

When the Town Clock struck twelve, the bubbly was opened and dispensed amongst great hilarity. This was followed by a series of rather drunken bicycle races up and down the High Street.

It was a lovely balmy night so the noise the Stotters and families made carried round the town. A passing police car briefly stopped, saw what was going on, wished Raeburn a happy birthday and told the crowd to make a noise more quietly. The police duly gave a wave and the celebrations carried on!

Hamish (Junior) and friend John Pauling who had been a Stirling Cup finalist that day, wet some heads by sprinkling well placed glasses of water from their top floor room in the Royal!

Willie Mackenzie was a tall bespectacled Glaswegian accountant who lived in Merrylee on the south side of Glasgow. He and his wife Jessie were great friends of Hamish and Helen Robertson.

Willie was another low handicap player with a booming drive and laugh.

His two sons Ian and Neil were regular visitors to Tain in the early years of the Stotters.

Tommy Young was born in Kilmacolm in 1914 and lived there all his life. He worked as a gardener and chauffeur and then became Head Greenkeeper at Kilmacolm Golf Club where he was a member, becoming an honorary member when he retired.

Tommy first came to Tain just before 1966, and was quickly absorbed into the Stotters. A small, athletic and weather-beaten character, he was the essence of politeness with a great sense of fun.

Frank says: "He was very quiet and sat in the background – a lovely man with a smile for everyone".

Tommy had a son also named Tommy, and two daughters – Tina (who married Stotter Andrew Urquhart and lives in Tain) and Barbara.

Tommy loved his golf and played off scratch for many years.

Tina remembers: "I lost track of how many clubs he broke with the amazing swing he had". Frank, who often played with him, confirms that Tommy had a unique swing – "possibly the fastest backswing in the game".

Tina also remembers time spent making the first Stotters' badges: "Dad was quite chuffed as the logo looked like his initials – TS with the upside-down glass as a Y".

Logos old and new are shown here.

Tommy's wife Liz (Elizabeth Mathie Young) passed away in March 2014 at the grand old age of 101. A small snappy dresser with a sharp wit, lively manner and ready humour, she and Hamish Senior used to joke with each other as to who was the older.

She won ultimately by 10 years.

Frank remembers his good friend Maurice Bembridge coming to Tain with his new bride, Susy, in the late 1960s, and enjoying some evenings with the Stotters.

Maurice played in the Ryder Cup four times, winning five matches, losing eight and halving three. He also represented England in the World Cup twice, and had 20 professional tournament victories.

MINUTES FROM THE 5ᵀᴴ MEETING OF THE STOTTERS HELD DURING GOLF WEEK AUGUST 1970

Held at the Royal Hotel, Tain.

The Fourth Match – the Stotters v Tain Golf Club – victory for the Stotters.

Mrs. D. Rutherford presented the cup to I. MacPherson.

Present: J. Houston, W. Kerr, R.F. Mackenzie, I. MacPherson, I. McColl, J.G. Robertson, W.R. Robertson, G. Tocher, I. Walkington and T.S. Young

APOLOGIES

H. Mitchell.

MINUTES

None.

CAPTAIN'S REMARKS

I. MacPherson, as Captain, expressed on behalf of all the Stotters their deep regret at the passing of 'Big Willie'.

Willie Mackenzie, a great competitor who loved life, loved Tain and golf, would be missed by all.

ELECTION OF OFFICE BEARERS

I. MacPherson proposed W.R. Robertson as Captain for 1971. This was agreed unanimously with an order for stotters all round. Having ordered the drink, W.R. Robertson proposed J.G. Robertson as Vice-Captain. This was agreed unanimously.

Some confusion arose about the subject of Minutes and amidst uproar and shouting J.G. Robertson proposed that the Stotters should appoint a Secretary and that W. Kerr was his nomination for the post.

There was a majority agreement for this proposal and nomination, with one objector (W. Kerr) and amidst further scenes of uproar and shouting, the proposal was carried and W. Kerr was appointed Secretary to the Stotters.

ANY OTHER COMPETENT BUSINESS

I. MacPherson proposed that the Stotters purchase a seat to be placed on Tain Golf Course in memory of Willie Mackenzie. This was seconded by R.F. Mackenzie and agreed unanimously. I. MacPherson undertook to do this.

Mr Frank Cougan had held a Shirt Auction in the Royal Hotel, the proceeds from which had been handed to the Secretary, amounting to seven pounds, with Frank Cougan's wish that this should go towards helping to defray the cost of the seat for Willie. This generous gift had been accepted.

W.R. Robertson then proposed that Frank Cougan be appointed Hon. Shirt Maker to the Stotters and be presented with the club tie. This was seconded by I. MacPherson, and agreed unanimously.

The day had, once more, been a great success.

Mrs D. Rutherford is Ann Chalk, now married to David Rutherford.

Frank Cougan played his first ever game for the Stotters after big Willie died – with Gilbert Tocher, then playing off 4 The format was foursomes, and as the lower handicapper, Gilbert had the honour of leading the pairing.

There was a group of four other Stotters standing on the first tee – clearly (no doubt deliberately) unsettling him, and suddenly, as Frank remembers: "Gilbert had a problem with balance; or a premonition of dementia; or perhaps glaucoma struck him as he made his swipe at the ball, so instead of this 4- handicapper hitting it straight down the middle, he swiped it into the ditch off a tree about 25 yards up to the right of the fairway".

As it was foursomes it was Frank's shot, and all he could do was knock it out into the middle of the fairway, still with over 300 yards to go to the green: "We got there comfortably in about 8 shots and lost the hole!"

It may or may not have been this year that Forbie was partnered with Davie Buchanan who had enjoyed "a modicum of the day's liquid gifts".

It was his turn to putt on the 18th green but Frank suggested Forbie putt, so they sat Davie at the wheel of his caddy car and proceeded to hole out.

After the shouts of "We won! We Won!" they went into the clubhouse, changed, and sat down at the window with their drinks.

Frank asked, "What's keeping Davie?"

Everyone looked out the window and there he was, still sitting in the buggy, asleep on the far side of the green.

The Stotters – 1970.

Back Row – L to R – Frank Cougan, Hamish Robertson Senior, Ian (Sport) Walkington, Raeburn Robertson, Ian MacPherson, Hammy Mitchell, Roddy Mackenzie, David Rutherford.

Front Row – Alan Robertson, Tommy Armstrong, Walter Kerr, Tommy Young, Gilbert Tocher.

Dr. John Houston and Frank Cougan.

Ian MacPherson and Dr. John.

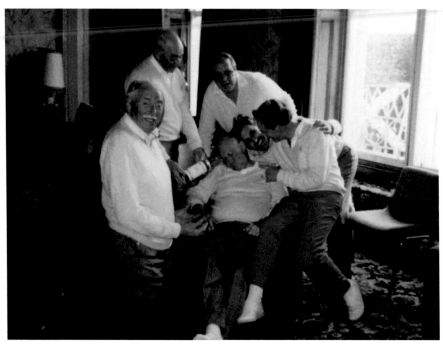

Attempt at Resuscitating Frank Cougan – L to R – Walter Kerr, Tommy Young, Wilson Kemp, Scott Ferguson and Forbie Urquhart.

Quartet – Frank(enstein) Cougan, Forbie Urquhart, Teddy Brookes and Tommy Young.

4 Stotters – with Hamish (Senior), Forbie and Dr. John.

MINUTES OF THE 6ᵀᴴ ANNUAL GENERAL MEETING OF THE STOTTERS – SUNDAY, 2ᴺᴰ AUGUST, 1971

Held at the Royal Hotel, Tain.

The Fifth Match – Tain Golf Club v the Stotters – victory for Tain Golf Club.
Mrs. W.R. Robertson presented the Cup to Mr R. Beveridge.

Captain W.R. Robertson in the Chair.

Present: Messrs R.F. Mackenzie, I. MacPherson, I. McColl, J.G. Robertson, G. Tocher, I. Walkington, T.S. Young and W. Kerr.

APOLOGIES

J. Houston.

Missing: H. Mitchell. The Captain ordered a search of bars, bedrooms and bathrooms. H. Mitchell was not to be found and the Captain ordered H. Mitchell be fined the usual penalty of drinks all round.

This was carried unanimously.

MINUTES OF THE PREVIOUS MEETING

The Minutes of the AGM held in August, 1970 were read, approved and signed by the Captain.

MATTERS ARISING FROM MINUTES

None.

CAPTAIN'S REPORT

Captain W.R. Robertson reported on the Annual Match against Tain Golf Club which resulted in a win for Tain (at this point uproar broke out, and when eventually order had been restored, Captain Robertson continued by pointing out the margin between the two sides had been small and a little more attention to handicaps might have brought a victory).

However, it had been a most enjoyable day with the weather at its best and everyone in good form, golf or otherwise.

The Captain was happy to report that the seat in memory of Big Willie was now in position at the Eleventh Tee and it was a truly magnificent one.

Captain Robertson expressed his thanks on behalf of both himself and all the members to Ian MacPherson for the generous effort made by him in providing the seat. This was greeted by much shouting and cries of "stotters all round". As no one seemed prepared to buy them, the Captain concluded by telling the meeting that Tain Golf Club had asked him to convey their thanks and appreciation for the seat.

Thanks to Frank Cougan, the Captain was able to report he had not seen such a well turned out 'shower' at Tain Golf Club for many a day.

Every Member was kitted out in pullovers provided by Frank at a small cost and further for 'free' (at this members went into delighted giggles) – shirts and ties for evening wear, which made them an even better evening 'shower'.

Captain Robertson expressed the thanks of all the Stotters which would duly be conveyed to Frank.

This concluded the Captain's Report which was acclaimed in the usual manner.

ELECTION OF OFFICE BEARERS

Captain W.R. Robertson in retiring from the Chair, proposed J.G. Robertson, at present Vice –Captain, as Captain for 1971/72 – this was agreed unanimously, and amidst much noise and furore, J.G. Robertson took the Chair as Captain of the Stotters.

Captain Robertson assured the members that he was very conscious of this high honour and would do his best to uphold the high standard set by the previous Captains.

At this point Captain Robertson was interrupted from the floor by a statement that went: 'never mind the f....... cackle, buy some drink'.

Ignoring the interruptions the Captain went on to congratulate the retiring Captain on his success in keeping such an unruly bunch in order, at the same time maintaining the dignity of the office, and that is was further to Raeburn Robertson's credit, having risen from his sick bed to take part in today's match, he had, with J.G. Robertson himself as his partner, recorded the highest winning score this day.

At this there was complete uproar and much shouting from the floor.

Captain Robertson assured members he would deal with 'Hammy' (still missing) when the time came, but turned down a suggestion from the floor, that: 'as it was now opening time, all members should search every bar in town for Hammy', because, being Sunday, none of his favourite bars were open, and with reluctance this explanation was accepted.

The Captain drew the attention of the meeting to a vacancy in the membership brought about by the death of W. Mackenzie, which had never been filled and he therefore proposed that Frank Cougan, at present Shirt Maker to the Stotters, be elected as a full member to fill the vacancy.

This proposal was carried unanimously.

At the same time the Captain felt Mr. Wilson Kemp, who had played in all the Stotters' matches with distinction, be elected as an Associate Member of the Stotters. This was also carried unanimously.

There then followed the 'tie' presentation ceremony when Frank was duly made a Stotter, and Wilson an Associate. Frank started to make a speech but was bluntly told: 'buy drink' and this was duly attended to.

The Captain asked that a vote of thanks be recorded to the Ladies for their sterling work, not only this year but in previous years also, in seeing that a Bar was set upon the course for the Annual Match, and thus saving many lives.

It was noted, with regret, that John Houston – 'Mr Wonderful Himself'– was not with us this year due to illness but word had been received that he was recovering and would be with us next year.

A suggestion that a basket of fruit be sent was turned down unanimously. However, all members wished him well.

The Secretary asked the members to accept his resignation, as from now. This was not accepted by a majority of nine to one. In fact some 'fruit' sounding like the Captain, suggested that W. Kerr hold the position for life.

The Secretary asked the meeting to consider once again his request for an Honorarium and the Captain interrupted saying as there was no further business he declared the meeting closed.

ADDENDUM

Presentation to Messrs. I. MacPherson and F. Cougan.

In the absence of both these named members, the Captain expressed what was the wish of all other members present, that some form of presentation be got up for Ian and Frank – Ian for his generosity in gifting of the seat now on the golf course and Frank for his shirts, now on our backs.

It was therefore agreed unanimously that Mrs Munro be asked to prepare two of her paintings for this purpose.

There being no further business the Captain declared the meeting closed.

The "Mrs Munro" referred to in the Addendum, was Winnie Munro, Sport's mother-in-law. She was a watercolourist of real distinction, having won a silver medal at the Scottish Royal Academy as a student.

As a footnote to the Stotters' bench, Ann Chalk was never formally elected as a Stotter, but still was recognized as their Honorary President. She is commemorated with a plaque on the Stotters' bench, the only female to have earned (!) that privilege, having passed away in May 1971.

The Minutes of 1971 are the first penned by Walter Kerr, so some shape begins to emerge for the AGM Minutes, despite his constant protestations. However there is also confusion in the Minutes as Frank Cougan is clearly not present but apparently starts to make a speech, so this was probably Wilson. Also Ian MacPherson must have gone missing during the meeting, another not unusual event.

Wilson Kemp – a larger than life character – here makes his first appearance in the Stotters' Minutes.

A jovial man with something of an underbelly presence, dark haired, bespectacled and of medium height, he soon became one of the backbones of the Stotters.

He was born in 1928 in the kitchen of the family home in Camelon. The youngest of seven children, he attended Carmuirs Primary School and Falkirk High School, where he became Captain of the School Football Team and went on to play at junior level with three well renowned teams – Camelon Juniors, Linlithgow Rose and Kilsyth Rangers.

He had a trial with the famous Queens Park FC, but lacked the enthusiasm for a full-time career in the sport.

He was also a first-class badminton player.

Hamish Junior remembers meeting him in 1966 at the newly opened Grangemouth Athletics Stadium, Britain's first all-weather track: "I remember his all-engulfing smile and zest for life".

He served from 1947 to 1949 in the Army based at Aldershot with the Royal Engineers as Lance Corporal – Ammunitions Examiner, and then started work as a Junior Civil Engineer with Falkirk Council, becoming a Civil Engineer.

He and Rita married in 1952 and had a daughter Janis a year later, but he contracted polio in 1954 and spent six months in Bannockburn Cottage Hospital.

He joined the civil service in 1968 where he eventually became a Senior Roads Engineer, and became a steward at the Ingliston Motor Racing Circuit.

Rita remembers, in summer 1969, reading an article in the Scottish Daily Express, written by one Roddy Mackenzie, about Tain Golf Week, and the Royal Hotel.

She suggested to Wilson they should go as he loved his golf, and Janis was away on a school trip.

They stayed at the Royal Hotel, where the Stotters were staying, and got chatting. Wilson had won a prize in the One Day Open and they all congratulated him in the bar.

After the Stotters' match on the Sunday, Pat Houston asked if Wilson and Rita would like to join the Stotters for dinner.

They all got on like a house on fire, and a new chapter began.

Wilson was a fine golfer. As Simon Houston was later to say, he was no Tiger Woods, but loved the game completely, and fitted perfectly into the Stotters' mould of good golfers, good drinkers and good friends.

He was to become the Stotters' Secretary, whose primary role was to fill the room with laughter at each AGM with his hilarious Minutes of the previous year's meeting.

Simon remembers: "He fulfilled this role with some aplomb. He was quite simply a genius with the written word. A very funny man.

And thanks to the wonders of television, the entire nation was treated to a glimpse of his comedy genius when he and Janis famously appeared on the Generation Game in the early 70s.

In round one he had to operate a ventriloquist's dummy and in the second round he had to create the perfect turban.

Was he successful? Well the fact that his hilarious efforts formed part of the title credits for an entire series should tell you all you need to know".

The amazing Wilson Kemp.

MINUTES OF THE 7ᵀᴴ ANNUAL GENERAL MEETING OF THE STOTTERS – SUNDAY 30ᵀᴴ JULY 1972

Held at the Royal Hotel, Tain.

The Sixth Match – the Stotters lost to Tain.
Mrs J.G. Robertson presented the Cup to Mr. Anderson.

Captain J.G.Robertson in the Chair.

All Stotters present and, in attendance, David Rutherford and Wilson Kemp.

MINUTES OF THE PREVIOUS MEETING

Previous Minutes of the AGM held on 2ⁿᵈ August, 1971 were read, approved and signed by the Captain.

MATTERS ARISING FROM MINUTES

Presentation to Ian MacPherson and Frank Cougan. Captain Robertson hoped that Frank and Ian now had their paintings, ordered at last year's meeting.

Both gentlemen reported having received same and expressed their thanks to the members for their kind thought.

Hamilton Mitchell apologised to the members for his absence from last year's meeting.

This he said was due to drink.

Captain Robertson, while accepting Hamilton's apology, felt that he had to levy a fine on him which he fixed at 50p. Plus a round of drinks. This delighted all the members.

CAPTAIN'S REMARKS

Captain Robertson, reporting on the Annual Match against Tain Golf Club which took place today in fine weather, said that it once more ended in failure as the Stotters lost again – but there had been a lot of tight games – very tight.

This didn't seem to worry the members as they were all happily consuming Hammy's drinks.

Captain Robertson didn't dwell too long on the Stotters' performance today – in fact he couldn't remember how the games had gone, but the margin of Tain's victory was not great. He was sure all the members would agree with him that it had been a successful day in all other respects.

The following members were fined by the Captain for being improperly dressed; i.e. not wearing the Stotters' tie when three or more of our members are gathered together. They were: J.G. Robertson – at this the meeting nearly broke up in uproar. With difficulty the Captain brought the meeting to order and then added to the list – Ian MacPherson and W. Kerr who were all guilty.

Uproar broke out again when he fixed a fine of 5p on all three. Members were not satisfied this was enough and at this point the meeting was nearly adjourned. But again order was restored with difficulty.

Continuing with fines, the Captain then fined David Rutherford 50p for failure to appear at the dinner on Sunday 2nd August 1972. This raised a further roar of protest and the Captain was heard to say David had also lost his Stotters' pullover on Sunday and was improperly dressed. The day was finally saved when an anonymous member ordered a round of drinks and peace descended on the meeting and David Rutherford, J. G. Robertson, I. MacPherson and W. Kerr all paid their fines.

The sum raised from last year's Shirt Auction was £27.00. This, the Captain reported, was the figure given to him by the Secretary. He had asked for audited accounts but alas the Secretary seemed reluctant to do this. This brought angry shouts once more from the members but the Secretary remained adamant that it was £27.00, audit or no audit, like it or lump it.

It was then put to the meeting that this money should be utilised to buy new ties for members. This was agreed unanimously and Ian MacPherson was instructed to attend to this.

It was further proposed by Captain Robertson, in view of the Secretary's reluctance to produce accounts, that any monies lying should be utilised in some fashion to prevent any further ugly scenes such as we had all just witnessed and to this end, any money from this year's Shirt Auction should be used to supply the drink at the 'Alps' in next year's match. The proposal was seconded by J. Houston and agreed unanimously by the members.

In closing, Captain Robertson asked members to show their appreciation to Tommy Young for the Badges, designed and made up by his daughter Christine (Tina) and gifted to the Stotters for wearing on their blazers. This was greeted with loud acclaim from all members.

Vote of Thanks continues:

To Ian Walkington for designing a Stotters' Flag which Tain Golf Club had agreed to fly at each year's annual match. All members showed their appreciation in the usual fashion.

ELECTION OF OFFICE BEARERS

Captain Robertson, in retiring from the Chair, proposed the present Vice-Captain, Tommy Young, as Captain for the year 1972/1973. This was agreed unanimously and amid the usual clamour Tommy Young took the Chair as Captain.

He thanked Hamish for the manner in which he carried out his duties and in the way he had conducted what could only be described as a difficult meeting. He thanked members for the honour, assured them he would do his best to uphold traditions, one of those being to buy drink and asked members to join him in partaking of the same. This brought the meeting alight and all members voted the Captain an instant success.

Captain Tommy Young had much pleasure in proposing Walter Kerr as his Vice-Captain for 1972/73. This was agreed by a majority vote.

Someone was heard to demand a recount – this was overruled.

ANY OTHER COMPETENT BUSINESS

It was proposed by J. Houston that the Stotters should entertain the Tain Team to lunch after the Sunday game – the idea being to continue the atmosphere of the match for a little longer than at present. This produced general discussion from the members in which opinion seemed to be equally divided for and against, and concluded in typical Stotters' fashion to take no decision and the matter was left in limbo – whatever that means.

In bringing the meeting to a close the Captain again thanked the Ladies for their help in setting up and attending to the Bar on the course.

There being no further business the Captain declared the meeting closed.

The fine on David Rutherford was rather strange as he can't have failed to appear at dinner on Sunday 2nd August as the day of the AGM was Sunday 30th July. The assumption is that the fine related to two year's previously in 1970 when Sunday was the 2nd August – but then again, who knows?

The Stotters – 1972 – Back Row – L to R – Roddy Mackenzie, Wilson Kemp, Sport, Walter Kerr, Dougie Torrance, Raeburn Robertson, Gilbert Tocher, Tommy Armstrong, Dr. John, Hammy Mitchell.

Front Row – L to R – Frank Cougan, Ian MacPherson, Tommy Young, Hamish Senior, David Rutherford

DINING AWAY FROM HOME

Forbie tells the story of dining away from home:

"I can't remember how it started, but I used to organise a meal out on the Monday night, laying on a bus for a 6 pm sharp pick-up at the front door of the Royal, taking Mrs Chalk with us as our guest which she looked on as a great treat.

One year we went to the "Cally" (Caledonian Hotel) in the "Port" (Portmahomack) where McManus looked after us very well and we had our drinks sitting out across the road overlooking the harbour. Then the next year it was to the Nigg Ferry Hotel where Peter Paterson also did us well and drinks again outside overlooking the Sutors (the two steep headlands marking the entrance to the Cromarty Firth; the northern one 151 metres high and the southern one 141 metres high – called "The Sutors" from an imagined resemblance to a couple of shoemakers (in Scots, *souters*) bent over their lasts).

But an outing with a difference was surely the one to a hotel above Culrain (north of Ardgay and Bonar Bridge) which involved taking a left turn opposite Culrain railway station and up the hill – I've seen better cart tracks!

Somehow the driver got us there – apparently the first time a bus had made it to the top – and we arrived safely. Fortunately there was enough room for it to turn for the return journey.

As we dismounted from the bus we were greeted by a thick-set man, in his 50s, dressed in a kilt, wearing full-sprung hill shoes, a heavy woollen jersey and, fore and aft, sporting a well-trimmed beard, reddish in colour.

We were ushered into a room where there were a few chairs, and a long rough finished sideboard on top of which was a stack of glasses. In the corner there were two shelves with various bottles, a big pitcher of peaty water and a notebook and pencil – an "honesty bar".

After we had a couple of drinks, a gong was sounded loudly just about deafening us, and we were led into another room where there was one long, rough finished table around which all 28 of us got seated comfortably. Everybody wondered what was next!

There was no menu as such. The man, his wife, and daughter all entered carrying large tureens of lovely homemade soup and ashets of pâté and homemade oatcakes. Jugs of water and bottles of wine were already on the table.

After this was cleared away, roasts of lamb, venison, beef and a whole salmon were laid on the sideboard with dishes of lovely vegetables put on the table. "Mine host" carved beautifully while his wife and daughter served with great skill. The main course was followed by cloutie dumpling, scotch trifle, fresh cream, ice cream, cheese and oatcakes. Finally, we had coffee, malt whisky, Drambuie and homemade shortbread.

Nothing fancy about this place but what an atmosphere and everything well cooked and served. A great, very enjoyable and very different night, fully deserving of the very nice tip we left".

While the Stotters enjoyed dining away from home, Florrie at the Royal Hotel – "the Aunt of the Stotters' children" – amused the children, and put them to bed.

There were also times when she probably put Ian MacPherson, Frank, and Hammie and a few others to bed after long nights!

This was not to be the last time the Stotters dined away from home.

Morangie House Hotel and Carnegie Lodge with The Wynne's great hospitality; and, in Portmahomack, The Castle Hotel and the Tee Up Café at the golf course, all welcoming (usually!) the Stotters en masse at various times during Golf Week.

On one of the occasions that the Castle was visited, as Frank remembers: "Dr. John was sitting at the bar when in walked Dods Mackay, one of Tain's renowned golfers and characters, whose hearing wasn't the best.

Dods said: "John Houston! How are you?" to which John jocularly replied: "Och I've got aids".

Dods replied: "Aye – I've aged masel!" "

On another occasion, Dr. John suggested to the Stotters that they go out after dinner for a wee dram. Before the breathalyser came on the scene, he drove 5 fellow Stotters, as Frank remembers: "In his clapped out Vauxhall Cresta," to a pub now long gone, up a steeply winding road. The car was full of cigarette smoke and chatter as the Stotters rattled onwards.

Suddenly they met a fast descending red Morris Cowley van.

Dr. John swerved to the left as did the van and they scraped past each other with a grinding screech of metal.

With chrome plating hanging off the car, the shout from the back seat rang out: "Keep going John!"

Both drivers did so, perhaps because the descending driver had just left the pub at the top of the hill, and the Stotters arrived safely to be poured their drams by a sour-faced Innkeeper who gazed bleakly at the half crowns tendered for their drams.

"Another close shave!" concludes Frank.

MINUTES OF THE 8TH GENERAL MEETING OF THE STOTTERS – SUNDAY AUGUST 5TH 1973

Held at the Royal Hotel, Tain.

The Seventh Match – the Stotters lost.
Mrs T. S. Young presented the Cup to Ian Anderson.

Captain T. S. Young in the chair.

All Stotters present with apologies from Frank Cougan and missing – Ian McColl.

MINUTES OF THE PREVIOUS MEETING

The minutes of the previous Meeting were read and disapproved and with great reluctance and amidst rising tensions were eventually signed by the Captain. He felt that the meeting would have to make it clear to the Secretary that at future meetings, because members didn't agree with his minutes, shouting 'get stuffed' and other rude words were to be deplored and not the Stotters' idea of conduct becoming a Secretary.

Before continuing with the Agenda, Captain Young felt it appropriate to pay tribute to Raeburn Robertson whose sudden death in May of this year had shocked us all.

Like Big Willie, Rae was a great competitor as well as a fine friend. Tain would not be quite the same again and he would be missed by us all. As a mark of respect Raeburn's name had been put on the seat at the 'Alps' beside Willie's.

Tommy Young thanked Ian MacPherson for attending to the plate. With glasses raised the Stotters downed a dram and prepared to tackle the agenda.

MATTERS ARISING FROM MINUTES

At the outset there was a delay – where was McColl?

The Captain felt this tendency of members to get lost before the AGM would have to stop – all agreed and downed another glass.

Once more to the Agenda.

Entertaining Tain Golf Club was John Houston's 'hobby horse' so once again off we went.

Alas, as usual there was little support for John's idea. There was a voice using dirty and four letter words and something to do with being a failure all his life, but the Secretary was unable to pinpoint the speaker and everyone else had their faces in glasses so it was agreed not to pursue the matter further.

The Captain drew the attention of the meeting to the fact that there was a vacancy in the membership and he therefore proposed our Associate Member, Wilson Kemp, to fill the vacancy. The proposal was moved by Gilbert Tocher, seconded by Ian Walkington and agreed unanimously by the members. With one accord the members held out the left hand of friendship to Wilson. They had empty glasses in their right hands and, of course, Wilson had the bottle.

Captain Young reported there was now a vacancy for an Associate Member and proposed Tommy Armstrong to fill the vacancy. A member, probably Mitchell, was heard to say at this juncture: "Never mind a proposer and seconder – we all agree – slap a tie round his neck and let him buy a round of drinks".

The Secretary, however, asked Hamish Robertson to move that Tommy Armstrong be admitted as an Associate, and this was seconded by Roddy Mackenzie. Agreed unanimously that Tommy was allowed to buy drinks.

CAPTAIN'S REPORT

Captain Young had nothing new to report on today's match. We got 'cuffed' again. God knows how we have tried, but this year failure once more. When asked the result of the match Captain Young could not remember and, as usual, the Secretary hadn't a clue. However it was felt the margin was not big and it had been a wonderful day.

Captain Young felt that some team trials should be carried out before next year or maybe pay some of the members to stay away. This remark didn't help much but in conclusion the Captain thanked all members for their support throughout his term of office.

ELECTION OF OFFICE BEARERS

Tommy Young is retiring from office and proposed Walter Kerr, the Secretary, at present Vice-Captain, for Captain 1973/74. This confused the meeting so Tommy tried again and a majority thought it would be OK.

Ian MacPherson then proposed Walter Kerr as Captain, seconded by J. Houston, and it was passed but not unanimously and, in a deadly silence, Walter Kerr took the Chair as Captain of the Stotters for 1973/74.

Because of the controversy over his election he refused to buy a drink but said he would do his best to uphold the dignity of the office. There continued to be a terrible silence. Captain Kerr congratulated the retiring Captain on his efforts on behalf of the Stotters and his successful year in office.

Amidst rising excitement and a hum of anticipation Captain Kerr proposed as Vice-Captain Hamilton Mitchell.

At this the meeting erupted.

Ian MacPherson quickly moved the proposal and equally as quickly was seconded by Hamish Robertson, and agreed unanimously with much cheering and shouting. Everyone prepared to retire to the bar and celebrate. However, the Secretary by threatening to fine everyone managed to call the meeting to order.

Ian McColl now joined the meeting and, quick as a flash, the Vice-Captain imposed a fine of 50p and would not accept any excuse.

The Captain thought it right to mention at this stage how disappointed we were that Frank Cougan could not make it this year and it was arranged to send him a postcard.

Our new Associate Member, as a mark of respect to the Stotters, proposed getting sports trousers made for members to be ready for next year's match provided he got the required measurements

At this proposal the meeting got completely out of hand. The Vice-Captain fined the following members: John Houston 5p; I MacPherson 10p; H Mitchell 10p; (how he fined himself I'll never know); and David Rutherford 5p.

Ian Walkington wanted the Secretary to be sacked for incompetence and failure to conduct the meeting properly and this was supported by Ian McColl still smarting over his fine. The Secretary in reply said it was the Captain's duty to conduct the meeting and not his.

R. F. Mackenzie asked who was going to take the inside leg measurements and the Vice-Captain fined him 5p for improper suggestions, and everyone agreed with Tommy's proposal but by this time Tommy was looking very apprehensive and sat, or rather fell down.

In bringing the meeting to some semblance of order the Captain thanked Tommy for his offer. All members were delighted. As everyone was by now terrified to open their mouth in case the Vice-Captain fined them, the Captain decided there being no further business to close the meeting.

Tommy Armstrong was a low handicap player who had become Captain of Turnberry GC during 1973 and continued his Captaincy until 1976. A slightly quiet though amusing character and of medium build, he loved a wee dram (no surprises there!).

Tommy was introduced to The Stotters by Hammie Mitchell who succeeded Tommy as Captain of Turnberry in 1976, serving 2 years in that role.

Tall and ruddy faced, Hammie was a Quarry Master and owner in Ayrshire. His strong bluff stern looks belied a man of charm, humour and warmth, with a very able drinking arm.

Hammy always came alone to Golf Week as his wife didn't keep good health and didn't appear to like golf. Despite this, he always appeared happy.

He was noted for mysteriously disappearing at times from social gatherings, an endearing Stotters' trait.

Bridget Ross – Ken Junior's wife – fondly remembers his kindness to her when she was pregnant, taking time to listen, talk and encourage.

MINUTES OF THE 9ᵀᴴ ANNUAL GENERAL MEETING OF THE STOTTERS – SUNDAY 4ᵀᴴ AUGUST 1974

Held at the Royal Hotel, Tain.

The Eighth Match – the Stotters won.
Miss Christina Young presented the cup to W. Kerr.

Captain Walter Kerr in the chair.

The AGM was due to start at 5pm, changed to 5.30 p.m. and probably started at 5.45 pm.

10 Stotters present (Ian MacPherson briefly) with T. S. Young in attendance.

Apologies from Ian Walkington.

Still missing – Ian McColl.

Before the Secretary could read the Minutes of the last AGM the Captain had great difficulty calling the meeting to order. J. Houston was taking the Lord's name in vain (this cost him 10p).

I. MacPherson was reported missing and was last seen in his bathing trunks heading for the local swimming pool chasing a couple of 'birds'.

H. Mitchell was hell-bent on going after him but was restrained and insisted that MacPherson be fined a 'fiver' when he returned. In the pandemonium that reigned it was only the Secretary threatening to resign and abandon the meeting that restored order and the following members were fined: J. Houston 10p; H. Mitchell 10p; J.G. Robertson 10p; R. F. Mackenzie 10p; Ian MacPherson to be decided.

MINUTES OF THE PREVIOUS MEETING

The Minutes of the last AGM were read, approved and signed by the Captain.

MATTERS ARISING FROM MINUTES

John Houston felt he must pursue his idea of entertaining Tain Golf Club after the Sunday game and the meeting reached boiling point once more. It had been agreed at the last meeting not to discuss this matter anymore and the majority of members were against it.

J. Houston was to be fined or buy a round of drinks but it was noticed that Houston had gone to sleep so drinks were ordered and it is unconfirmed as to whether these were charged to his account.

It was apparent that T. Armstrong, on being questioned, had done nothing about his suggestion to get trousers made for next year's game.

An altercation took place between the Vice-Captain and our new Associate Member and the rest of the meeting sat back. He was fined 10p for his lack of initiative and the members seemed to lose interest in the subject so the matter was put in abeyance.

CAPTAIN'S REPORT

The Captain (W. Kerr) reported that he had received instructions from the Secretary (W. Kerr) to be brief and he – the Captain- felt that this, coming from the finest Secretary the Stotters were ever liable to have, had to be adhered to. He promptly reprimanded W. Kemp for saying: 'Thank God' but he thanked all present and the other players we had incorporated into today's game for bringing home a victory.

A number of the members awoke at this time and congratulated each other in a manner not quite in keeping with the idea of the club. All seemed to lose their place at this stage and what followed is not really known.

The Captain remembered to thank Christina Young for accepting the cup on his behalf and also thanked the ladies for helping out at the Alps. Sadly, it had to be explained to some members, in reply to "what help?" – the reply was "the drink you fools"; and that they, the ladies, had served it to all and sundry.

In closing, the Captain thanked the Vice-Captain for his support not only today but throughout the year – each time they met they needed it – however today had passed off without incident.

The Captain asked members to spare a thought for Ian Walkington who because of affairs of state was unable to join them – whether he be in Nicosia or Kyrenia wasn't clear but R. Mackenzie was able to help by assuring all that he was in Cheltenham very much wrapped up in the Turkish/Cypriot war.

It was agreed to send the usual 'haste ye back' card and hoped that once he had settled the international situation he would be able to attend a much more important one – Tain Golf Week.

At this point MacPherson joined the meeting, properly dressed – if you consider bathing trunks and a towel 'nicked' from his bedroom as being properly dressed.

There was uproar, the Vice-Captain wanting to fine him a fiver but being told he wasn't Captain yet and he'd be fined himself if he didn't control himself. J.G. Robertson decided he'd been silent too long and decided he wanted to be heard. Gilbert Tocher asked what the row was all about and that drinks should be called for. Frank Cougan remarked that this was worse than 'bloody Ireland' and W. Kemp was heard to say out loud: 'how did I get involved with a shower like this?'

T. Armstrong was heard to shout at Houston: 'how could he ever have thought of supplying trousers to such a useless shower of ......'.

Finally the Secretary took control, reduced MacPherson's fine to £1 but thought an explanation might not be out of place. I'm afraid the explanation was so vague and garbled it was in effect no explanation. How the meeting accepted this was beyond me, writes the Secretary.

It was noted with satisfaction that Frank Cougan was able to be with the Stotters this year which was evident from the new shirts members had begged, borrowed or stolen from him but, this apart, everyone was glad to see him back.

J. Houston thought that as a gesture Frank should buy a drink. Asked what he meant by a gesture John replied with usual bedside manner: 'Any ...... gesture'.

However, someone pressed the bell and the Secretary asked Frank if he knew that he was taking a size 16 in shirts now.

ELECTION OF OFFICE BEARERS

Walter Kerr retires from office and proposed that Hamilton Mitchell, presently Vice-Captain, be elected Captain for 1974/75. Ian MacPherson objected for no better reason than having lost his lighter.

This once more brought heated discussion between the Captain elect and MacPherson; however order was restored and R. Mackenzie agreed to second the proposal. By a majority decision H. Mitchell was elected Captain of the Stotters for 1974/75.

This was met with many comments in coarse, hearty humour. In taking the chair Captain Mitchell thanked the members for their faith in electing him to this high office and he promptly fined T. Armstrong for remarking that 'faith had nothing to do with it.'

Captain Mitchell continued with the usual remarks, carrying out his duties etc. and went on to propose Gilbert Tocher as his Vice-Captain.

This was a popular choice with members on their feet shouting: 'Wake up Gilbert, your turn to buy a round', and Gilbert, bless his heart, agreed but it was left to J.G. Robertson, as always great on protocol due to his classical education, to point out that before Gilbert bought anything it gave him pleasure to second him as Vice-Captain, and before things became too complicated it was agreed unanimously – another record.

The Captain thanked Frank Cougan for supplying the sports shirts for today's game, all the members being happy to get a 'handout' as their stock of shirts was running low.

Frank suggested he might take over from T. Armstrong and get trousers for next year's match. The usual conversations regarding measurement of inside legs, etc. ensued.

Ian MacPherson was still demanding to know what had happened to his lighter – by this time he had the couch upside down, but this interruption brought strength from the new Captain and he fined MacPherson and threatened to have him ejected.

There was discussion, at length, introduced by T. Armstrong as to whether Stotters would be prepared to steward a hole during the Open at Turnberry in 1977.

Tommy would give members more information and explain what was involved. At this stage MacPherson came out from under the couch saying 'Ehh?'

Once more details were available the members agreed to consider his proposal next year.

The new Captain felt that something would have to be done about Ian McColl's absence as he had given no explanation as to why he had not turned up for these last two years. It was decided that the Secretary would write to him and ask him what his intentions were and the meeting was in agreement with this.

Unanimously decided that Doug Torrance become an Associate Member and Doug was asked to present himself before the members with tray in hand, loaded with drink, and for this little service he was presented with a tie.

In the process he nearly fell over MacPherson who was still looking for his lighter.

At this point the Captain was in full flight and took J.G. Robertson to task for making Forbie Urquhart an Associate 'out of the goodness of his heart or through drink'. He had no objection, far from it – he was delighted but as Captain he must insist that matters be conducted through the proper channels.

It was agreed that I. MacPherson would get the cup engraved with today's victory noted. He requested permission to put a base plate round the cup with the original Stotters' names on it, including Ann Chalk. This was agreed.

The meeting was closed, there being no further business.

Doug or Dougie Torrance was a dentist from Kilmacolm.

Walter Kerr and Ian MacPherson introduced him to Tain. Not noted for his golfing prowess, he loved the holiday and the company.

Doug was a bachelor, small, and balding with a healthy red complexion. He had a wicked sense of humour especially when whisky was involved, and was noted for going to Tain GC for a sandwich hoping he wouldn't spill it like he did his soup!

Forbie remembers: "He went to Dornoch for a day trip one year, got 'fu and couldn't remember where he was staying. The police got involved as he was "lost". He mentioned the Stotters and they said: "Ahh, it'll be the Royal in Tain".

MINUTES OF THE 10ᵀᴴ ANNUAL GENERAL MEETING OF THE STOTTERS – SUNDAY 3ᴿᴰ AUGUST 1975

Held at the Royal Hotel, Tain.

The Ninth Match – Stotters versus Tain Golf Club: the Stotters won.

Miss Christina Young accepted the Cup from Roy Mackenzie, Captain of Tain on behalf of Hamilton Mitchell.

Captain Hamilton Mitchell in the chair.

All Stotters in attendance – absent I. McColl.

Also in attendance T. Armstrong and D. Torrance – Associate Stotters.

Before opening the meeting Captain Mitchell expressed on behalf of all of the Stotters their deep regrets at the passing of Alan Robertson, our Pharmaceutical Advisor. His sudden death last year was a great shock to us all.

Despite his long struggle against ill health, Alan's cheerfulness, wit and love of life would remain as an inspiration to us all. He would be sadly missed.

MINUTES OF THE PREVIOUS MEETING

The Minutes of the AGM held on 4ᵗʰ August, 1974 were read, approved and signed by the Captain.

Before the meeting could get underway, T.S. Young raised a point of order which was – the legality of the meeting. This had never happened before and the members were completely at sea.

T.S. Young's point was that this meeting had been called for 5 p.m. and only he, Wilson Kemp and R.J. Mackenzie had appeared at the appointed time.

As it was now nearly 6 pm he felt the meeting should be abandoned and members retire to the bar as a lot of valuable drinking time had been lost and he was also thirsty.

The Captain promptly fined T.S. Young for making facetious statements but was ruled out of order as it was pointed out it was the Secretary's duty to see all were assembled at the proper time. The Captain then fined the Secretary who promptly tendered his resignation.

By now the meeting was completely out of hand so the Captain withdrew his fines and agreed that the practice of being late should cease and, if it happened again, action would be taken against the offenders. This was agreed unanimously and T.S. Young withdrew his complaint.

MATTERS ARISING FROM MINUTES

J. Houston felt a full turn-out of the Stotters at the Alps on the first Saturday evening in August to pay our respects to absent friends, should be carried out. Only he and Tommy Young made the effort this year.

It was pointed out to J. Houston from the Chair that it was a good job only two members attended because the mess of tyre tracks these two had left on the 18th fairway would remain as an eyesore for the rest of the week.

The excuse offered by Houston and Young was that they had got lost. How in the name of God they got lost and ended up on the 18th fairway was beyond anyone. The only conclusion the Captain could arrive at was that they were both drunk.

Gilbert Tocher felt the two members should have been breathalysed but despite all of this J. Houston demanded that all the Stotters appear for the ceremony. He and the Captain then had a long argument over the use of the word 'demanded' and it all ended without a decision being taken.

The Captain welcomed back Ian Walkington. He was delighted to see that at least one of the members was able to help solve an international situation instead of creating one. This was too deep for the rest of the members who were by now demanding an interval for drinks.

The Captain promptly fined Ian MacPherson, Hamish Robertson, R.J. Mackenzie and Frank Cougan for not addressing the meeting through the Chair. This brought silence, it being a new approach to running a meeting.

Frank Cougan intimated that he was negotiating to get new jerseys for next year's tournament and assured members this would cost them plenty this time.

Once more there was silence brought about over the question of cost, but smiles returned to members' faces when Wilson Kemp suggested there might be a discount.

But Cougan would not budge. It was going to cost us all plenty. It was with reluctance that the meeting agreed to let Frank carry on with the order.

The Secretary was asked what action had been taken as instructed at the last meeting about Ian McColl's membership, and when he replied – nothing – it was unanimously agreed the Secretary be sacked, fined or buy a round of drinks.

The Secretary ignored the resolution and it was eventually agreed to leave Ian McColl's membership in abeyance.

Ian MacPherson asked T. Armstrong, Captain of Turnberry, if he still wanted the Stotters to steward a hole at Turnberry in the 1977 Open. T. Armstrong did not recall asking the Stotters to do this. This didn't go down at all well.

MacPherson demanded a £5 fine on Armstrong who, in turn, appealed to the Captain who was not at all sympathetic and thought the fine should be larger. Houston was, once more, heard appealing to the Deity and Hamish Robertson was – for once – speechless.

Order was eventually restored when Armstrong was heard to apologise and he thought he had better buy a round of drinks and the angry members reluctantly returned to their seats pacified.

It was unanimously agreed that the Stotters would steward a hole at Turnberry with the following conditions: there would be free car parking; free meals and drinks with entry to the clubhouse; and the Captain of Turnberry might consider a free dinner in the evening in the Hotel. The Captain of Turnberry's reply is unprintable.

CAPTAIN'S REPORT

Before making his Report the Captain left the meeting and was immediately censured. MacPherson and Robertson felt he should be fined at least £10. At this point the Captain returned claiming immunity.

The Captain was delighted to report that he had led his side to victory against Tain today. He thought the conduct of the members was up to standard. He personally did not recall much of the events but he had a vague idea, remembering Tina Young accepting the cup on his behalf.

He trusted he had made a suitable speech. As none of the members had heard a word he said, it was agreed it must have been suitable. He thanked Florrie and the Stotters' wives and friends for dispensing drinks at the Alps. That, he the Captain, did remember, and altogether hoped everyone had enjoyed the day.

ELECTION OF OFFICE BEARERS

Mr. Mitchell had the pleasure of proposing Gilbert Tocher, at present Vice- Captain, to be Captain for 1976. This was seconded by J.G. Robertson and agreed unanimously by the members.

Captain Tocher in taking the chair thanked H. Mitchell for his fine efforts during his year of office, which did not seem to meet with the members' approval and it was with difficulty that the new Captain restored order. He appealed against the use of what he could only describe as 'appalling language' and asked members to respect the Chair.

This brought the members into line, as being asked to show respect to anything was new to them. Continuing, the Captain now came to the appointment of his Vice-Captain and had pleasure in proposing I. Walkington to fill the position. This was seconded by R. J. Mackenzie – agreed unanimously.

The members were so delighted at the selection of Vice-Captain that they called for the raising of the Stotters' flag, and raising of glasses that turned out to be empty and demanded that Ian press the bell and put matters right. This was duly done with much ceremony.

Captain Tocher was conscious of the high honour that had been placed upon him and would do his best, with the help of his Vice, to uphold the tradition set by his predecessor.

ANY OTHER COMPETENT BUSINESS

Hamish Robertson proposed – to fill the vacancy as Pharmaceutical Advisor caused by the death of Alan – that his son, David Robertson, be approached to take over this duty. This was seconded by Ian MacPherson and agreed unanimously.

Tommy Young asked the meeting to consider holding the AGM at 6.30 p.m. in future as it seemed impossible to get the Members out of bed and sobered up in time to attend a meeting at 5 p.m. The Captain asked for members' views on this and the response was tragic.

All sorts of rubbish were talked about and the Secretary, who was nearly asleep, had to be forced to pay attention and promptly then asked if the members would consider voting.

The Captain reminded the Secretary that he was in the Chair and that if anyone was going to ask for a vote on a motion he would do it.

Calling for a vote, Captain Tocher, after counting those for and against, came up with the result: For T. S. Young's motion – 4; Against – 17; which to say the least was impossible as there were only 11 members present.

Rather than have a recount it was agreed to hold the matter over.

J. Houston proposed that the next match against Tain should be a Greensomes instead of a 2-ball Foursome. There were so many members against this that Houston had to admit he was wrong again but felt that if he persisted he would eventually get one of his resolutions adopted.

The rest of the members had their doubts.

Never daunted, Houston tried again.

This time his resolution was that a full turnout of the Stotters make their way to the 10th tee on Saturday 31st July, 1976 before dinner, and have a dram at the seat, in memory of absent friends.

He even volunteered to polish the name plates. This was freely discussed but alas no decision was taken much to Houston's disappointment.

Ian MacPherson drew the meeting's attention to the present day value of the Rose Bowl.

He recalled that he and Hammy had purchased it on the Stotters' behalf in 1966 for £24.00. Its present day value, which he had received, was now £124 so it could be considered a good buy. This was agreed and despite calls of 'flog it' and 'melt it down', Ian thought the question of insurance be looked at. The Captain agreed that this was a valid point and as the Cup was always kept by Tain GC he thought this should be brought to their notice for consideration as they were bound to have insurance cover on the other club trophies.

There being no further business the Chairman declared the meeting closed.

The section in the Minutes about the Captain of Turnberry giving the Stotters preferential treatment at the Open in 1977 is significant of course, as Hammy Mitchell, the 1974/5 Stotters' Captain, was to be Captain of Turnberry in 1976/77.

The appointment of David Robertson as Hon. Pharmaceutical Advisor appears to have disappeared from the Stollers' annals – unsurprisingly, as David was not a golfer. He took over from his father running the David A Ross & Co. Chemist's shop, no small task considering Alan's local reputation.

On one occasion in the early 1970s The Sunday Post ran a centre-page human interest story of an American who sent Alan a postcard.

Addressed only to:

Shake

Tain

Shake denoted the Chemist nickname: "shake the bottle".

It duly arrived 2 weeks after posting!

MINUTES OF THE 11ᵀᴴ ANNUAL GENERAL MEETING OF THE STOTTERS – SUNDAY 1ˢᵀ AUGUST 1976

Held at the Royal Hotel, Tain.

Captain Gilbert Tocher in the chair.

The Tenth Match result – the Stotters won.
Captain Tocher accepted the cup from Captain Urquhart.
The cup then being duly filled and emptied in the accepted style.

Present: Ten Stotters.
In attendance: Messrs T. Armstrong and D. Torrance.

APOLOGIES

The Secretary intimated that apologies for absence had been received from the Vice-Captain, Ian Walkington. As was to be expected, this news was received in stony silence until it dawned on members what had happened, and in the resulting unseemly outburst members quite forgot themselves to such an extent that the Captain adjourned the meeting for refreshments.

In re-convening the meeting it was agreed that the absent Vice-Captain be fined the substantial amount of £5 plus God knows how many drinks.

MINUTES OF THE PREVIOUS MEETING

The Minutes of the AGM held on the 3ʳᵈ August, 1975 in the Royal Hotel, Tain were read, not approved and signed reluctantly by the Captain.

MATTERS ARISING FROM MINUTES

The Captain was delighted to see that members had made the effort to be in time for the AGM after last year's protests from T.S. Young because he was kept hanging about. The members present all looked blank about this because they hadn't a clue what the Captain was on about.

The Captain reported that all members, with the exception of one, had reported at the Alps on Friday evening for the polishing ceremony as proposed by J. Houston last year.

To the demands of the members as to who was the missing member the Captain admitted – it was himself.

When order had been restored Hamish Robertson rose to his feet to admit that he had also missed the ceremony whereupon J. Houston, in his usual eloquent manner, demanded both members be fined £1.

Both the Captain and H. Robertson refused to pay on the grounds of victimisation and once more, in the ensuing uproar, the meeting was adjourned for a short interval.

Suitably refreshed, the Captain reconvened the meeting and both he and Hamish agreed to pay the fine.

The Captain thanked F. Cougan for providing new pullovers and, on advising the members of the cost, the atmosphere again became tense.

Both Wilson Kemp and R. Mackenzie were heard to demand that this should go to the Pricing Commission but eventually members agreed that Frank had done us proud and paid up.

Vacancy – as Ian McColl had withdrawn as an active member of the Stotters a vacancy now existed and the Secretary asked members for their views on the subject, and promptly wished he had not bothered!

But slowly, ever so slowly, it appeared that T. Armstrong would be invited to fill the vacancy.

Electing new members is never taken lightly by the Stotters as all kinds of pros and cons, too numerous to mention, are gone into.

Eventually Captain Tocher made a proposal that T. Armstrong be invited to become a member of the Stotters and this was seconded by Ian MacPherson and agreed unanimously with Messrs. Houston, Mackenzie and Mitchell giving a standing ovation. Their idea of a standing ovation was an empty glass in their hands, shouting 'Fill them'.

This the new member did and there was a short and happy interval for refreshments.

Revived, the members went on to discuss the Open at Turnberry next year.

Ian MacPherson offered the services of the members of Kilmacolm Golf Club to steward a hole, provided it was the 18th at a point near, if not in the clubhouse. This, T. Armstrong, endearing himself to the meeting, said was impossible or to quote his exact words: 'Not bloody likely'.

H. Mitchell, not to be outdone, said he was not prepared to provide free car park passes, free entry tickets to the course or club house and certainly no drinks to any of the Stotters coming to the Open.

Without hesitation at this remark Captain Tocher adjourned the meeting, thus preventing a riot.

Eventually, after order was restored, all the members wished Hamilton and Tommy all success with the Open albeit without much enthusiasm.

CAPTAIN'S REPORT

Captain Tocher thanked the members for their support during his year of office. He was sorry Ian Walkington could not be with us but he was prepared, at least, to be charitable and forgive him. He was glad to have captained yet another winning team and, in asking the Secretary for the final result of today's match, was shocked to hear, once more, that he did not know.

Undaunted, Gilbert then asked the Secretary for a financial report and to his surprise was told that he had one to give, whereupon the Captain called upon the Secretary to give the financial report.

The Secretary said it would be brief.

In short, 'we were skint'.

Whereupon the Secretary was immediately fined 50p for being facetious and he promptly resigned, and not for the first time at this meeting uproar broke out. Rising to his feet R. F. Mackenzie suggested we might retire for dinner as by now he was not only hungry but very thirsty, but Hamish Robertson pointed out that we were still awaiting the completion of the Captain's Report.

Captain Tocher, still retaining his dignity, continued by thanking the ladies for once more attending to our needs at the Alps.

At this point J. Houston interrupted by asking the Captain to enlarge on the term 'attending to our needs', and before the Captain could reply H. Mitchell gave J. Houston a suitable answer in his usual charming manner.

In conclusion Captain Tocher thanked F. Cougan for acting on behalf of the absent Vice-Captain today.

ELECTION OF OFFICE BEARERS

Captain Tocher had much pleasure in proposing F. Cougan as Captain for the 1977 season. This was seconded by Wilson Kemp and approved unanimously. Captain Cougan, in taking the chair, thanked the retiring Captain for his efforts during his year of office and he hoped that he would be able to carry on in the same tradition.

At this point R. F. Mackenzie, still insisting he was thirsty, said it was high time the new Captain stood a bloody drink.

After a short interval Captain Cougan proposed Ian Walkington as Vice-Captain for 1977. At this, points of order flew about and it took the calming influence of the Secretary to remind members that we had no bloody constitution, and to elect Ian as Vice-Captain in his absence, and to get on with it.

Whereupon T.S. Young seconded the Captain's proposal and it was carried unanimously.

ANY OTHER COMPETENT BUSINESS

The Captain drew members' attention to a strange request that had filtered back from Tain Golf Club during the year – that perhaps there was too much drink being consumed on the course during the annual match, and if this could be cut out, more support for the match would come from the Tain members.

It had therefore been agreed by the Stotters during the year, with reservations, to agree to this and Captain Urquhart had been duly informed. But after today's game a peculiar situation had arisen.

The Stotters finished the match sober and Tain finished it 'plastered'.

The Captain, in light of this, asked members for their views as to future tactics. Unfortunately for him, the members having finished the match sober, had made up for lost time and were incapable of making a decision. So the matter was held over.

J. Houston wished the new Captain every success in his year of office and took the opportunity of making a proposal which he had made last year, and like all his last proposals had been thrown out, which was that the annual match be played as a Greensomes.

Now it must go on record that for the first time in the history of the club R. J. Mackenzie agreed, and seconded J. Houston's proposal.

Houston was speechless and furthermore it was agreed unanimously.

It must further go on record that never had a Stotters' meeting ended in such harmony, not only agreeing to John's proposal but agreeing the Captain should arrange this.

Thanking the Captain for chairing the meeting all retired to the bar tired and happy.

It is evident that, through the years since inception, at least two personal themes emerge repeatedly.

One is that Walter Kerr was a (tongue-in-cheek) reluctant Secretary who consistently tried to resign, and who consistently was refused this option.

The second is Dr John's series of proposals which – perversely – the Stotters always refused to accept – until now!

His proposal to adopt a Greensomes format has remained extremely successful through the succeeding years.

Frank Cougan is convinced that the main reason for the change was to give both sides two chances of playing off the first tee, given the vagaries of early Sunday morning 1ˢᵗ Tee drives.

MISS WORLD IN THE CLUBHOUSE --1976

In 1976, for entertainment, Forbie suggested a Miss World Competition, having taken part in a similar event (as Miss Havana) while on holiday in Corfu just before Golf Week.

Tina Urquhart, Tommy Young's daughter remembers this as "an amazing night".

There was a panel of judges made up of Hamish Robertson's wife Helen (representing the Stotters), Alistair Fleming (Tain GC) and Big Fred McLennan (Stornoway); and as Club Entertainments Convener, it was Forbie's job to compere the show.

Unfortunately, he had managed to break his ankle taking part in the Corfu hotel version, and was on crutches with his leg in plaster.

However: "The show must go on," and he managed to get into his dinner suit to look the part.

A fine bevy of beauties had entered the competition, all eager to win the coveted title of "Miss World" – Tain style. The line-up was:

Miss Switzerland – Tommy Young – clad in clogs, tights, short skirt, cute bonnet, and a frilly apron.

Miss Abbi Dabbi – Walter Kerr – bare legs & feet, Arab jellaba, rope head dress and chiffon over his face.

Miss Hawaii – Ian MacPherson – grass skirt and head dress, with two oranges in a brassiere.

Miss Bogside – Frank Coggan – Lyle stockings, floral overall and scarf, complete with fag in side of mouth.

Miss Carriage – Dr. John – in pram, wearing baby hat and nappy with large safety pin and sporting dummy in his mouth, plus crying toy.

Two Tain characters – Martin Ryan and Davie "Chimp" Ross;

And two Stornoway lads also took part.

Forbie describes the carnage which ensued:

"We had a very fine organist to play the music of the country each beauty represented, as they paraded round the "arena", and who played them off after answering the judges' questions.

As you can imagine some of the questions and answers were hilarious. Last one on was Dr John who brought the house down especially when his pram broke a spring before leaving the arena!

After the finale of the prize giving, Dr. John took me to the bar, bought me a drink and got me comfortable on my crutches with glass in hand.

He then called for silence and began, in his "down in his boots" voice: "We cannot let this successful night's entertainment pass without thanking the compere and organiser of it all etc., etc".

He rambled on and on, finally shaking me by my free hand, whereupon he took the jug of water from the bar behind me and poured it down my trousers!"

Martin Ryan, 40 years later, remembers that he was the winner – as Miss Christmas Island.

"I can't remember much more, other than that strong drink was involved!"

And the night was clearly traumatic for fag-in-mouth Frank Cougan as he stopped smoking the following year.

Miss World – Frank (Miss Bogside) and Forbie.

Miss World – Tommy Young as Miss Switzerland leads the parade with Miss Bogside bringing up the rear.

MINUTES OF THE 12ᵀᴴ ANNUAL GENERAL MEETING OF THE STOTTERS – SUNDAY 31ˢᵀ JULY 1977

Held at the Royal Hotel, Tain.

The Eleventh Match – the Stotters v Tain Golf Club – the Stotters won (the margin in dispute).

Captain Frank Cougan accepted the cup from Captain Urquhart and the scene was quite undignified as the pair of them were far from sober.

Captain Frank Cougan in the chair.

Seven Stotters present.

APOLOGIES

The Secretary intimated he had received apologies for absence from the following – Messrs. H. Mitchell, R. J. Mackenzie, Ian Walkington and Gilbert Tocher.

MINUTES OF THE PREVIOUS MEETING

The Minutes of the Meeting held on the 1ˢᵗ August 1976 were read, approved and should have been signed by the Captain but he was at this stage involved in arguments with the members over the absences; and before the Captain could sort himself out T. Armstrong proposed a vote of thanks to the Secretary for reading the Minutes so successfully which was seconded by T. S. Young, naturally much to the Secretary's delight but not to the Captain's, and in the ensuing uproar it was never made clear if the meeting approved this proposal or not.

CAPTAIN'S REPORT

At last Captain Cougan got a grip on the meeting and right away proposed that all the absentees be fined £1 except H. Mitchell. In his case the fine should be £3.

The Secretary pointed out to the Captain that if he had listened to the Secretary's remarks he would have realised apologies had been received from all concerned. The Captain promptly fined the Secretary 50p for being facetious whereupon the Secretary resigned. As nobody knew what to do next W. Kemp pressed the bell and ordered drinks.

This naturally, as always, restored peace.

The Captain continued to press for a vote on his proposal but never to be quiet for long, H. Robertson put forward a counter proposal – not to fine the absent members, and was promptly fined 50p by the Captain for no good reason.

The meeting however carried H. Robertson's proposal unanimously and in the jubilation that followed no-one bothered about the Secretary and his resignation, and the meeting continued.

However, it was noticed that members were not keen to catch the Captain's eye as he was in a fining mood. In fact, this was going to be the 'Year of the Fines' and also the year that the 'Troubles Came to Tain'.

The rest of the Captain's report was taken up by a series of fines and are as follows:

To every member who failed to wear the official shirt for Sunday's match – fine £1. Caught in this net were W. Kerr and I. MacPherson. At this, MacPherson was just caught at the door and brought back protesting that he was sure the Secretary had 'nicked his shirt' and he was 'only going to check'.

The Secretary simply ignored his remarks and the fines stood.

Ian MacPherson, by this time in a really happy mood, proposed that mine host – D. Rutherford – who incidentally had gone missing – be fined £1 for not engraving the Cup as promised. This was seconded by T.S. Young.

At this point T. Armstrong, who had fallen asleep, awoke saying: 'Who's filling the Cup?'

The members thought this was a good idea, and it was with difficulty that the Captain eventually got unanimous approval for the original proposal.

How the fine was to be collected was never cleared up.

J. Houston and H. Robertson brought the meeting to a halt over the question of drink.

Houston maintained that he had been waiting for over 23 minutes for a drink from Robertson who rejected this statement and, as would be expected, an argument broke out.

But quick as a flash the Captain 'nailed' them both by fining them £1 each for diverting the course of the meeting, later reducing the fine to 50p muttering something about 'respect for senior citizens'.

The following members were fined 50p for not attending the Seat Polishing ceremony on Friday evening: W. Kerr, I. MacPherson, T. S. Young, H. Robertson and T. Armstrong, and a further fine was made on W. Kemp who had attended the ceremony but, in the Captain's opinion, had not polished the seat properly, and this included Scott Ferguson, who was not even a member and who, at this point, took it upon himself to address the meeting and had to be forcibly restrained, not understanding the Captain's rough justice.

As expected this took a long time to sort out but in the end the fines were paid much to J. Houston's delight.

A fine on the Captain of £1 was proposed unanimously by all the members for 'buggering about'. A further fine of 50p to J. Houston for trying to reduce the Captain's fine to 50p. This restored a lot of the members' confidence.

T. Armstrong rose to his feet and proposed a vote of no confidence in the Captain. This was immediately vetoed by the Captain who fined T. Armstrong 50p for speaking out of turn and not addressing the meeting through the Chair.

By unanimous decision J. Houston was fined 50p for leaving the room without permission – he was fined at the same time as above.

The Captain then decided to fine Ian MacPherson 50p for holding up the proceedings.

T. S. Young was fined 50p for complaining that members no longer wore the Stotters' badge on their riding habit.

By this time the Captain and the members were exhausted.

As stated at the outset this was proposed as the 'Year of the Fines' and the 'Troubles', but in conclusion the Captain's proposal was agreed unanimously and the fines were collected to go a favourite kid's charity; and then, more as an afterthought, he fined T. Armstrong 50p for not attending the Team Trial in the Spring at Kilmacolm.

The Captain thought fit to have it put on record that the only proposal J. Houston had ever managed to get the members to agree to, namely that the Sunday match played against Tain should take the form of a Greensomes, had proved to be a great success.

With this all agreed and Houston was speechless.

As always the Captain proposed a vote of thanks to the ladies for looking after the Bar at the Alps. This was agreed unanimously.

This concluded the Captain's Report such as it was, and he thanked the members for their support throughout the year and particularly as he had to do without the services of his Vice-Captain, but had been ably supported by Wilson Kemp who had stepped into the breach.

APPOINTMENT OF OFFICE BEARERS

Captain Cougan had much pleasure in proposing Wilson Kemp to be Captain for 1978. This was seconded by Ian MacPherson and agreed unanimously. Wilson Kemp, accepting office, made the usual foolish statements that all previous Captains of the Stotters have made; i.e., to uphold the dignity of the Club etc.

But he quickly got the members' attention by simply producing a bottle of whisky and one could hear remarks being bandied about like: 'this looks like the best Captain we have ever had'.

H. Robertson proposed a vote of thanks to the retiring Captain for chairing the meeting. This was greeted with silence.

After this interruption by H. Robertson, Captain Kemp now took over the chair and thanked the retiring Captain for his efforts during a difficult year. He had much pleasure in proposing T. Armstrong as Vice-Captain for the ensuing year. This was seconded by J. Houston and agreed unanimously. Ian MacPherson wished both Wilson and Tommy every success in the coming year, and then collapsed.

It was proposed by Captain Kemp, and seconded by W. Kerr, that Scott Ferguson be admitted to the Stotters as an Associate. This was agreed unanimously and Scott was duly presented with a tie.

Unfortunately Scott thought fit to address the meeting, but received the usual treatment given to members when such an occurrence takes place – namely: 'Sit down and buy a round of drinks'.

This was duly done.

There being no further business the Captain declared the meeting closed despite difficulty from Houston who wanted a motion discussed about drinking on the course and as usual no-one paid a blind bit of attention.

Scott Ferguson makes his Stotters' debut this year.

Having gone to school with Wilson Kemp, he was his golf partner.

An Educationalist, Scott was headmaster of Limerigg Primary School then Laurieston Primary and latterly Bantaskin Primary in Falkirk before retirement.

He and his wife Christine, with their son Ian, used to holiday in Buchanhaven (Peterhead) during the second week in August, and Wilson suggested to Scott that they come to Tain for Golf Week before going on to Buchanhaven.

The Fergusons subsequently caravanned at Portmahomack with Wilson and Rita year after year.

Scott was dapper and dark haired, sporting a miniature Turkish-style moustache and eyebrows. After one AGM he was put to bed as per the norm (!) and Pat Houston and Rita decided to go upstairs and shave a chunk of his moustache off!

He was an outgoing friendly character, with a beautiful singing voice. He and Wilson sang "My Brother Sylveste" every year, in the style of Little and Large, who had performed it as a comedy duet.

See Appendix 1 for the words of this classic Irish song, penned by an unknown songwriter.

He tried and tried to qualify for the match play stages of Golf Week, but Simon Houston remembers – as his caddy – that he never quite made it.

Scott inevitably fell asleep during almost every Stotters' AGM, and also achieved infamy for running through The Royal in his underpants after most meetings.

MINUTES OF THE 13TH ANNUAL GENERAL MEETING OF THE STOTTERS – SUNDAY 30TH JULY 1978

Held at the Royal Hotel, Tain.

The Twelfth Match – the Stotters v Tain Golf Club – the Stotters won (the margin was once more in dispute).

Captain W. Kemp accepted the Cup from Captain John Urquhart amidst the usual cat calls and boos from the assembled company.

Captain Wilson Kemp in the chair.

Present: All Stotters including I. MacPherson (from his bed of pain) and Scott Ferguson and J. Campbell in attendance.

APOLOGIES

The Secretary intimated, after a great deal of needless prompting, that he had received apologies from R. F. Mackenzie and I. Walkington.

MINUTES OF THE PREVIOUS MEETING

The Minutes of the last AGM held on 31st July 1977 were read, with a great many interruptions from members who seemed disenchanted with the Secretary; approved; and as usual ignored by the Captain.

CAPTAIN'S REPORT

Captain Kemp in his opening remarks, asked members to be upstanding which, at this stage, was impossible; fill their glasses – which resulted in an unholy scramble; and to drink a toast to absent friends, and in particular to Roddy Mackenzie who was having a rough time recovering from his operation.

Now there is nothing like a sentimental toast of this nature to set the Stotters off in all kinds of directions, but arising from all this verbal garbage it was proposed, in their usual generous manner to send Roddy and Helen a postcard wishing them well.

Captain Kemp drew the meeting's attention to the absence, once more, of Ian Walkington.

Immediately a change of scene, back to their old ways – muttering and points of order – demands for his resignation, all quite unseemly and undignified, and in the end it took all Captain Kemp's charm and ability to keep the meeting in order.

God knows how many persons were fined. It appears everyone present was fined £1. Incidentally it should be noted that before the meeting finished the fines amounted to £17 – an all-time record.

Back to the Meeting – the attitude of the members so incensed the Secretary that he lost the place and pointed out that Ian Walkington was the only member who had shown any respect for him and was the only Stotter to have written to the Secretary regretting his inability to attend.

Captain Kemp fined the Secretary £1 for not addressing the company through the Chair and for seeking self-glorification by making such statements in front of members.

The Captain congratulated Ian MacPherson on coming through his operation successfully and then fined J. Houston for making some offensive remark. He also fined H. Mitchell £1 for carrying on a conversation with Houston whilst he was addressing the meeting.

The Captain thanked the members for their support in today's match.

While the result was always in dispute, the fact that we had won the Cup was enough for him. J. Houston felt that it was intolerable that year after year no-one was ever sure of the score and he called for a vote of censure on the Secretary for not recording the results properly.

This was seconded by T. Armstrong, whereupon the Secretary immediately resigned.

The Captain fined Houston and Armstrong £1 each for conducting a vendetta against the Secretary but agreed that the Secretary was lacking in his duty and fined the Secretary £1 for resigning.

Fortunately for everyone concerned, Scott Ferguson decided to speak and was fined £1 for so doing, the Captain pointing out that as an Associate he was not allowed to make comments.

The usual rumpus ensued and by the time everyone calmed down the Secretary episode had been forgotten.

The Captain thanked F. Cougan for providing new pullovers and shirts and thought this was the best turned out Stotters' team to have played at Tain. This cut no ice with Frank for he asked members for £8 each for the pullovers.

What a transformation took place! Even Gilbert woke up.

Ian MacPherson suggested that the cost be defrayed out of the Stotters' fund to which the Secretary replied: 'What fund?'

A demand for a financial statement also evoked the same response from the Secretary.

A short adjournment for drinks calmed everyone down and it was agreed that each member would stump up the £8.

The Secretary informed members that Dr Roy Mackenzie had personally restored the seat to its former glory, and as this had entailed a great deal of hard work it would be fitting if the Stotters presented Dr Roy with a small token of their esteem for his work. It was also noted that the seat was now situated at the Clubhouse.

This led J. Houston on to his annual crusade regarding the ceremony at the seat. It was not clear from his remarks whether anyone had attended this year but he was as usual keen to fine everyone.

The members asked if Tain could be approached to put the seat on the 17th tee which would cut out the long trek out to the Alps and might prevent some of the disasters of previous years, i.e. T. Young and J. Houston driving a car down the middle of the 18th fairway, getting bogged down, and leaving tyre marks there for the rest of Tournament Week.

In conclusion the Captain thanked members for support during his term of office, the ladies attending to the bar at the 11th which for many is the highlight of the game, whilst to others it is the 'kiss of death'.

At this point Ian MacPherson thought it was time everyone had a drink and encouraged by all, made it to the bell, and everyone at last relaxed.

APPOINTMENT OF OFFICE BEARERS

Wilson Kemp had much pleasure in proposing T. Armstrong as Captain for 1979. T. S. Young seconded the proposal and this was carried unanimously,

H. Mitchell being caught unawares as his face was buried in a glass.

T. Armstrong, in accepting office, felt that there was little doubt that he would bring dignity and decorum to the Captaincy which he felt had been lacking in past Captains.

Before the members could gather their wits, he proposed that Ian Walkington, in his absence, be appointed Vice-Captain, which Gilbert Tocher, still in a daze, seconded and then all hell broke loose.

Having been promised another drink by the Captain, the members agreed to the Captain's proposal and Ian Walkington was appointed Vice-Captain.

Captain Armstrong, before closing the meeting, raised the question of our annual match with Tain in light of the Sunday Tournament which had started this year, resulting in the Stotters' match being played between the 1st and 2nd rounds of the event.

As he could see problems in the future, he wondered what the feelings of the members were on this matter. There followed a full and frank discussion on the question in which a number of alternatives were put forward, but in the end it was agreed to leave any decision on the matter to Tain Golf Club.

There being no further business the Captain drew the meeting to a close with a vote of thanks to W. Kemp for handling the earlier stormy part of the meeting with his usual aplomb.

This Meeting was one of the stormiest in Stotters' history as the record £17 worth of fines indicates. It is also the precursor to the change in venue for the match which the Sunday Tournament precipitated.

MINUTES OF THE 14TH ANNUAL GENERAL MEETING OF THE STOTTERS – SUNDAY 3RD AUGUST 1979

Held at the Royal Hotel, Tain.

The Thirteenth Annual Match – The Stotters v Tain Golf Club – the Stotters won the trophy on a split decision.

Captain Armstrong accepted the cup from Captain Urquhart and made his usual polished speech which nobody listened to.

Captain Tommy Armstrong in the chair.

Present – All Stotters, except that apologies for absence had been received from F. Cougan.

In attendance S. Ferguson and J. Campbell.

MINUTES OF THE PREVIOUS MEETING

The minutes of the AGM held on 31st July 1978 were read and eventually approved after what the Secretary termed 'harassment'; not signed by the

Captain as he claimed that he had not made all the outrageous statements attributed to him; and for the 13th time the Secretary resigned.

While order was being restored Ian MacPherson complained about the lack of drink and was promptly supported by J. G. Robertson who proposed a vote of censure on the Captain because – as he and MacPherson had travelled from Portmahomack – they should not be subjected to such treatment.

Eventually the Captain calmed the two gentlemen by ordering refreshments. The vote of censure was withdrawn and the Secretary was told to 'get on with it and not be bloody stupid'.

CAPTAIN'S REPORT

Captain Armstrong, at the outset, felt that the members would wish to pay tribute to Gilbert Tocher, whose sudden death in the spring of the year had come as a shock to everyone.

Gilbert, a founder member of the Stotters, had been a friend to all of us.

No words could convey the high esteem in which he was held and he would be greatly missed. Mary, Gilbert's wife, had written to the Secretary offering a trophy to be played for annually by the Stotters and a cheque for £15.00 to buy the members a drink or use it as they saw fit.

Hamish Robertson had brought the trophy to Tain, a delightful thistle-shaped cup, and the Captain felt an appropriate name would be 'Gilbert's Goblet'. This was agreed unanimously and the Secretary was asked to write to Mary expressing the members' appreciation of her gesture.

In conclusion the members agreed that the lowest score on Monday's tournament round would be declared the winner of Gilbert's Goblet.

One feels that Gilbert would have been highly amused at the various ideas which were put forward by members on how to compete for his trophy.

Captain Armstrong, continuing, felt sure he spoke for everyone in expressing our regret that F. Cougan could not make Tain this year due to illness and asked that a message be sent to Belfast conveying our best wishes.

Houston wanted to add a 'wee note' about shirts, as he had always relied on Frank to keep his stock up declaring that 'Cougan's shirts were better than the ones he had been forced to get at Oxfam this year'.

R. F. Mackenzie took a poor view of this as he was sure Frank would have more on his mind than shirts at this moment but was forced to agree that the shirt auction would be missed.

Reporting on the Match against Tain, which was once more reduced to 14 holes and played in appalling weather, the Captain felt that the Stotters had put up a fair performance considering the conditions.

At this, Scott Ferguson, despite being told again that he had no voice as an Associate, ignored everyone and asked: 'Where the hell is Ian Walkington – Vice-Captain?'

At this H Mitchell asked the Secretary: 'What was he up to, and had he forgotten to read out an apology for absence?'

The Secretary replied: 'I never got one' and was promptly decried by W. Kemp and R. F. Mackenzie. At this point the meeting once again disintegrated into a shambles.

Ian MacPherson did not help matters by declaring that he always knew that the Secretary was 'a bloody failure'; and John Campbell, a dazed look on his face, asked the Captain if this was how Stotters' meetings were normally conducted whereupon the Captain said 'yes' and fined the following members:-

S. Ferguson for talking and starting the rumpus.

H. Mitchell for aiding and abetting.

R. F. Mackenzie and W. Kemp for doubting the Secretary, although Captain Armstrong felt they had some grounds for so doing.

Ian MacPherson for putting the meeting into chaos.

John Campbell for not being any help.

J.G. Robertson for being silent.

J. Houston for complaining too much.

T. Young for going on about Walkington.

- And finally, the Secretary for incompetence.

All were fined £1.

When order was restored the Captain continued with his Report – he felt that the future of the Sunday match was more than ever in doubt because of the one day competitions still being held over Saturday and Sunday and asked for members' views on this.

This was a mistake … for what followed was completely incomprehensible and impossible to minute. Seeing he was getting nowhere the Captain decided to pause for drinks and, as has happened in the past, the Meeting settled down to business as soon as drink was supplied.

The Captain, having got no help from members as to the future of the annual match, gave up and suggested leaving it to next year's Captain to sort out. This just made matters worse.

Between Ian MacPherson wanting to melt down the cup for money, and at the same time, threatening to tell Tain Golf Club to stick their empire where the sun don't shine, and Houston wanting to invite the Walker Cup team to play us, resulted in the whole meeting becoming bogged down and it was only saved from complete disarray by the Captain announcing that he had concluded his Report.

ELECTION OF OFFICE BEARERS

The Captain thanked the members for their usual non co-operation during his term of office and was hurt that no-one had had the decency to thank him for arranging our very successful team trial over Western Gailes – whereupon T. S. Young cast doubt on this by asking: 'Who had come up with a trophy for the Spring Meeting? – Wilson Kemp'.

MacPherson then asked: 'Who had won the b----- thing?'

No one could remember, but the Secretary, ever alert, said it had been won by MacPherson and Kerr.

R. F. Mackenzie, rising somewhat unsteadily to his feet, proposed a vote of thanks for Wilson for providing 'The Hic-Cup' and implored the Captain to speed up the meeting.

At this Captain Armstrong proposed J. Houston as Captain for the incoming year, and there being no seconders, promptly declared that J. Houston was elected.

Houston, on accepting office and judging the feeling of the meeting to a nicety, forgot to elect a Vice-Captain, or if he did, the Secretary can't remember who it was.

Captain Houston thought fit to address the Meeting in his usual erudite manner but once more failed miserably.

As soon as he opened his mouth MacPherson was threatening him with all sorts of dire consequences if he didn't get the Tain problem sorted out. Order was only restored when he asked the members to consider filling the vacancies caused by:

1) Gilbert's unfortunate death.

2) The unanimous conclusion that Ian Walkington would not be likely to appear again during Tain week.

He proposed that S. Ferguson and J. Campbell be elected as full Stotters. The proposal was carried unanimously whereupon Scott got to his feet saying: 'I would like' -- only to be told by the Captain to: 'Sit down Scott – you've said enough'.

John Campbell, still looking dazed, remarked that he could not make head or tail of any of this – with which the Captain agreed.

ANY OTHER COMPETENT BUSINESS

T. Armstrong asked the Captain to accept his resignation from the Stotters and for once Captain Houston was at a loss for words. The resignation was accepted with regret.

There being no further business the meeting was closed.

1979 was something of a landmark year.

Gilbert's sad demise was part of this, noted as he was for saying, on more than one occasion: "I'll stay up drinking until I fall over!" – and once, when at the burn at the 17th, he tried to retrieve his ball from the water – and ended up in it himself.

The Tommy Armstrong resignation was unique, and there is a lingering suspicion that this may have had something to do with some form of confrontation with Hammy Mitchell, and the perceived lack of appreciation for his organising Stotters' team trials.

As well as the appearance of Gilbert's Goblet, the Hic-Cup emerges thanks to the munificence of Wilson Kemp. It was introduced for the Stotters' Spring Meeting which was played initially at Kilmacolm, with the winning pair getting the cup.

The Stotters referred to the meeting as the Spring 'trials' before the team was picked for Golf Week. Given there were only 12 Stotters it has to be said that team selection was something of a foregone conclusion!

John Campbell, a tall, quiet dark-haired character, was a banker and Sheena Gillies' brother.

Sheena and her husband Bill used to holiday in a cottage in Tain which they rented from a Dr. McTaggart who lived in Balintore. In the early 70s they brought John up, and he stayed in the Mansfield Castle Hotel.

That year, he played with Ken Galloway from the Stornoway contingent, and became a regular visitor, whilst Dr. McTaggart played with one of the Robertson brothers; and through this connection John met and mingled with the Stotters.

As a very good golfer (playing off 2/3), he always qualified for the knock-out stages of Golf Week and with his fabulously dry sense of humour, he was a natural fit with the Stotters.

Forbie beat him at the 18th in an early round of the Stirling Cup, and felt "real chuffed!"

John was President of Glenbervie Golf Club where John Panton was Club Professional for over 40 years, John being a 3-times Ryder Cup player, who in 1967 famously beat the legendary Sam Snead to become World Seniors Champion.

He only once brought his very stylish wife to Tain but unusually (!) she seemed not to enjoy Golf Week.

Sport was not at 1979's AGM.

Hugh remembers:

"He nearly met his Waterloo during the Mixed Foursomes in 1979".

He was partnering Nell Mackenzie, and Hugh was caddying.

"He started to feel pain and breathlessness on the 6th/7th fairway, and had to stop playing and start walking in with me.

At the 15th tee he couldn't walk any further, so I ran to the clubhouse to find someone with a car to collect him.

Gilbert Tocher diagnosed a heart attack (fortunately incorrectly) – it was a collapsed lung. He was rushed to Raigmore Hospital in Inverness, where they promptly ruptured a blood vessel, necessitating a dash by ambulance to Forester Hill in Aberdeen.

Sport had vivid memories of blood pouring into him at one end through a drip, while it poured out of him at the other end.

Ten miles out of Aberdeen, the ambulance caught fire!

A reserve ambulance was rushed out of the city and Sport entered Aberdeen under full police escort, blue lights flashing, sirens blaring ... even though by this stage he was past caring.

Fortunately he lived to tell the tale, but it was a very near thing".

1980-1984

The Minutes Book records the following for these years:

"Unfortunately no Minutes for the AGMs of the above years are available.

In 1980 Tain Golf Club decided that, because of the huge entry for the Sunday One Day Open, it was impossible to continue the match against the Stotters.

It was decided therefore the game should be played over Invergordon Golf Club, and for the years noted above the Stotters are extremely grateful to Invergordon Golf Club, and especially to those friends from Tain Golf Club who forsook the Sunday Open so that the challenge match could be kept alive.

The results of the matches are recorded below:

1980	Stotters won	(14th match)
1981	Tain won	(15th match)
1982	Tain won	(16th match)
1983	Tain won	(17th match)
1984	Stotters won	(18th match)".

The Invergordon years were initiated by Raymond Cameron (formally of Shandwick Inn) who at that time ran the Royal Hotel in Tain.

During these years a number of debutants appeared.

Andrew Urquhart, Tommy Young's son-in-law, played for Tain against Hamish Junior (drafted in at the last minute). Neither of the two remembers which year nor who they played with, but both are confident they triumphed!

Hamish remembers struggling to keep his drives out of woods and houses bordering various fairways. He also remembers that it was his job to drive Hamish Senior and others home for obvious reasons.

Andrew was born in Cadboll House in1945. His father was a farm grieve (manager or overseer).

He went to Hilton School, leaving at 15 to complete a five year joinery apprenticeship with A. Morrison in Tain. He worked as a joiner for a few years till deciding to take his HGV licence, driving with A. and J. Fraser of Portmahomack till 1986.

He then went back to joinery until he had a serious accident. He was working with David Ross, a stalwart for many years in the Tain team, at Golf Club Secretary – Magi's – house opposite the St. Duthus Hotel (formerly a blacksmith's smiddy).

Andrew fell from a roof and broke both ankles.

He resumed his driving, this time with Bannerman of Tain, and was with them till he retired.

He met Tina, Tommy's daughter, in 1981, and they married in 1982.

He played for Tain against the Stotters until he became an Associate Stotter after Tommy's death in 1994.

During the Invergordon years, there was one death-defying car trip when Andrew and the late Derek Mackenzie drew the short straw and headed to Invergordon with Teddy Brookes in the driving seat. The journey time was half what it should have been but all arrived safely, though in real terms never ready to play golf.

Derek and Andrew were paired together, and they met up with Donnie Mackay (DM28 car reg) who knew the Stotters and had a bottle ready for them.

Through politeness (!) they accepted his offer of a dram.

Some two hours later all reappeared with a glow on to resume their round of golf with nobody quite knowing where they had left off in relation to the holes or the score.

Andrew vaguely remembers being a passenger in Teddy Brookes' car coming back from Invergordon, and without doubt nobody was particularly sober, but Walter Kerr, for some reason, actually drove.

"Walter was swaying to the classical music he was playing in the car approaching the car park at the Royal. Florrie spotted Walter and I, so went over and told Walter he was drunk.

Walter's calm reply was: "Thank God for that – I thought there was something wrong with the steering!""

Also during these years, the legendary figure of George "The Wig" Raeside appears, reaching the dizzy heights of Stotters' Captaincy in 1984.

He was a friend of Dr John's.

During his first year, he was called up for duty on the Sunday morning, and as everyone was gathered around the first tee, he slipped off to the practice area to hit some shots.

He was soon spotted amidst much jeering and general hilarity. Dr John was appalled, and son Simon says this has never happened before or since.

Allegedly, George was very fond of Florrie at the Royal Hotel. He was more often not at Tain than at Tain and apparently went off to South Africa without any of the Stotters knowing.

Another debutant during the Invergordon years was Johnny Houston Junior who remembers the experience: "My first Stotters' match as a player was during the time we were "banished" to Invergordon.

It was a huge thrill to play in my first game but I have to say it was not the same with it not being Tain.

I always remember how seriously we took the match as kids when we were caddying and genuinely did see the Tain team as the enemy (!).

We would always try to give the Tain guys more drink but this had limited success. If the Stotters lost we were really upset and would hold caddies' inquests but with all the other fun that didn't last long.

The first Sunday in August has always been my favourite day of the year".

How true.

As new names emerge on the Stotters' scene, the sad death of Tommy Armstrong in 1981 creates an opportunity for new blood.

Forbie Urquhart appears to have activated his somewhat dormant Associate Stottership bestowed upon him in 1974 by Hamish (Senior), and played for the Stotters during these years.

Frank Cougan fondly remembers another story involving the Irish: "In 1981, the Home International matches were held at Royal Dornoch. The Kilmacolm Team had gone up to play against Tain the previous weekend.

I persuaded three of my pals from Shandon Park to come over, so two carloads arrived in Tain – four of them stayed in the Royal and the other four wherever they could get their heads down.

A great day and night was had. Suffice to say the three teams played, but some of the Belfast boys were not used to the fact you had to fortify yourself before going out on the course, and then to maintain the alcohol/blood level throughout 18 holes!

During the round, one of the Belfast golfers pulled a caddy car with a squeaky wheel which was really irritating – till the 16th or 17th hole when one of the Tain members relieved himself on the offending wheel – this cured the squeak".

This may or may not have been the same year as the Irish helped Forbie open his safe.

Dr. John was apparently a big supporter of the K method promoted by Bernard Gallagher, as his letter with attachment to Forbie and Margaret illustrates.

John Houston

M.B., Ch.B., D.R.C.O.G.

NETHER JOHNSTONE HOUSE
BY JOHNSTONE
Telephone: Johnstone 29320

27th September, 1984.

Dear Forbie and Margaret,

While perusing September's Golf Monthly, I came across a photograph and article by Bernard Gallacher, which demonstrates, to my mind, the K method with which I have been boring you for some time.

The moment I looked at it my thoughts were transformed to some future date when the stentorial voice of the starter calls, "And on the tee representing Great Britain and Ireland, FORBIE URQUHART", and as this young, lythe, athletic figure leaps to the tee, the fluency of his swing is surpassed only by the scintillating and captivating smile which he throws in abundance to the admiring multitude.

As I follow this figure after striking his shot some 300 yards down the fairway, I trip over a beer can and am rudely awakened, still gazing at this picture, which I am sure Forbie you will find informative.

I have taken the liberty of making a tracing of my K method and, superimposed on Barnard Gallacher, it demonstrates what I mean, and if you will notice the slight inclination of his right foot at address, the lower leg of the K is actually a line drawn through his right shin bone.

Trusting this information will lead you to new fields of glory.

Yours Aye,

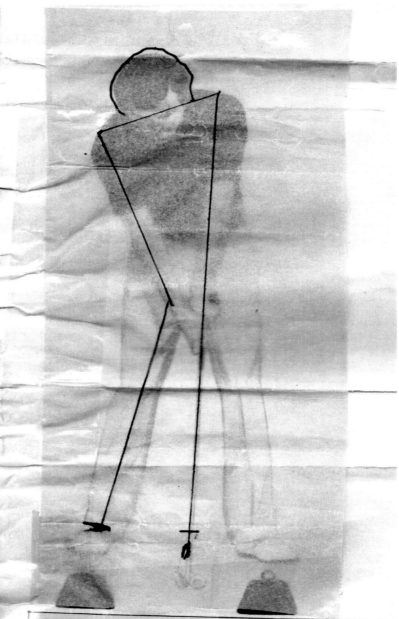

ADDRESS
At address I try to have my weight distributed
equally between the right foot and the left
foot. From this position it is much easier to
move into the correct backswing weight
transfer than it is if you have a preponderance
of weight on either the left foot or the right
foot.

MINUTES OF THE 20ᵀᴴ ANNUAL GENERAL MEETING OF THE STOTTERS – SUNDAY 3ᴿᴰ AUGUST 1985

Held at the Morangie House Hotel, Tain.

Result of the nineteenth annual match – the Stotters v Tain Golf Club – the Stotters won the cup.

Vice-Captain W. Kemp was in the chair due to the absence of Captain George Raeside who was fined £5 for dereliction of duty and £5 for lack of an acceptable excuse.

The fines were imposed only after considerable discussion and a majority verdict. They may be waived next year if G. Raeside produces a bottle of whisky.

Before the meeting degenerated into its usual disgusting drinking session, several motions were put forward for discussion but as none of the proposers could speak coherently none of the proposals was recorded.

W. Kemp appointed himself Captain, not in any show of megalomania but because no-one else was prepared to do so.

Mr. J. H. MacPherson then proposed F. Urquhart as Vice-Captain, and after considerable discussion on F. Urquhart's suitability for this demanding post the motion was seconded by J. G. Robertson and unanimously approved.

Mr. Urquhart accepted the post with suitable nauseating blandishments, but his oratorial style was quickly forgiven and forgotten when he produced a bottle of Grouse and dispersed drinks all round.

This settled the company down and it was agreed that Forbie would be the Stotters' local representative. He was requested to make arrangements for soup and sandwiches after the game which it is hoped will be held, once more, over Tain Golf Club.

The post of Secretary once more raised its ugly head. W. Kerr again refused to take over. As no one was willing to take the post it fell to the Captain to take these Minutes.

Mr J.G. Robertson asked that a vote of thanks be recorded for Walter's sterling work as Secretary since the Stotters' inception. This recommendation was agreed unanimously.

There being no competent business, or indeed a sober Stotter, the meeting ended in utter confusion at 4 p.m.

Walter Kerr's ultimate and final resignation ended one era, but ushered in another secretarially as the legendary Wilson Kemp penned these, his first Stotters' Minutes.

MINUTES OF THE 21ST ANNUAL GENERAL MEETING OF THE STOTTERS – SUNDAY 3RD AUGUST 1986

Held at the Royal Hotel, Tain,

The Twentieth Match – the Stotters v Tain – Tain won the cup (margin of victory unknown).

APOLOGIES

H. Mitchell, F. Cougan, J. Campbell and R Mackenzie.

MINUTES OF THE PREVIOUS MEETING

The Minutes of the last AGM were read, and because none of the members present could remember anything that had been discussed, were approved unanimously.

CAPTAIN'S REPORT

Captain W. Kemp thanked everyone for their support during the past year but felt he had been let down by members in the game against Tain this morning. He considered it was disgraceful that, considering the drinking practice the Stotters put in on the Saturday night, they were unable to match Tain not only at golf but in the drinking stakes as well.

These remarks did not go down too well with the members present and the Captain hurriedly moved on to the next item.

ELECTION OF OFFICER BEARERS

The Election of Office Bearers was carried out in its normal meticulous, ruthless, fashion.

Mr Kemp's previous remarks and inability to captain the Stotters' team to a victory in the match led to his replacement by F. Urquhart. To everyone's delight he celebrated his appointment in time honoured fashion i.e., he supplied a bottle of whisky.

F. Urquhart proposed G. Raeside as his Vice-Captain but this did not meet with instant approval and there was a strong lobby for Mr. Raeside to sign an undertaking that he would be available to carry out his duties. The Captain stood firm in the face of mounting criticism and Mr. Raeside's nomination was finally accepted.

Mr W. Kemp was demoted to Permanent Secretary.

ANY OTHER COMPETENT BUSINESS

The Secretary was asked to record in the Minutes how pleased the Stotters were to be playing the Annual Match over Tain Golf Club again.

The number of holes played was ideal in that not one member of either team was the 'worse for wear' and all the participants were off the course before the One Day tournament started.

It was also significant that there were more Tain members participating this year and it is hoped that this trend would continue.

The food provided by Jean and David Geekie was more than adequate and the Stotters hoped that this arrangement would also continue in the future.

The Secretary was also asked to write to Invergordon Golf Club and express our gratitude for putting up with us in previous years.

A heated discussion on the status of a Stotter developed and the Captain showed a total lack of control by allowing the protagonists to escape without being fined.

After impassioned speeches on the subject by Dr. J. Houston and Mr. MacPherson, the Captain decided enough was enough and called a halt to this non-productive topic.

It was at this point in the proceedings that Mr. MacPherson fell asleep. His incapacity to make his usual inflammatory remarks was much appreciated by the rest of the company.

It was agreed that the annual Stotters' trial match be held each year at Kilmacolm on the last Sunday in April. It was also agreed that Mr. MacPherson try to arrange this year's game for September.

After the Captain poured everyone another dram, which action effectively stopped further discussion, the Captain closed the meeting and a cacophony of cheers, catcalls and snores could be heard.

This was the year that Claire Cougan, one of Frank's two daughters, remembers caddying for her dad when he was playing with (or against!) Bob Beveridge.

Bob shouted over: "We got a birdie!"

Needless to say they were swinging a dead seagull round their heads.

MINUTES OF THE 22ND ANNUAL GENERAL MEETING OF THE STOTTERS – SUNDAY 2ND AUGUST 1987

Possibly held at the Royal Hotel, Tain.

The twenty-first annual match – the Stotters v Tain Golf club – won by the Stotters.

Captain F. Urquhart in the chair.

APOLOGIES

Received from G. Raeside, R. Mackenzie and J. Campbell.

MINUTES OF THE PREVIOUS MEETING

These were read to the assembled company and unanimously approved only because none of those present could remember what had been discussed.

SECRETARY'S REPORT

The game against Tain Golf Club on the Sunday preceding Golf Week was won by the Stotters and once again everyone involved had thoroughly enjoyed themselves. The format of playing 10 ½ holes seems ideal for our ageing band of warriors and the shortened course allows players to get back to the club house more-or-less sober.

Dr. John apologised profusely for 'f---ing up' the arrangements for the April Hic-Cup date and his apology was met with the normal polite reprimands. Mr. MacPherson then said he would look after the arrangements for next year's game and this announcement was greeted with astounded looks amid real silence.

ELECTION OF OFFICE BEARERS

The election of a Captain was fraught with difficulty.

There was no Vice-Captain present to assume the responsibility and the members were so incensed by G. Raeside's absence that the wish was expressed to strike him off the membership.

The Captain, however, retained a calming sough and managed to restore order. When asked if he could face another year in office Mr. Urquhart accepted this onerous task with complete aplomb and even bought a flock of haufs.

The Captain was urged to select as Vice-Captain someone who was certain to be present next year and if S. Ferguson had not been sleeping then this honourable post would have been his.

The Captain therefore proposed F. Cougan as Vice-Captain and this was accepted unanimously. Mr Cougan accepted the post with his usual humility.

W. Kemp was again forced to accept the post of Secretary.

ANY OTHER COMPETENT BUSINESS

The question of how many playing Stotters was examined, and it was agreed that numbers were becoming dangerously low.

J. G. Robertson proposed Dr. K. Greig be elected to the company and this was seconded by F. Cougan and agreed unanimously.

Dr. John, during one of his dissertations on the vicissitudes of, among other things, Aids, somehow or other proposed R. Towart also be elected as a Stotter and even more surprisingly, this was seconded by I. MacPherson. This motion was carried also without dissention.

Mr. Robertson stirred himself once again and put forward the proposal that J. Houston Junior be elected an Associate Stotter and that if I. Walkington showed no sign of returning to the fold then J. Houston Junior be asked to fill the position. F. Cougan seconded the proposal and it was carried unanimously. The new Stotters celebrated their election by producing bottles of whisky.

This additional supply rendered almost everyone comatose and when the Captain saw S. Ferguson showing signs of revival, deemed it politic to end this meeting on a peaceful note and this he did at approximately 5.15 p.m.

A vote of thanks to the Chair was proposed by I. MacPherson.

The reference to playing ten and a half holes arose because of the Sunday competition and the demand for tee off times. The Stotters' match was reduced to playing holes 1 to 5 and then playing from the 6th tee to the 10th green, stopping of course for Florrie's bar, and, suitably refreshed, proceeding "through the jungle" to the 14th tee to play the closing 5 holes.

Ken Greig was an Obstetrician/ Gynaecologist from Paisley. He was a keen golfer but a high handicapper, and a great friend of Hamish Robertson's.

Dr. John used to send him all his gynaecological patients and they carried out joint domiciliary visits in the evenings, after which Ken "would end up at ours for a few drams", as daughter Deen remembers.

A quiet, good natured man, he loved Dr John's outrageousness.

John invited him up one year in the 80s and he came regularly with his wife May, cheerfully featuring for the Stotters for 12 years.

May was a bit different from most of the Stotters and their wives in that she was teetotal and, as Forbie remembers: "Tended to come across as a bit quiet. I used to make a special non-alcoholic drink, complete with a fancy cocktail stick and a cherry for her at the Gilbert Goblet gatherings. She loved the bit of fuss and it usually got a smile out of her".

Robert Towart was married to Anne Houston, Dr John's eldest child.

His verbose comments at AGMs were particularly sleep-inducing (!).

John Houston Junior, born in the Stotters' inaugural year of 1966, is the elder of Dr John's 2 sons.

Born in Elderslie, appropriately the birthplace of William Wallace, John lives in Glasgow with Angela and their lovely daughter Eilidh.

Having worked in the Financial Sector for a number of years he now supports adults with learning difficulties, a brave switch of roles he often wishes he'd made much earlier.

A member of Hilton Park on the outskirts of Glasgow, he plays off 5 or 6 depending on how often in a year he plays, and was off 3 at his best.

Having come to Tain Golf Week every year since he was born, he grew up "surrounded by so many characters in the yellow it was a real honour to be elected as an Associate Stotter...and somewhat daunting I have to say".

For a few years Johnny wasn't a member of a Golf Club but he still came to Tain "for the craic".

He first played in Golf Week aged fourteen and qualified with two 87's (net 74's).

Having always caddied for Hammy Mitchell, it was a lovely touch by Hammy to reverse the roles and caddy for him in the first round.

Johnny says: "Unfortunately nerves got the better of me and I got slaughtered 7 and 6 by a local lad, Jamie Scott, who was two or three years older".

Fate, however, took a hand in that he and Jamie struck up a friendship, and Jamie even played for the Stotters once when they were short of numbers. Despite leaving for the States in the 90s, he still keeps in touch and once attended The Stotters' Saturday night dinner with his wife, son, and father who still lives in Tain.

Two years after Johnny's first entry he won the Munro Rosebowl in 1982, and then won it again 25 years later in 2007, going on to win the McVitie and Price in 2014, 54 years after his father, who also won the Munro in 1970.

Johnny then made history by winning the Munro again in 2015 and the Stirling Challenge Cup in 2016 – an incredible hat-trick of Tain trophies.

Johnny has many memories of playing at Tain: "There was the time when Hamish Munro, playing for the Stotters I think for the first time, didn't make it past the 8th.

He lay his clubs in a hut which was then at the side of the green and fell asleep on top of them! Someone, I can't recall who, drove out there that night to collect him and he was still lying out for the count.

I also recall having to make two speeches as the Stotters' Captain at the prize-giving as my counterpart from Tain, Ross Campbell, had lost the ability to speak so I had to do so for him".

One of the nicest tributes to Tain comes from Johnny: "I always remember my Dad driving us up as kids and saying that he always felt the hair on the back of his neck stand up as we passed Stepps on the way out of Glasgow to head north for Golf Week and it was the same every year.

I still get the exact same feeling even after all these years".

Ken Ross echoes this: "Even today my excitement rises as we pass Alness and approach Tain knowing that it is going to be another year of unpredictable fun".

MINUTES OF THE 23RD ANNUAL GENERAL MEETING OF THE STOTTERS – SUNDAY 31ST JULY 1988

Held in the Royal Hotel, Tain.

The 22nd Annual Match – the Stotters v Tain – won by Tain Golf Club.

Captain F. Urquhart in the chair.

APOLOGIES

R. Mackenzie and H. Mitchell.

MINUTES OF THE PREVIOUS MEETING

The Minutes were read to the assembled company and several members tried to raise various topics from these Minutes but as the presentation of the items was so incoherent and unintelligible, the Captain instructed the Secretary not to record any such drivel.

The Captain proposed the acceptance of the Minutes as read. This was seconded by F. Cougan and carried unanimously.

SECRETARY'S REPORT

The game against the club on Sunday ended in victory for Tain.

The arrangements made by F. Urquhart in the clubhouse after the game were the highlight of the day as far as the Stotters were concerned and Forbie was thanked for his part in making the day bearable.

ELECTION OF OFFICE BEARERS

Captain Urquhart thanked everyone for having helped him through his 2nd year of office and quickly proposed F. Cougan as Captain. The proposal was seconded by S. Ferguson and approved without dissent. F. Cougan took over the chair and much to the delight of the members produced a bottle and gave everyone a hauf.

The new Captain then proposed that as 1990 would be Tain Golf Club's centenary it would be most appropriate if J. G. Robertson was appointed Vice- Captain as this would mean that J. G. R. would be Captain of the Stotters during the Centenary year.

No one could quite understand the reasoning behind this and the Captain was unable to expand on his idea.

Nevertheless the appointment was approved unanimously.

W. Kemp was again appointed Secretary and it shows how popular he is when he was not opposed for the post.

ANY OTHER COMPETENT BUSINESS

Mr I. MacPherson pointed out that Ian Walkington had been present but that he had not played for the Stotters and asked the reason for this. The Captain explained that Ian had not been keen to play but would have filled in if required. Captain Cougan stated that whilst he agreed with the maxim 'once a Stotter always a Stotter' he felt that the club needed 12 *active* members.

One of the company, who shall be nameless, was heard to mutter: 'If that's the case we had better recruit 10 new bodies'. This remark was ignored and T. Young proposed that J. Houston Junior be appointed a full Stotter. This was seconded by J. G. Robertson and J. Houston Junior was duly elected.

It was decided after much discussion that the Hic-Cup game at Kilmacolm should be used to form the basis of the team for Tain: i.e., the pairings for the Hic-Cup should be retained unless there was a case of complete incompatibility. It was also agreed that the date for the Hic-Cup be the last Sunday in April.

It was at this point that S. Ferguson fell asleep and the Vice-Captain went for a pee.

There was no objection to the Vice-Captain's action but as this was the 5th consecutive year that Ferguson had fallen asleep the Captain decided to impose a £5 fine.

The next topic for discussion was regarding a new Stotters' jersey. The Vice-Captain proposed that the new jersey should be blue and this was seconded by I. MacPherson.

Dr. Houston immediately proposed that the colour should remain as is and was seconded by F. Urquhart. On a show of hands the counter proposal was carried by 10 votes to 2. The new jersey is to be available for the Stotters' Match in 1990 and Mr Cougan to arrange this.

The Captain raised the subject of what the Stotters should do for Tain's centenary year. He felt it would be politic to show our continuing support for the club in some tangible form and asked members for any suggestions.

Plenty of these were forthcoming but Ian MacPherson won the loudest applause by saying that: 'Whilst I don't think we should do anything, I am not averse to doing something'.

The Captain felt we should present the club with a suitable gift and asked the members to think about it and give him suggestions at the Spring Meeting at Kilmacolm.

Dr. Houston pointed out that T. Armstrong's name was not yet on the seat and asked if he could make the necessary arrangements. This suggestion was met without dissent.

Mr. Urquhart informed the members that 'The Safe' was up for grabs and a Minute's silence was observed for the demise of this Stotters' institution.

As S. Ferguson showed some signs of reviving the Captain hurriedly closed the meeting at approximately 5.15 p.m.

The proposal to change the Stotters' jersey from yellow to blue, though perhaps raised frivolously in true Stotters' style, was hastily beaten back.

The announcement by Forbie that his shop was for sale was indeed a major milestone in Stotters' tradition.

MINUTES OF THE 24TH ANNUAL GENERAL MEETING OF THE STOTTERS – SUNDAY 3RD JULY 1989

Held at the Royal Hotel, Tain.

The twenty-third annual match – the Stotters v Tain Golf Club – won by the Stotters (margin unknown).

Captain Frank Cougan in the chair.

MINUTES OF THE PREVIOUS MEETING

These were read to the assembled company by the Secretary and to everyone's surprise Dr. Ken Greig asked a question – what is happening in regard to the trophy the Stotters were going to present to Tain Golf Club to mark their centenary?

This gave the Captain a chance to illustrate his verbosity, but after about 10 minutes of futile talk he was asked if he had a concrete proposal to put before the members.

He then proposed a crystal goblet with the Stotters' emblem thereon and the date would be very appropriate. He asked if there were any other suggestions and as none were forthcoming it was agreed that the goblet be ordered up with one proviso – that the total cost be £150 – anything over this would be paid by F. Cougan.

Hamish Robertson Senior will present the memento at the Centenary Dinner.

The Captain proposed the adoption of the Minutes seconded by I. MacPherson and this was unanimously agreed.

SECRETARY'S REPORT

The annual match had been won by the Stotters and victory was achieved by Ken Greig sinking a vital putt on the last green in the last match.

The catering arrangements in the club house again were excellent and thanks are once again due to Forbie for doing the needful.

Another of the original Stotters, Ian McColl, had passed away and both his and Tommy Armstrong's plaques were now on the seat.

ELECTION OF OFFICE BEARERS

Captain Cougan proposed J. G. Robertson as Captain and this proposal was seconded by F. Urquhart and carried unanimously.

J. G. Robertson took the chair and immediately a semblance of order was restored with the members becoming strangely subdued by the aura of authority emanating from the chair. Whether the effect on the members was caused by the smoke from his pipe or his whisky breath is difficult to say.

The new Captain proposed K. Greig as his Vice-Captain and the proposal was acclaimed with delight by the assembled company.

W. Kemp was again proposed as Secretary and this was unanimously accepted.

ANY OTHER COMPETENT BUSINESS

S. Ferguson asked what was to be done about the £25 that had been collected in fines and proposed that this should be put to John Fraser's retirement fund. That S. Ferguson was still awake so surprised everyone that no dissenting voice was raised and the proposal was carried unanimously.

Mr. MacPherson asked why we only played 10 holes in the Sunday match and asked if the fixture could be extended to 15 or 18 holes.

F. Cougan said that the atmosphere in the clubhouse seemed to indicate there would be no objections to 15 holes being played. Captain Robertson asked if the matter could be left in his hands and this was agreed to by the Company.

The Secretary was asked to note in the Minutes that W. Kerr is due a vote of thanks for keeping Mr. Ferguson awake for the duration of the meeting – a feat which had not been achieved during the past five years.

W. Kerr proposed that Simon Houston be appointed an Associate Stotter and this was seconded by S. Ferguson and carried unanimously.

There being no other business the meeting closed harmoniously at 3.15p.m.

Walter Kerr won Gilbert's Goblet this year, as Johnny Houston remembers: "I loved the time big Walter won and was basking in the glory of it all but when I pointed out he was in a prime position to qualify he turned white and told me that would be the ultimate disaster – needless to say, he didn't make the cut!"

Simon Houston, the youngest of Dr John's 5 children, was born in 1968 in Johnstone, Renfrewshire, and lives in Glasgow with his wife, Lynn. Their three children, Tori, Sam and Anna, like most of the Stotters' families, are regulars at Tain during Golf Week.

Simon's Stotter career began: "As a young caddie, initially for Tommy Armstrong before establishing myself as Scott Ferguson's bag man. Scott was less than impressed on my debut because every time he stopped at his ball, he looked round to find me 50 yards behind, practising my swing!"

One of his early memories is of father John" thinning a bunker shot at the 18th and the ball clearing the clubhouse and landing in the car park.

He made a speech afterwards and said he was delighted he got the ball back because it was fresh out of the wrapper six months earlier!"

Simon is Content Editor at the Scottish Sun newspaper, having previously been a journalist at the Scottish Daily Mail, Daily Record, and Sunday Times.

He comments: "Very much office based nowadays, but my career has taken me to some amazing and dangerous places. Managed to narrowly escape death in the line of duty – much to the frustration of those who are bored listening to my stories!"

He was a regular broadcaster from the first war in Iraq.

Like Johnny, he is a member of Hilton Park in Glasgow, playing off 8, and also like Johnny, has been to Tain for Golf Week virtually every year of his life.

He says of his election to Associate Stotter status: "As my father was a founder member, I was always going to follow in his footsteps and join the 'family business' as it were".

His journalistic career was to prepare him for "15 years of pleasure serving as the Stotters' third secretary, after Walter Kerr and Wilson Kemp".

His acerbic wit never fails to energise Stotters' AGMs.

Simon reached the final of the Brookes Trophy in 2006, and the semi-final of the Munro Rose Bowl in2009.

"There was also the year that might have been when Alan Gordon and I crept in as final qualifiers but nobody told us so we forfeited our first-round ties while fast asleep. That was a hard pill to swallow".

He is very proud of his son Sam winning the Teddy Brookes Trophy in 2015.

MINUTES OF THE 25ᵀᴴ ANNUAL GENERAL MEETING OF THE STOTTERS – SUNDAY 5ᵀᴴ AUGUST 1990

Probably held at the Royal Hotel, Tain.

The twenty-fourth annual match – the Stotters v Tain Golf Club – Tain Golf Club won – no figures given.

Captain J. G. Robertson in the chair

MINUTES OF THE PREVIOUS MEETING

These were read to the assembled company and to the astonishment of the Secretary, one of the Stotters actually had a question to ask about the Minutes.

Ian MacPherson asked why we had not played 15 or 18 holes.

Captain Robertson replied that when he had sounded out the Club on this proposal it was the Club's feeling that 10 holes were sufficient.

The Captain then read out a letter from the Captain of Tain Golf Club thanking the Stotters for both attending the Centenary Dinner in such large numbers and for the Stotters' goblet.

The Captain also asked that it be noted in the Minutes that Tony Watson made a most acceptable speech after the Match and such is the Captain's power of oratory there was scarce a dry eye in the house 'ere he finished.

ELECTION OF OFFICE BEARERS

Captain Robertson proposed Ken Greig to be Captain of the Stotters and the appointment was ratified unanimously.

The new Captain for his opening address delivered a homily on osteoporosis, and after expounding expansively on this theme acknowledged that the immediate past Captain proved his theories on the subject a load of crap.

The assembled company sat bemused throughout the speech and at least three-quarters of them appeared to have contracted the disease by the time the Captain had finished.

However, all was forgiven when Ken produced a 'flock of haufs'.

Captain Greig proposed S. Ferguson as his Vice-Captain. There were no objections to this proposal.

Mr. Ferguson was installed as Vice-Captain and immediately launched into an exemplary display of his command of the English language. He was halted in his tracks when the company advised him to sit down and shut his f------ mouth.

ANY OTHER COMPETENT BUSINESS

Ian Walkington, whom we were all pleased to see, asked what had happened to the Stotters' flag. F. Urquhart suggested he be allowed to make enquiries on its whereabouts. F. Cougan proposed that if the flag is found it should be displayed during Golf Week either on the buggy or attached to the Pro Shop.

Walter Kerr requested it to be recorded in the Minutes that Dr. John had risen from his sick bed to be at Tain to support the Stotters. This was accepted without dissent and the Captain thanked John very much for his support.

Frank Cougan proposed that a new Stotters' jersey was urgently required as the team was looking rather ragged on the 1st tee. W. Kemp seconded this. Mr MacPherson proposed nothing to be done about new jerseys, and this was seconded by J. G. Robertson.

The counter-motion was carried despite an eloquent diatribe on the subject by Dr. J. Houston who although speaking for some time said little new on the subject.

F. Urquhart mentioned that he hoped the Stotters would wear the yellow jerseys on the qualifying days because many people in Tain look forward to seeing the Stotters during Golf Week. The Captain asked everyone to follow this suggestion in 1991.

Hic-Cup – date to be left to Ian MacPherson who will try for 1st Sunday in April.

Frank Cougan proposed Ken Ross be elected as an Associate Stotter. J. G. Robertson also mentioned that H. Robertson (Junior) could be keen on becoming a member. Simon Houston ventured the opinion that at least two Associate Stotters are required and if we can elect younger members such as those mentioned, so much the better.

The general atmosphere of the meeting was that J. G. Robertson sound out the people mentioned and report back to the Captain.

No other business was raised and the meeting closed at 3.25 p.m.

Letter from Tony Watson – Captain Tain Golf Club (see above) – 3rd April 1990

To: The Stotters' Captain

Dear Frank,

To you, Frank, and the rest of the Stotters, my sincere thanks to you all for your magnificent gift presented on the evening of our Club's centenary. We all felt that the evening was complemented by such a loyal turnout from the Stotters and it was only fitting that a group such as yours, who have been such good supporters of Tain Golf Club over the years, should be there. Thank you for coming.

Once again, many thanks.

My best wishes to you and all your fellow reprobates for the season ahead.

Haste ye back.

Yours sincerely,

Tony Watson

1990 marked Tain Golf Cub's centenary and Past Captain Ian McGregor (Glenmorangie) compiled and edited a brilliant booklet, "Tain Golf Club 1890-1990", to celebrate the occasion.

Hamish Robertson wrote a President's Message as a Foreword, saying:

"Tain Golf Course has a beautiful setting – where is there a more magnificent view than from the twelfth tee? On a clear day one may see the coastline from the Kyle of Sutherland to the Ord of Caithness. It is kept in first class condition – not too long by present day standards, but difficult enough – a perfect Course for enjoyable Golf at all times and particularly holiday Golf. It has drawn me back every year since 1933 with the exception of War years and each year I see improvements on the Course and in the Clubhouse amenities, thanks to successive forward looking Committees".

Simon's tongue in cheek comment about "younger members" amuses as both Hamish and Ken are over 20 years older than him.

However, Ken and Hamish Junior – second cousins – appear on the Stotters' stage formally for the first time in 1990, but both had been coming to Tain for a long time with their parents – Hamish almost from birth and Ken since he was eleven.

He recalls: "I couldn't play in the tournament but I remember going out onto the course in the evening and playing with Big Willy Mackenzie's two sons, Ian and Neil, who like me were lodged in the attic rooms at The Royal. Our parents were cheerfully consuming large drams in the clubhouse.

Ian nearly holed in one at the sixth. However, it was his drive from the junior tee at the seventh. It's the only time I have seen someone hit a drive through his legs!"

The following year, Ken achieved notoriety as the "wee bairn who broke his arm outside the Clubhouse".

In attempting to vault the white railings then marking out-of-bounds, he misjudged the one handed vault – chaos ensued and Ken remembers his parents coming out of the clubhouse with glasses of whisky in hand.

"So off we go to Inverness in the Bentley, the three of us on the large front seat, my mother supporting my arm and my father at the wheel. If breathalysers had existed they would have exploded with the fumes.

Bentleys need a lot of petrol and petrol costs money, and at 8 pm near Alness we discovered we had neither.

It was 64 miles from Tain to Inverness via Dingwall in the days before the Kessock Bridge. We stopped at a garage fortuitously still open and my father explained the predicament to the proprietor who regarded these sassenachs in a guzzling limousine with marked suspicion.

Dad mentioned his cousin Shake the Chemist in Tain and immediately our credit was good".

Mr Murray, the Consultant, duly operated and fixed Ken's arm in Raigmore Hospital.

Sharing a room one year with his parents, Ken remembers the door suddenly opening at about 2am and in coming Shake and his brothers, Hamish and Raeburn, "brandishing a vacuum cleaner with which they attacked my father apparently by way of revenge for some misdemeanours he had rendered them many years before!"

Tain aerodrome played a pivotal role in Ken learning to drive when very young (probably aged about 11). Cousin Ross Robertson recalls Ken Senior tossing the keys to his Bentley to him and telling him to teach Ken to drive, with Ken only able to see over the steering wheel by sitting on a cushion.

Ken continues: "Later when I was taller, Ross allowed me to illicitly drive Uncle Raeburn's Rover 75 to Portmahomack and back. The nearest police station was at Dingwall and we had no fear of the law, and of course our parents were setting a good example by drinking in the club or local taverns well after closing time!"

Brought up in Tunbridge Wells, Ken plays most of his golf at East Sussex National and has been in single figures since teenage days. He was the proud winner of the Munro Rose Bowl in 1972.

An orthopaedic surgeon based in Eastbourne, he splits his near-retirement time between there and his house in South Africa with his golfing wife, Golf Week caddy, and Stotters' Minutes typist Bridget.

Their 2 sons, George and Simon were both to become Stotters.

Hamish, born in Edinburgh in 1947 and three weeks older than Ken, started his career with Rolls-Royce in Industrial Relations, and then worked in three other Industries – Clothing Manufacture, Food Manufacture, and Retailing with John Menzies, joining them in the 70s.

With them, he headed up their embryonic HR Function, then was Regional Manager for the Scottish Stores and Bookstalls for seven years, before becoming Music, Video and Multimedia Manager, "the most sociable job on the planet", with launches of new CD's, DVD's and Computer Games taking him to London every week and abroad frequently.

Before his liver could rot completely however (excellent preparation for Stotter-ship), he transitioned back into HR as HR Director, until WH Smith took Menzies over.

For the next 14 years, till retirement in 2013, he facilitated Leadership Learning and Development work and Executive Coaching as an Independent Consultant.

In sport, he jumped for Scotland – Long and Triple Jump – for about 12 years, holding the Scottish records for most of that time, also jumping for Great Britain with Lynn Davies.

He came 8th in the 1970 Commonwealth Games Long Jump, and 13th in the Triple Jump, and is very proud that his school record for the triple jump still stands after 52 years.

Married to Shirley, who faithfully but mainly fruitlessly, caddies for him, Hamish's sons, Dale and Scott, and five grandchildren, know Golf Week well, but more often prop up the two family fours who play each May/June in Tain for the Hamish Robertson Texas Scramble Trophy, which the family put up for Competition in 2005 after Hamish Senior's death.

Hamish plays off an erratic 14, and always reserves his best golf for the Stotters'
Sunday morning match and his worst golf for the 4 Day Tournament.

He did qualify once for the Stirling Cup and won one match before being knocked out,
and came close to qualifying in 2013 when he had a fine 27 holes but took 9 off the tee
at the 10th and failed to qualify by two shots.

He is the author of The Timetrippers, the children's equivalent of James Redfield's
Celestine Prophecies, and authored this book with a lot of help from fellow Stotters,
families and Tain stalwarts.

MINUTES OF THE 26ᵀᴴ ANNUAL GENERAL MEETING OF THE STOTTERS – SUNDAY 4ᵀᴴ AUGUST 1991

Held in the Royal Hotel, Tain.

The twenty-fifth annual match – the Stotters v Tain Golf Club – a victory for Tain Golf Club, a sad result for the Stotters as this year is their silver anniversary.

Captain Ken Greig in the chair.

APOLOGIES

Received from H. Mitchell and I. Walkington.

The Captain said how saddened he had been by the deaths of John Campbell and Dr. John Houston and asked members to observe a minute's silence. After this had been observed John Houston Junior commented that his father would have appreciated the whisky glasses being raised and this was done to the toast of 'absent friends'.

MINUTES OF THE PREVIOUS MEETING

These were read to the assembled company and as there were no corrections, omissions or deletions, the Minutes were approved on a motion proposed by J. G. Robertson and seconded by W. Kerr.

MATTERS ARISING FROM THE MINUTES

F. Urquhart reported that he had made enquiries into the Stotters' flag but he was sorry to report that it was in tatters and not suitable for display, and there were mutterings that some of the Stotters were suitably described by that phrase.

Forbie suggested that matters be left in his hands to see what could be done. As no-one else wanted anything to do with this matter his suggestion was quickly accepted.

ELECTION OF OFFICE BEARERS

Captain – Ken Greig said how proud and honoured he had been in being Captain for the past year and thanked everyone for providing the support needed to carry out the arduous duties the position necessitated. After a few more minutes of similarly nauseating comments he was asked to 'shut his mouth and get on with it'.

He proposed S. Ferguson as Captain and as there were no dissenting voices Mr. Ferguson took the chair.

To everyone's surprise his acceptance speech was brief and to the company's delight he celebrated his appointment in the time honoured manner.

Vice-Captain – Mr. Ferguson proposed R. Towart as his Vice-Captain and on this proposal being accepted Mr. Towart made his acceptance speech in a manner very reminiscent of his late father-in-law, Dr. John – i.e., funny but totally incomprehensible.

Secretary – W. Kemp was again proposed as Secretary by the Captain and despite protests from Mr. Kemp he was once again elected Secretary.

Just after his appointment, the Secretary lost all interest in the proceedings and the remainder of the Minutes have been compiled from hearsay and very hazy recollections of some of the 'goings-on'.

ANY OTHER COMPETENT BUSINESS

Mr. Urquhart asked if the après match arrangements had been satisfactory.

The answer to this was a resounding "yes", and Forbie was asked if he would make the necessary arrangements for next year. He was also thanked for cleaning the plaques on the seat. He said he was quite happy to carry on with these tasks.

J. Houston Junior said it was nice to see Ken Ross back again and proposed that Ken be made an Associate Stotter. This was seconded by F. Cougan and approved unanimously.

The Captain, following up S. Houston's remarks last year that at least two Associates were required to keep numbers up, said it gave him great pleasure to propose H. Robertson Junior and R. Robertson as Associate Stotters. The proposal was seconded by the Vice-Captain and carried without dissent.

J. Houston Junior intimated that the Houston family wished to donate a Dr. John trophy to be played for during Golf Week.

After considerable discussion it was decided that the Trophy be awarded to the player with the best net score over the two qualifying rounds during Golf Week.

The Trophies up for grabs in 1992 are:

Gilbert's Goblet – best net score on Monday.

Dr. John Trophy – best net aggregate on Monday and Tuesday.

J.G. Robertson wished to record in the Minutes the Stotters' appreciation to Forbie and Margaret for entertaining us so royally on Monday evening but wondered if we were not imposing too much on their friendship and hospitality. Mr. Urquhart replied that he and Margaret were delighted to do the honours that night – but what he muttered under his breath has not been reported to me.

Fines were imposed as follows: S. Ferguson – £5 for not wearing a Stotters' jersey; F. Cougan – £5 for not having the Hic-Cup.

J.G. Robertson expressed the desire that the old Minute Book kept so assiduously by W. Kerr during his term of office be handed over to the present Secretary so that it can be brought up to date.

At this juncture Captain Ferguson fell asleep, and as the Secretary was also comatose it is assumed the meeting ended in pure disorder.

Hamish's younger brother, Roddy, now joins the ranks of The Stotters.

3 years younger than Hamish, but at 6ft 2, 4 inches taller, Roddy was also born in Edinburgh but brought up in Glasgow after Hamish Senior moved there with the Bank.

He had a world-travelling career, predominately with Metcom, a Glasgow based training and trade association organisation. Organising and speaking at International conferences, he was Chairman, Secretary, Director and Committee member of a number of British and European bath, sink and other Trade organisations.

An extremely good hurdler, photographer and Indian culinary expert, he married Alice and they had 3 children – Shona, Michael and Gail.

Sadly, Roddy never lived to see seven grandchildren arrive as he had a major brain haemorrhage in 1997, and recovery was slow due to other medical complications.

Almost miraculously he fought through the difficulties, which included massive memory loss and coordination problems, with the help of his family and Rehab Scotland.

Deen remembers the year when he returned to play in the 4 Day Open:

"He was standing at the 4-day score-sheets after the second round and someone said: "look at that score ha ha ha – 136!"

Roddy, standing behind them said: "I know, and I birdied the 18th!"

During his comeback he had to ask his fellow players to help him remember his score, though brother Hamish reckons this was a ploy to see if he could squeeze a shot or two off his actual score.

He took a bet one year with Ian (Murd) Ross when staying at Murd and Ray's Golf View House that he would beat Murd in the first round.

Roddy scored 112 nett, but won the money as Murd no returned!

He managed a virtual full return to work as Project Coordinator with the Glasgow Playschemes Association, much to the astonishment of medical staff and family alike, and walked the 96 miles of the West Highland Way in an astonishing 5 days to raise funds for Rehab Scotland, raising £1400 in the process.

Unfortunately, a second haemorrhage struck from which he was unable to recover, passing away in May 2006.

However, his memory lingers on – on the Sunday morning of the Stotters v Tain Match, a silver tray, presented by Alice and family, bearing the legend "Roddy's Round" appears, laden with whisky for everyone, and the traditional toast to Absent Friends remembers Roddy and the others who have become etched in the memory and on the Stotters' bench outside the Pro's shop.

MINUTES OF THE 27ᵀᴴ ANNUAL GENERAL MEETING OF THE STOTTERS – SUNDAY, 2ᴺᴰ AUGUST, 1992

Held in the Royal Hotel, Tain.

The twenty sixth annual match – the Stotters v Tain Golf Club – ended in victory for the Stotters.

Captain Scott Ferguson in the Chair.

MINUTES OF THE PREVIOUS MEETING

These were read to the assembled company and Mr. Cougan proposed that they be accepted as a true record of the proceedings. This was seconded by Dr. Greig and unanimously agreed.

This was exceedingly strange to the Secretary who could not even read his notes, let alone remember what took place.

MATTERS ARISING FROM MINUTES

Stotters' flag: F. Urquhart informed the members that he could not trace the flag and to make sure everyone understood what that meant the Captain stated: 'the f...... thing has been lost'.

The perennial question of 'who is a Stotter?' was again raised with the following points worthy of note:

1) Tommy Young feels that anyone who stays away for years is obviously not interested and should be struck off.

2) Ken Ross pointed out that in the early days the number of visitors was relatively small, but nowadays the entry is much greater and, when the time comes, it may be the Stotters will have to invite outsiders to play in the annual match.

He also wondered if the Stotters are perhaps becoming inbred.

3) Frank Cougan maintained that: 'Once a Stotter always a Stotter' should be the norm and asked how a new Stotter is elected to this office. J.G

Robertson stated that appointment is by invitation only.

4) The Vice-Captain said that keeping numbers up should be a top priority and wondered how an increase in numbers would affect the Sunday game. Mr. Urquhart said that he felt that Tain would always accommodate the numbers wishing to play.

5) Mr. Robertson Senior stated that he had been coming up to Tain for forty years and the Stotters to him symbolise the spirit of Golf Week. He also felt that if less than 12 Stotters fail to turn up then the Associates should be drafted in.

F. Cougan pointed out that G. Raeside had returned to the fold this year and hoped he would be back next year.

Ken Ross hoped that no decision will be taken on this subject as he had thoroughly enjoyed the lively discussion that the topic had provided. He also thanked Ian MacPherson for mentioning absent friends and bringing back childhood memories.

On this maudlin note the Captain decided enough was enough and proceeded to the next item on the Agenda.

Mr. Urquhart reported that the £5 charge on Sunday covered soup, sandwiches and a dram and hoped everyone was happy with the arrangements. The Captain thanked Forbie for his work and expressed the wish that these arrangements be made for the next year.

Mr. Cougan recalled that years ago the Stotters had a cash fund, mainly realised through the sale of shirts, the swearbox, fines and the children's' party and wondered if we should again start such a fund and use the proceeds to do something for the Club.

Mr. Ross stated that he felt very strongly that today epitomised the spirit of Golf Week and agreed with Mr. Cougan that the Stotters should do something for the Club and suggested that the Men's Changing Room exterior should be painted to blend in with the rest of the Clubhouse. The Captain thought the proposal was admirable but was wary of treading on the Club's toes by telling it how to spend any donation it received from the Stotters.

Mr. Urquhart agreed with Mr. Ross's sentiments but felt the Captain was right to point out the pitfalls.

The members were clearly becoming restless and as there was no whisky left to pacify them the Captain closed the meeting at 3.50 p.m.

A vote of thanks to the Chair was proposed by J.G. Robertson.

These Minutes are notable for the omission of the election of Office Bearers. Robert Tomant, however, was elected Captain, John Houston Junior became Vice-Captain, and of course, Wilson Kemp continued as Secretary.

The comment Hamish Senior makes about coming up to Tain for 40 years is strange given that he was born in Tain in 1913 and had been almost every year except for the War Years.

MINUTES OF THE 28ᵀᴴ ANNUAL GENERAL MEETING OF THE STOTTERS – SUNDAY, 1ˢᵀ AUGUST 1993

Held in the dining room of the Golf View Guest House (courtesy of Mr. (Murd) and Mrs. I. Ross).

The twenty-seventh annual match – the Stotters v Tain Golf Club ended in victory for the Stotters.

Captain R. Towart in the Chair.

MINUTES OF THE PREVIOUS MEETING

These were read, not approved, and only accepted when the Secretary threatened to resign. Mr. Urquhart proposed their acceptance and this was seconded by S. Ferguson. Amidst rising tensions and much muttering the Minutes were finally accepted.

MATTERS ARISING FROM MINUTES

Mr. MacPherson made an impassioned plea to Mr. K. Ross and Mr. S. Ferguson to curtail their comments adding that this would effectively cut the time of the meeting by half.

Ken Ross was fined £5 by the Captain for not appearing from Hong Kong on satellite television to address the Stotters.

The Captain intimated that he had spoken to the Club and that they had intimated that another Stotters' seat would be appreciated.

Mr. MacPherson interjected that the Stotters had done a lot for the Club over the years and he was backed up by J.G. Robertson and F. Urquhart.

After several minutes of fruitless discussion it was agreed to leave the matter in abeyance especially when it was pointed out by someone that there were no funds available anyway.

The question of the buggy was raised by J. Houston Junior and whether the Club were maintaining it properly.

Mr. MacPherson said that the buggers were notoriously unreliable and that to maintain it properly could cost the club £120 per year. He felt we should perhaps gift any funds raised to 'the buggy fund' and help the Club maintain it. Can we approach the Club to find out if this would be acceptable?

Mr. Cougan apologised for not providing a flag and Mr. MacPherson astounded everybody by saying that he would get a flag made.

ELECTION OF OFFICE BEARERS

Captain Towart thanked everyone for their support during the year and without further ado proposed his Vice-Captain, John Houston Junior, as Captain. The recommendation was accepted unanimously.

Captain Houston took the chair and immediately fined S. Ferguson £5 for not wearing proper Stotters' apparel.

The Captain took himself off for a pee and J.G. Robertson immediately proposed a £1 fine on the Captain for dereliction of duty.

Vice-Captain – the Captain said he had pencilled in Ken Ross as his Vice-Captain but as he was in Hong Kong he therefore proposed S. Houston as Vice-Captain. Mr MacPherson said that as long as Simon followed Dr. John Houston's advice to 'keep his bowels open and his mouth shut' then he would second the proposal. The proposal was accepted unanimously.

Secretary – W. Kemp was again returned to the post unopposed which just goes to show that a penchant for writing a load of crap is one of the prerequisites for a Stotters' secretary.

ANY OTHER COMPETENT BUSINESS

Hamish Robertson Junior asked if he could be provided with a Stotters' jersey and this seemed to propose no problem at all.

Forbie regretfully announced that he and Margaret would be unable to entertain the Stotters on Monday night. J.G. Robertson expressed the view that Forbie and Margaret had entertained the Stotters royally for many years and expressed our thanks to them for putting up with us for so long.

The Secretary was asked if any alternative arrangements could be made and it was left to the Secretary to do something.

Spring Meeting for the Hic-Cup: Try for the last Sunday in April.

F. Urquhart asked if we were happy with the arrangements for the Stotters in the clubhouse. The Captain thanked Forbie for his efforts and hoped he would continue as the Stotters' PR man in Tain.

Mr. Ferguson asked that as the Royal Hotel has lost favour with the Stotters would it be possible to have future AGMs at Golf View.

J.G. Robertson said he would make enquiries and expressed our thanks to Murd for being so generous this year.

The Captain proposed a toast to absent friends and on this maudlin note the proceedings ended at 15.40 hours.

Mr. MacPherson proposed a vote of thanks to the Chair.

This relatively tame meeting had one peculiar note in that Ian MacPherson pleaded for Ken Ross and Scott Ferguson to curtail their comments, even though Ken was in Hong Kong at the time, thus also missing out on being elected as Vice-Captain.

MINUTES OF THE 29ᵀᴴ ANNUAL GENERAL MEETING OF THE STOTTERS – 31ˢᵀ JULY, 1994

Held in the Dining Room of the Golf View Guest House – courtesy of Mr. and Mrs. I. Ross.

Twenty-eighth match – the Stotters v Tain Golf Club ended in victory for the Stotters, and considering he could hardly stand, the Captain of Tain made a remarkable presentation of the Cup to Captain Houston.

Captain John Houston in the chair.

MINUTES OF THE PREVIOUS MEETING

These were read to the assembled company and proposed for adoption by H. Robertson Junior and seconded by R. Towart. Their adoption was passed unanimously.

MATTERS ARISING FROM MINUTES

Mr. MacPherson had produced a magnificent Stotters' flag and the Captain expressed everyone's appreciation for this gesture.

It was even more enthusiastically received when Mr. MacPherson refused any recompense for the flag.

ELECTION OF OFFICE BEARERS

Captain Houston said how saddened everybody was at the deaths of Walter Kerr and Scott Ferguson during the year and asked everyone to observe a minute's silence.

He thanked everyone for their support during the year and said that he was delighted that Andrew Urquhart had decided to throw in his lot with the Stotters, and welcomed him to the meeting. He then proposed Simon Houston (present Vice-Captain) as Captain and his recommendation was accepted unanimously.

Captain Simon Houston took the chair and expressed the deep honour he felt at being elevated to such high position and prattled on in like vein for a minute or so. The speech was greeted with total silence and the Stotters wondered what they had let themselves in for.

Worse was to follow however, because Captain Houston proposed K. Ross as his Vice-Captain. R. Towart seconded this and before any of the assembled company could voice acceptance or otherwise, the Captain promptly appointed Mr Ross Vice-Captain.

Secretary – W. Kemp was again appointed Secretary on a proposal by the Captain and seconded by everyone.

ANY OTHER COMPETENT BUSINESS

The Secretary stated that today had been an historic one in the history of the Annual Match as a lady, one Morag Sutherland, had taken part, playing for Tain.

The Secretary expressed the wish that this was a one-off occurrence and that in future the teams would revert to gentlemen only. He was immediately labelled a 'sexist old b------' by some of the younger Stotters but as the Secretary thought that they had called him a 'sexy old b------' the meeting carried on without further acrimony.

Robert Towart asked if the Captain had sole discretion to appoint Stotters.

He had it pointed out to him, in no uncertain terms by the older members, that membership was by invitation only and invites were only given out if the existing Stotters were convinced that the person concerned would be a regular attender at Golf Week.

The Vice-Captain asked if 12 was a sacrosanct number and felt that we should extend the pool.

Captain Simon Houston felt that by expanding the numbers we could create a monster and pointed out that at the last two meetings it was agreed that the membership should be 12 full Stotters and two Associates.

John Houston and I. MacPherson agreed we should continue to be very selective and asked that the present format should be adhered to: i.e., 12 full Stotters and membership by invitation only.

Andrew Urquhart also felt that the Stotters should remain 'an exclusive club'.

R. Towart felt that there had been a different atmosphere during the match and afterwards in the Clubhouse, and the Secretary agreed that it had indeed been like an old time Stotters versus Tain match.

W. Kemp proposed Ian Ferguson be made an Associate Stotter. This was seconded by the Captain and approved unanimously.

I. Ferguson accepted his appointment and stated that he intended being at Tain for Golf Week in future years and thanked the Stotters for accepting him.

Ian MacPherson proposed Andrew Urquhart as an Associate Stotter and this was seconded by H. Robertson. The proposal was accepted unanimously.

The Captain proposed G. Ross as an Associate Stotter. This was seconded by R. Towart and again accepted unanimously.

Mr. Urquhart and Mr. Ross both expressed their thanks for having been accepted into such a stalwart band, and the Stotters were much relieved to discover that G. Ross does not have his father's propensity for speech making.

R. Towart again proposed that the Captain should pick the team for Sunday's match on the Saturday when he knew who would be available. It was agreed that this was a sensible suggestion.

I. MacPherson wondered if the dates of death should be engraved on the plaques on the Stotters seat.

What a can of worms this opened up!

F. Urquhart agreed this should be done.

Then the Vice-Captain threw the whole question into the melting pot by asking if the dates would be from inception as a Stotter until death. I. MacPherson wanted just the date of death, and as he had supplied the seat he should have the first say.

The Vice-Captain ignored this remark and asked the company to consider the following options:

a) Date of Death only.

b) Date of inception as Stotter – Date of Death.

c) Date of Birth – Death.

After long, and occasionally heated, discussion it was agreed that proposal b.) was desirable.

The Secretary is to provide F. Urquhart with the necessary details and also collect money from the members to reimburse him for the work. It was also agreed that a plaque 'The Stotters – formed 1966' be put on the seat. Mr. Urquhart said he would attend to this.

The Vice-Captain also felt that the Stotters should provide a small seat at the 8th tee because there was always a hold up there during tournament week. This suggestion did not raise much enthusiasm and no decision was taken.

There being no further business, no drink and no prospects of any more, the Captain closed the meeting.

Mr. MacPherson proposed a vote of thanks to the chair and the meeting ended at approximately 4.05 p.m.

There is a lovely irony in the election of three Associate Stotters, just after apparent agreement that there should only be two.

It is fitting that Scott's son, Ian Ferguson, was proposed as an Associate Stotter in the year of Scott's sad demise. Ian had been a regular visitor to Tain with his parents since the late 1970s.

Born in Falkirk in 1960 and still living there, Ian was to become a Chartered Modern Language Teacher (French and German) – currently at Craigmount High School in Edinburgh, having previously worked in Wallace High School, Stirling; Elgin High School; and at Aston University, Birmingham as an Overseas Placements Officer.

A quiet individual, and small in stature, Johnny Houston claims that he used to play with ladies' clubs ("well, certainly ladies' woods!").

However, Ian is quite clear that he didn't ("though at some point I may have had a ladies' driver for a few months, whether at Tain or not I don't know").

Ian won the Teddy Brookes trophy in 1979 when only 17, and whilst Johnny remembers caddying for him at some stage, it was actually Dr. John who was on his bag.

"He was pulling my trolley at one point in heavy rain with no waterproofs of any sort, his trousers soaking and just flip-flops on his feet. Every time I stood over my ball on the fairway wondering what to play, he would immediately hand me my 4-wood.

He knew better than I did that each time I used it the ball would land on or close to the green. Most memorably, during my final match after I'd hit another 4-wood on to the green around the 15th, he pointed it at me and announced loudly: "that's who you should have married!""

His involvement with the Stotters was to be all too short because of his other interests: "Probably the main reason I didn't continue to visit Tain (and I regret it, but you can't do everything) was that as a passionate student of French (and German) my French friends weren't on holiday until the end of July/beginning of August and if I wanted to be able to spend any time in France with them it was during that time before I went back to work – and of course that coincides with the Stotters and Tain golf week".

Despite not being able to return regularly, Ian has some very fond memories of Tain, including: "MacPhearson being swapped for a teddy bear; Geraldine Houston caddying and shouting before tee-shots were played at the 16th:"bags I fish it out of the burn!"; Tommy Armstrong in the match-play stage of the tournament after a breakfast of a double-gin, standing at the ninth tee in the pouring rain – 6 down – asking: "is anybody enjoying this?""

Ian now plays his golf at Falkirk G C, off 15, but is still ever hopeful that this can come back down.

George William Aird Ross, Ken's elder son, also emerges in 1994.

Born in 1977 in London and living in Walton-on-Thames, George is married to Sandra, and they have three children – Oliver, Emily-Anna, and Zachary.

After graduating in Physics at the University of Bath, he trained as an ACA, joining the Structured Finance team of Merrill Lynch, but claims he "didn't single-handedly start the financial crisis as my father would have you believe".

He survived the acquisition by Bank of America in 2009, becoming a Director and working with them for seven years.

He joined the investment arm of RBS, (now NatWest Markets) in early 2017 to head up coverage in the Financial Institutions Origination and Solutions area in the UK and Ireland for Building Societies, Challenger Banks, Specialist Lenders, Fintech and Asset Based Lending.

Playing off 10 at the Berkshire Golf Club, George doesn't get the time to play frequently enough, hence "my golf is rather volatile though not quite so much as the Capital Markets in 2008".

In his early years, he was a regular visitor to Tain with Ken and Bridget, but work and family commitments limited his visits in the early years of the millennium.

"However, in 2013 I returned bringing my family of 4 (at that time) and extended family members, and we have never looked back".

He remembers being very keen at the age of 17 "to see first-hand whether the AGMs really were as debaucherous as I'd been led to believe!"

He soon was to acquire the characteristic Stotter vagueness about years and events during Golf Week. "I'm slightly hazy about dates but have eased my way well into the normal rigmarole of the AGMs, so most years merge into one!"

This vagueness is well characterised by the tale George was told as a boy.

It's actually the story of the epic 18th hole incident involving Alan Robertson and Cecil Philip, but it was told to George as follows:

"In an early Stotters' match when whisky had obviously been consumed and the foursome had reached the 18th, a Tain gentleman was due to putt from quite a distance across the green and it appeared he was either short-sighted or under the influence.

He asked for the Stotter to be a good fellow and attend the pin for him. The Stotter, being an exemplary member, held the pin, albeit he moved it two or three feet to the side of where the actual hole was positioned.

The people sitting outside the clubhouse were in on the joke and everything was quiet as the Tain gent motioned to play. He gave it his best attempt and it disappeared three foot left of the tended pin much to his miscomprehension.

He holed it!

There was raucous amusement from the galleries and what made it worse was that this apparently led to the loss of the match by the Stotters on the last!"

The reality of the tale may differ, but George prefers the way he remembers it.

George has twice lost in the final of the Brookes cup, both times in the mid-90s. "The last time I lost on the 19th by missing a 2-foot putt – a brutal way to go".

He is also a beaten finalist in the Stirling.

Geraldine Houston has always caddied for him – "which has been great, if not also drink fuelled".

He remembers some memorable matches against Gary and Craig "resulting in us tacking down the 18th, criss-crossing the fairway in an attempt to find the green".

"It has been great to play against Donald, Graham, Sugar and many others over the years. Rarely has the sun not shined, the whisky not flowed and the earth not moved!"

George loves coming to Tain: "It's beautiful – the camaraderie of the Stotters and extended family and friends; my Tain relatives and local friends established over many years of playing; the course, which is truly an absolute gem, a term very befitting of this course but so often overused; and the memories of all those hard fought rounds and Stotters' matches".

The Stotters' Bench

Golf View AGM – 1995 – L to R – Robert Towart, Hamish Senior, Wilson Kemp, Frank Cougan, Hector MacIntyre, Sport, George Ross, Simon Houston, Forbie (shielding Andrew Urquhart), Ken Ross, Johnny Houston

MINUTES OF THE 30TH ANNUAL GENERAL MEETING OF THE STOTTERS – SUNDAY 30TH JULY, 1995

The AGM held 'alfresco' at Golf View Guest House courtesy of Mr. and Mrs. Ian Ross.

The twenty-ninth annual match between the Stotters and Tain Golf Club ended in victory for the Stotters, and the Captain accepted the trophy for the 4th year in a row.

Captain Simon Houston in the chair.

MINUTES OF THE PREVIOUS MEETING

These were read to the Members by the Secretary and it was pointed out that the Secretary had, at last, got it wrong.

J.G. Robertson was not present and therefore could not have approved the adoption of the Minutes. The Secretary was fined £5 for this gross error. The Secretary amended the Minutes and these were then proposed for adoption by J.G. Robertson and seconded by R. Towart. This was carried unanimously.

CAPTAIN'S REMARKS

Captain Houston thanked Murd and Ray Ross for again allowing us to use Golf View for our meeting and expressed the hope that this arrangement could be continued.

He then asked everyone to observe a minute's silence for Ian MacPherson and Tommy Young – two of the original band who had sadly passed away in 1994.

APPOINTMENT OF OFFICE BEARERS

Captain Houston proposed K. Ross as the Captain and the proposal was adopted unanimously.

Ken Ross took the chair.

His first word was 'Gentlemen' – this threw the meeting into such confusion that it was several minutes before order was restored and some of the older members had to be revived by passing a glass of whisky under their noses.

The Captain said it was a great honour to be elected Captain of such a prestigious club and hoped he would carry out his duties in a manner befitting the position.

He then warbled on about how valuable a good Secretary was and this gave W. Kemp hope that he would at last be replaced.

However, both Captain and Secretary were brought down to earth when a disembodied voice told the Captain to 'shut his f...ing mouth and get on with the meeting'.

Captain Ross proposed H. Robertson Junior as Vice-Captain and this proposal was accepted unanimously.

Captain Ross proposed W. Kemp as Secretary and this was also accepted unanimously.

ANY OTHER COMPETENT BUSINESS

F. Cougan pointed out that the plaques on the seat had not been altered as agreed at last year's AGM. The Secretary took the blame for this and admitted he had not provided Forbie with the necessary details to allow new plaques to be made.

The Secretary was fined another £5 for dereliction of duty.

The Captain then pointed out that there are now only 11 full members. Simon Houston immediately proposed I. Ferguson as a full Stotter and this was seconded by J. Houston and carried unanimously. The Vice-Captain asked if 12 full members was the agreed limit and the elder members confirmed this to be the case.

John Houston pointed out that the number of players available for the game seemed to vary daily from the Friday we arrived until the game took place. He said we should ignore G. Raeside as he had again let us down and asked everyone to let the Secretary know in plenty of time if they intended being in Tain.

The Captain pointed out that this year we had 12 full Stotters and two outsiders, and paid tribute to Hector MacIntyre for never having lost his

Stotters' match. It was agreed that 14 should be a maximum as any additional players might start to cause interference with the Sunday Open Tournament.

F. Cougan pointed out that there was a decided scarcity of drink and the Captain hurriedly left the meeting to remedy the situation.

The Vice-Captain queried if we needed more Associate members or if our present complement of 12 full and two Associates was ample.

The Captain said that as there had recently been an influx of younger members he saw no need for a further increase. F. Cougan and H. Robertson felt that invitations should only be issued sparingly and felt that Associates should serve an apprenticeship though they were reluctant to say how long the apprenticeship should be.

These last statements were generally agreed and it was the feeling of the meeting that the numbers we have at this point in time are the maximum required.

The Captain then broached the subject of the proposed new Clubhouse at Tain and felt that the Stotters should perhaps be doing something about it. Simon Houston supported Captain Ross on this issue and felt that we should make representations to the Club before anything serious happens.

F. Urquhart suggested that we leave this topic until next year when any proposals should be known. J.G. Robertson submitted that it matters not one whit what the Stotters think, Tain Golf Club would go their own way.

This sober statement killed any further discussion on this topic.

The Captain felt that perhaps the social events of the week should be looked at to see if the company could get together more often and asked members to put forward suggestions for discussion next year.

By this time, as drink was getting low, shadows getting long, and eyes beginning to close, the Captain decided that enough was enough and thanked everyone for their forbearance in listening to his rhetoric, asked the Secretary to arrange for flowers to be delivered to Ray and closed the meeting.

J.G. Robertson asked for a vote of thanks for the chair and the meeting closed at 16.25 hours.

George Ross remembers an incident during this AGM: "In a recess moment, Johnny Houston turned to talk to me and asked "Ai, err, bleee blah root ta neb, Tam,

Simeon, a no lassie? Ar yee gee?"

I had no idea what he had just said, so I obligingly just nodded my head and said, "Yes".

Next he rolled back, looking startled and said, "Feck me, ur GAY!"

I connected the previous sentences and figured out what had been said. Next year I brought Sandra!"

Hector Michael MacIntyre (no relation of the comedian, though he could learn from Hector's irrepressible enthusiasm!) was indeed noted for not having lost his match, but as he made his debut the previous year this was not exactly outstanding.

Hector remembers: "Due to shortages of Stotters, I played in the match in 1994 with Ken Ross against Stuart Thomson (Distillery manager) and Craig (Watson). We won with ease, Stuart collapsing on the 17th tee".

Hector's soft lilting accent marks him out as hailing from Benbecula, though he now lives in Glasgow, married to Maggie with two children – Greg and Laurie.

As a Sales Director in the engineering sector, he has travelled extensively working in the Oil & Gas, Power and Chemical industries. He includes in his itinerary the Americas, Africa, Europe, the Middle East and Asia.

Hector plays off 21 at Hilton Park and Benbecula.

Johnny Houston remembers how the Stotters' connection began: "Jamie Scott from Tain went to study Mechanical Engineering at Paisley Tech, close to where we lived, and in 1982 introduced us to this lad from the halls of residence (the former Thornly Park approved school), with a full sweeping head of hair – from Benbecula – by the name of Hector MacIntyre. The rest, as they say, is history".

Sadly, Hector's hair has now gone leaving him with a shining dome to match his forehead.

He first came to Tain in 1983 and fell down the stairs at the Railway Inn, a pattern familiar to many Stotters

After his Stotters' debut, he was soon to join the Stotters' ranks.

Hector was proud to qualify from the 4 Day Open in 2014 for the first time, but has many excuses for failing to qualify in other years, summarised in his own words as follows:

"Hungover.

Taking a 13 at the 17th when I could have taken a penalty drop out of the river.

Waiting 30 minutes to play my second shot at the 18th –ended up with an 8, and failed to qualify by one shot.

A jet making me five-putt at the 15th.

Playing with Simon Houston".

He rues: "Most qualification failures have happened on the 2nd hole first round and the 11th hole second round".

Hector, to many people's confusion on the tee, is a left-handed player, though some say changing to right-handed would massively improve his Handicap.

He fondly remembers Gary Tonge twice falling into the river at the 17th :

"He took his practice shot, lost his balance and fell back into the river. He was fished out after much hilarity and eventually played his shot only to fall right back in again".

Liam Hughes also remembers this: "We very nearly fell off the bridge laughing to join him".

Not so fondly, he also remembers partnering Andy Robertson (Tricia Houston's former husband) and "getting slaughtered – lost every hole".

Like all of the Stotters, Hector has come back year after year to Tain because of "the people, the course and the friendships".

MINUTES OF THE 31ST ANNUAL GENERAL MEETING OF THE STOTTERS – SUNDAY 4TH AUGUST 1996

Held at Golf View Guest House, Tain.

The thirtieth match between the Stotters and Tain Golf Club resulted in a Stotters' victory, and the Captain congratulated his team on making it five victories in a row.

Captain Ken Ross in the chair.

APOLOGIES

Apologies for non-attendance were received from F. Cougan and I. Ferguson.

CAPTAIN'S REMARKS

Ken Ross said it was gratifying to see 10 full Stotters and one Associate Stotter in attendance, and was pleased that Hector MacIntyre was also in attendance as: 'a kind of NATO observer – to oversee the meeting, make a lot of useless observations and be totally ignored by any warring factions'.

He thanked Forbie for the marvellous job he had made of the Stotters' seat and thanked the Secretary for his marvellous minutes.

The Captain was interrupted in full flow by I. Walkington wishing to make a point of order

Amid a deafening silence, Ian pointed out that George Ross's fly was undone, but as George was a relative newcomer and had little to show he did not propose a fine.

I. Walkington was promptly fined £1 for being too frivolous and daring to interrupt the Captain.

Forbie Urquhart stated that Derek Mackenzie had stripped, sealed and varnished the seat on a materials only basis and the work had cost £15.

The plaques were £38 and he hoped everyone was satisfied with the result. The Secretary had already given Forbie money to cover the outlay and he had spare cash to hand back.

The Captain asked if Rita and Christine would use the extra to buy flowers for Ray Ross.

The Captain stated that he had had no formal offer from the Factor re the proposal of a Skibo v Stotters' match and asked the company if the proposal should be pursued.

John and Simon Houston felt that if the Stotters were to receive the courtesy of the course then the matter should certainly be pursued. George Ross felt the game, if it could be arranged, would add another dimension to the Stotters' sojourn in Tain. R. Towart agreed wholeheartedly and, if it was a freebie, definitely go for it.

J. Houston and the Captain pointed out that the whole essence of the Stotters is Tain Golf Week and that their association has been and always will be with Tain.

The Captain next raised the question of what the Stotters could or should do, re the new clubhouse. J. Houston felt the club should be approached to see what it felt the Stotters could reasonably do to help in any way.

F. Urquhart felt that nothing should be done at this point in time.

Hamish Robertson Senior opined that the Stotters should do nothing until Tain had made up its mind on final proposals. This judgement from the President of Tain Golf Club effectively ended further discussion on the topic.

ELECTION OF OFFICE BEARERS

Ken Ross proposed H. Robertson Junior as Captain and, as no dissenting voices were raised, the appointment was approved unanimously.

Hamish took the chair and thanked Ken for doing such a good job in his year as Captain. He felt privileged to follow such illustrious Captains as Dr. J. Houston, G. Tocher etc., and hoped he would be able to carry out his duties as ably as they had.

A disembodied voice interrupted and asked if a Vice-Captain were to be appointed before it became dark and a chastened Captain hurriedly proposed I. Walkington as his Vice-Captain. The proposal was accepted unanimously and I. Walkington accepted the position in his inimitable fashion.

W. Kemp was again proposed as Secretary and, there being no other nominations, he agreed to carry on for another year.

ANY OTHER COMPETENT BUSINESS

Captain Robertson said that the people on the fringes of the Stotters, like the lads who came up with the Houstons, should be made welcome as we needed them to become interested in the Stotters because in due course they may be required to keep the Stotters going.

The company agreed that this was an excellent sentiment. Ken Ross pointed out that Hector MacIntyre was a perfect example of what the Captain was saying and proposed Hector as an Associate Stotter. The proposal was accepted and Hector accepted his election with delight.

Someone pointed out that the Captain was not wearing a Stotters' jersey and should be fined accordingly.

As the Stotters had not had new jerseys for some considerable time the company felt it was unfair to impose any penalty but he was warned to rectify the situation for next year.

Forbie said that the Golf Club and indeed a lot of townspeople recognised the yellow jersey as the Stotters' colour and felt we should wear the colours during Golf Week.

The Secretary announced that arrangements had been made to play over Portmahomack on Wednesday 7th August for the Hic-Cup, the format being Stableford score over 9 holes. The participating members to repair to the Castle Hotel for the presentation.

J. Houston announced a barbeque at the caravan site on Monday 5th – 7.30 for 8.

J. Houston asked for a minute's silence for absent friends.

The Captain wished the Members good luck in the 4 day Tournament and thanked Ian and Ray for allowing us the use of the facilities at Golf View.

This was much appreciated and he hoped we would be allowed to hold next year's AGM at the same venue.

K. Greig congratulated the Captain on his handling of the meeting and on this happy note the Captain closed the meeting at 17.05.

MINUTES OF THE 32ND ANNUAL GENERAL MEETING OF THE STOTTERS – 3RD AUGUST 1997

Held at Golf View Guest House, Tain.

The Thirty-First Match between the Stotters and Tain Golf Club. The Stotters won.

Captain Ian Walkington in the Chair.

APOLOGIES
Received from Ian Ferguson, Ken Greig and H. Robertson Junior.

MINUTES OF THE PREVIOUS MEETING
These were read by the Secretary and as no dissenting voices were heard were adopted as correct – Proposal S. Houston and seconded by K. Ross.

CAPTAIN'S REMARKS
Captain Walkington asked for a minute's silence to be observed for Roderick F. Mackenzie who had embodied all the qualities which made a Stotter.

After the minute's silence the Captain thanked his team for once again recording a victory in the annual match against Tain, and felt that he himself had contributed greatly by recording an 8 and 7 victory thus uplifting the team's spirits by such sterling leadership.

This self-effacing statement caused most of the members to choke on their drinks and the Captain was asked to shut up and get on with the business of the Meeting.

Happily the Captain took the hint and moved on to the next item.

ELECTION OF OFFICE BEARERS
Captain Walkington said that due to unforeseen circumstances, the Vice-Captain could not manage to be present and this being so, the Captain

proposed himself. This caused considerable uproar and catcalls of "big headed be whiskered b------" could be heard loud and clear.

The Captain ignored the disturbance and there being no other nominations his proposal was accepted.

Vice-Captain Ken Ross proposed that H. Robertson Junior should be elected Vice-Captain and this was seconded by S. Houston. The proposal was carried unanimously.

Secretary – W. Kemp was again elected unanimously.

ANY OTHER COMPETENT BUSINESS

Once again the problem of 'sleepers' arose. K. Ross stated that people elected as Stotters should at least show some vestige of loyalty towards the Club and for anyone to ignore the ideals of the Stotters was a major sin and they should be excommunicated.

The Captain asked if G. Raeside should still be afforded the title of 'Stotter' and felt that the 'The Wig' had not been a role model. F. Urquhart agreed with the Captain and the members decided that G. Raeside should be struck off.

Frank Cougan pointed out that it had been agreed many moons ago that 'once a Stotter always a Stotter' but accepted that in G. Raeside's case his attendance record and attitude fell far below the accepted standards.

Ken Ross then asked why the game against Tain had to start at 8 a.m.

Forbie said that the Club felt that the match should be over before the Sunday One Day event got underway.

The views were expressed that the matches were more or less on time and that nowadays we do not wander down the 18th fairway with glasses in hand. Because they had changed the time, is there a faction within the Club against the match taking place?

Hamish Robertson Senior said he would have a quiet word with the Captain of Tain about the early start.

Ken Ross asked what had happened to the flag this year.

The Secretary apologised profusely for forgetting to raise the flag, but as he had difficulty in raising anything these days the slight matter of the flag fades into insignificance. Notwithstanding this explanation the Secretary was fined £5.

Bob Meikle had been ashamed that no acknowledgement of the Stotters' donation to repair Houston's buggy had been given and rectified this by presenting the Secretary with a handwritten apology.

Frank Cougan felt that if the club had been told the buggy was knackered it would have been better to have written it off. The point was also raised enquiring whether the money had actually been spent on the buggy. As far as the Secretary knew it had, but he would make discreet enquiries re this.

K. Ross asked if now was the time for the Stotters to make a contribution to the new Clubhouse.

Hamish Robertson Senior said the time was now right.

After some discussion it was agreed that we present Tain Golf Club with a new Trophy Cabinet and it was left to the Secretary to organise this.

K. Ross asked about the origin of the Hic-Cup.

Once this was explained the Captain rose to close the meeting but Hamish Robertson Senior interrupted and asked that the Stotters should be reminded that at official dinners or outings Stotters' shirts and ties are 'de rigeur' and the only acceptable dress.

The Captain asked the members to note this 'diktat' and vowed heavy fines for anyone transgressing the code.

He then closed the meeting at 16.46 hours.

TAIN GOLF CLUB
Letter from Bob Meikle   2ND August, 1997

Dear Wilson,

As you know, I was appalled to learn today that the superb contribution from 'the Stotters' towards the refurbishment of the 'buggy' had not been formally acknowledged by the Club.

Casting no aspersion in relation to this dreadful, unfeeling omission, but keenly aware of both my responsibility in all matters pertaining to Tain Golf Club, and of our delight, I now write to express the Members' and Management Committee's warmest appreciation for your Members' much valued gift. Without it, we would not have embarked upon refurnishing the vehicle.

Sadly, a saga of inexplicable engine failure, starter, fuel mixture imbalance and sand in the works inter alia, means that the buggy 'ne va pas', but ongoing investigation will hopefully bear fruit, ultimately!

I have arranged for a buggy from David's stable to be at the Stotters' disposal during Golf Week 1997 in compensation.

Again, sincere apologies and much thanks to you all!

Sincerely,

Bob Meikle – Captain

This year, Hector MacIntyre won Gilbert's Goblet as Johnny Houston remembers: "The Bull had a fine round of a net 69 after he had been out of his tree on the Sunday. Taking it easy and early to bed on the Monday night resulted only in a horror show on the Tuesday, and Tain almost had to set up a sub-committee to count his score!"

Hamish is Tain's number one fan

Veteran pledges to continue his annual pilgrimage to Royal Burgh

an visitor: Hamish Robertson pictured outside Golf View House, Tain, overlooking Tain Golf Course

HAMISH Robertson must surely hold the record for being Tain's most faithful tourist.

For Mr Robertson (85) has been making the summer pilgrimage to his old home town every year without fail since 1934, with the exception of the war years.

Not for Hamish the exotic delights of foreign travel, or coach holidays around the country.

Every August for nearly 60 years he has headed for Tain – with his wife Helen and family in the early days, then as a couple, and latterly sadly alone after his wife's death two years ago.

"I have a great fondness for the place, as did my wife and family," said Mr Robertson who is honorary president of Tain Golf Club and thrice the winner of the club's annual tournament.

"I wouldn't consider going anywhere else, although I'm afraid all my contemporaries have gone and there's hardly anyone left in Tain that I know.

"I am now the oldest member of Tain Golf Club,

and I enjoy coming up for the annual tournament."

Mr Robertson's nephews David, who owns the chemist's shop, and retired tea planter Ross, still live in the town and he enjoys get-togethers with them during his annual fortnight, his golf and a few drams each evening.

Born and brought up in Tain, Mr Robertson joined the Commercial Bank from school as a teenager in 1928 when George D Gill was manager.

He moved to the bank's head office Edinburgh when he was 21, where he worked until the outbreak of war.

As an Argyll and Sutherland Highlander he saw active service in Africa, Italy, Egypt and Palestine, moving up through the ranks and finishing the war as a major.

But after the war, he resumed his job with the bank and it was back to Tain each year for summer holidays.

He recalls when all the main roads were subject to a 30mph limit and police

"speed traps" took the form of a local bobby leaping out from behind a bush waving a white hanky.

"It's all change now," laughed Mr Robertson. "When we used to drive up in the early days, we used to go through all the villages and towns along the way. Now you don't go through a single village.

"But I think the biggest change is the influx of people to the area from various places.

"When I left it was a sleepy town of around 1,500, and now it's around 3-4,000.

Mr Robertson retired 25 years ago, having risen to area general manager with the bank, which latterly became The Royal Bank of Scotland, in Glasgow.

He now lives in Newton Mearns, outside Glasgow, and has three sons, eight grandchildren and a great grand-daughter.

But he pledges that every year "so long as I'm not cripple," he will make the pilgrimage to the Royal Burgh.

MINUTES OF THE 33RD ANNUAL GENERAL MEETING OF THE STOTTERS – SUNDAY 2ND AUGUST 1998

Held at Golf View Guest House.

The thirty-second annual match between The Stotters and Tain Golf Club. The Stotters won by 1 hole, despite the gallant efforts of Hector MacIntyre and Andrew Robertson.

Captain Ian Walkington in the chair – once again.

APOLOGIES

Received from K. Ross, F. Cougan and I. Ferguson.

MINUTES OF THE PREVIOUS MEETING

With the relaxed approach of someone who knew in advance that it was the last time he would have to produce this annual bullshit, the Secretary was in typically fine form as he delivered what would be his final set of Minutes.

As they were the first pair to waken up, R. Towart and K. Greig felt duty bound to propose and second the minutes respectively.

CAPTAIN'S REMARKS

Captain Walkington congratulated the Secretary for his excellent performance, and the rest of the gathering for yet another superb victory against Tain.

MATTERS ARISING FROM MINUTES

Sadly it was not long before the meeting threatened to descend into anarchy. The guilty party was one H. MacIntyre who mistook the term 'matters arising' for an opportunity to launch a scathing tirade against the 'useless fat b' who was posing as his partner in a nine down defeat two hours earlier.

Somewhat deflated and miffed at the manner of his defeat, MacIntyre demanded that only real golfers be allowed to participate in the Stotters' match as opposed to dummy rubber versions.

He was politely told by J. Houston and R. Towart to 'shut the f… up'

as this was a matter which should be addressed under Any Other Competent Business. MacIntyre offered a contemptuous 'Err' and took comfort from a nearby bottle of Glenmorangie.

H. Robertson Junior asked if the meeting could move on.

Simon Houston raised 'The Wig', prompting the annual meeting of the 'when is a Stotter not a Stotter' debating society.

The Minutes had recorded that G. Raeside had been struck off the list and R. Towart reminded those present that he had argued against the deletion of his name.

Dr K. Greig said that the Secretary had been too blunt with the term 'struck off' (that's struck off) and asked that the phrase be amended to 'relinquished'.

The Secretary took umbrage at this, and insisted that if 'struck off' was the term agreed at the previous meeting then 'struck off' it would remain.

He added that anyone who disagreed would quite simply be 'struck off'.

ELECTION OF OFFICE BEARERS

Captain Walkington proposed H. Robertson Junior as his successor. This was seconded by J. Houston and carried unanimously.

The outgoing Captain vacated his chair with the time honoured bullshit.

His dashing young successor accepted the role, albeit twelve months late, before thanking the immediate past Captain for his vote of confidence, and reminding his Dad that he would need some extra pocket money to buy everybody a celebratory drink.

The Captain then proposed George Ross as his Vice-Captain. This was seconded by H. MacIntyre, who had just emerged somewhat battered and bruised from his twelve round bout with the aforementioned bottle of Glenmorangie.

As no other nominations were forwarded, George Ross happily accepted the role.

With speed that would put Linford Christie to shame, W. Kemp proposed S. Houston as the new Secretary. With speed that would put Agatha Christie to shame this was seconded by H. Robertson Senior. The proposal was accepted unanimously.

And there it was.

In a brief moment, twenty years of brilliant history had come to an end.

Golf View, nae Tain itself, was smothered by an outbreak of impassioned applause as the outgoing Secretary passed on the tools of his trade to his successor.

And through the bedlam a quiet Falkirk accent could be quite clearly heard uttering the words 'Thank Christ for that!'

A piss break was declared in celebration.

ANY OTHER COMPETENT BUSINESS

Captain Robertson asked that members should discuss only competent business with a capital 'C'.

It took R. Towart only 10 seconds to break the Captain's directive. The subject of Andrew Robertson's less than breath-taking performance that afternoon was up for discussion.

Delighted at the chance to finally put forward his argument, H. MacIntyre said 'Err', before becoming re-acquainted with the Land of Nod.

W. Kemp apologised for failing to include Simon Ross in the line-up, but said he had assumed that Simon would be playing in the One Day instead. It was agreed that an accidental and unfortunate oversight had occurred.

However, as the debate had highlighted a potential shortage of Stotters' manpower, the Captain suggested that perhaps the family should be extended. W. Kemp said that as the introduction of new Stotters was by invitation, then such an approach should be made to Donald Sutherland, to become an Associate.

Recognising Donald's loyalty to the match and support of the Stotters over the years, the move received a warm welcome.

A second proposal to approach and sound out Donald Sutherland about the possibility of him becoming an Honorary Stotter was moved by W. Kemp and seconded by R. Towart. It was agreed that such an appointment would allow Donald to wear the yellow jersey and attend the AGM, but would not carry voting rights.

A first move to have Simon Ross instated as an Associate Stotter was proposed by R. Towart and seconded by H. MacIntyre.

Ian Walkington then moved that Murd and Ray Ross should also be offered honorary positions as they had provided the Stotters with excellent facilities over recent years. Although this was not accepted, the meeting agreed that it was a matter which should be revisited next year.

For the time being, a resolution to send Ray a bouquet of flowers, purchased from Stotters' funds, was passed.

W. Kemp was then fined £5 for turning up at the meeting in a shirt which was not of the Stotters' wardrobe.

£1 fines were imposed on R. Towart, G. Ross, H. MacIntyre, A. Urquhart and Dr. K. Greig for appearing for dinner the previous Friday night without Stotters' ties.

£2 fines were imposed on H. Robertson Senior and Junior for not turning up at all.

At this stage I. Walkington, clearly tickled by events, attempted to move the debate on to a higher intellectual plane by announcing to the meeting something not fit to print.

The meeting was closed at 16.41 p.m. and given that lengthy bursts of rancid hot air had been the order of the meeting, it seemed more than appropriate to call a halt to proceedings on that somewhat flatulent note.

Andrew Robertson, Tricia Houston's ex-husband, here steps into and immediately out of the Stotters' story. Formerly in the Royal Navy, he wasn't perhaps the best of golfers (though not necessarily because of that). Andrew was drafted in at short notice to play and clearly did not fare well. He and Tricia have three daughters – Rachel, Amanda and Julia.

Donald Sutherland's election as an Honorary Stotter was extremely well-earned and well-timed as he, along with Forbie Urquhart, was to become a key figure in the relationship between Tain and the Stotters.

Born in Dingwall in 1950, Donald had played for Tain against The Stotters for almost 20 years, and he describes the Stotters' matches as his favourite games of golf. Alarmingly, he says: "It's a great privilege to play in these matches and meet up each year with everybody associated with the Stotters – a great bunch of people".

Married to Morag, another great Tain and Stotters-associated stalwart, they have two daughters, Yvonne and Donna, and three grandchildren, Erin, Jack and Lucy.

His bearded visage and trademark self deprecating smile belie a thoughtful and considerate man who continues to be a hugely valuable link between Tain and The Stotters.

Playing now off 18, a slow climb up from an all-time low of 10, Donald is an ever-present and extremely competitive combatant.

He says of his matches: "All great memories of my matches. In my early days my regular opponents were Wilson Kemp and Scott Ferguson, and after Scott's passing it was Wilson and Forbie. In the last few years it's been mainly against Johnny and partner, always good fun. My most regular partner has been Gordon Bannerman, and during one match against Wilson and Forbie, Gordon was making a big fuss about breaking his tee.

You should have seen his face when Forbie produced sellotape and repaired it – priceless!"

Another tip he got from Forbie was how to avoid losing his tee – Forbie used to tie a weight to his tee to stop it flying away.

The furthest Donald managed in the 4-Day Open was to the semi-final of the Stirling Cup: "And I managed to throw away a substantial lead to lose that one".

He was Captain of Tain GC in 1995/6, and for many years served on the Committee of Management.

Simon Ross makes his first named appearance in 1998, four years after his older brother George was elected as an Associate Stotter.

Simon Raeburn Aird Ross was born in Watford in 1980, and now lives in London, married to Rebecca and with a daughter, Isabella (her name a delightful synchronistic echo of Isabella, the eldest of George Ross's children, born in 1840).

Simon's film star good looks fit him perfectly for his work in the film industry as a Commercials Director, and he has worked worldwide in this capacity. Amongst his major Stotter achievements are the creation of the excellent 2016 Clubhouse photographic montage, and the design of this book's cover.

Playing his golf at Royal Eastbourne, like his brother and father, he currently plays off 11 and earned his subsequent Associate Stotter status by "caddying for Stotters for many years thus proving my drinking credentials".

Whilst Simon reached the second round of the Stirling Tournament in 1992, he still claims his best round at Tain was 12 over par when he was 12.

When asked what brings him back to Tain, he usually replies: "I'm forced to go".

As a footnote to the AGM, Sport, after handing the reins of office to Hamish, wrote to him in September, copying all the Stotters, and Stotters' widows, saying:

"THIRTY YEARS ON------

Dear Captain,

As some hurtle and others shuffle towards the Millennium, and to brighten the autumn days, I enclose a couple of "archive" items and a happy picture.

This August, Hamish Senior produced a well-worn "snap" of the Stotters gathered by the first tee in 1972. I unwisely suggested that I might get it enlarged – and the blow up job has worked. One sad note is the absence of "big" Willie Mackenzie, our first casualty of the original playing twelve. And of those now, alas, but three remain.

My swansong as Captain.

With best wishes/love, as appropriate,

Ian (Sport) W".

Attached was a copy of the People's Journal Article from September 1968, and the photo he describes.

1972 STOTTERS' PHOTOGRAPH

KEY

1. Big Roddy Mackenzie (F)   6. Raeburn Robertson (F)   11. Frank Congan
2. Wilson Kemp   7. Gilbert Tocher (F)   12. Ian Macpherson (F)
3. Ian Walkington (F)   8. Ian McCall (F)   13. Tommy Young (F)
4. Walter Kerr (F)   9. John Houston (F)   14. Hamish Robertson (F)
5. Dougie Torrance   10. Hammy Mitchell (F)   15. David Rutherford

(F) Founder Members

In 1998, Tain's rebuilt Clubhouse was officially opened by Sir Michael Bonallack OBE, Secretary of the Royal and Ancient Golf Club of St. Andrews.

THE WILLIE ROSTOCK CLUBHOUSE SHOT

One of the Tain regulars until he had a serious accident affecting his legs was Willie Rostock, whose son is a talented local football player.

Willie used to be a fisherman plying the Dornoch Firth mussel beds. A cheerful character who (amazingly) enjoys a dram from time to time, he featured in one of the most memorable Stotters' match moments, as Donald Sutherland remembers:

"Willie Rostock, Bob Bev and I were playing in a three at the end (I think because the Stotters were struggling for numbers – hard to believe when you see it now).

Bob drove at the last, I duffed the second shot into the ditch area and Willie absolutely thinned the third shot – it somehow missed everybody standing outside the clubhouse, went through an open window and finished in the Clubhouse.

At this time the Clubhouse was not out of bounds, so Bob got his wedge out ready to play the next shot back through the open window amidst much hilarity. Surprisingly though, someone showed some common sense and decreed that we could have a free drop outside the Clubhouse.

To this day I still regret that bit of common sense as I would love to have seen Bev's attempt to play it back to the green – don't ask me who won the match, I suspect it was the Stotters though because I don't think anyone else would have shown the generosity to give us a free drop if the match hinged on it!"

Johnny Houston remembers the occasion well, as the ball sailed through the open clubhouse window and landed in his mum – Pat's – lap as she was enjoying her dram!

Hamish Robertson's memory differs slightly from Donald's in that he thinks he played in this match.

"It was a beautiful sunny Sunday, hence all the clubhouse windows were open, as a rather worse for-wear Willie lined up his wedge shot to the green. As he hit it, he fell over and didn't see the ball sail into the clubhouse.

The resulting hoo-ha took some time, and Bev's dropped ball outside the Clubhouse was conducted with grave ceremony watched by a tottering Willie and a huge crowd of laughing onlookers!"

Willie himself adds: "Well at least I shouted "fore"!"

MINUTES OF THE 34ᵀᴴ ANNUAL GENERAL MEETING OF THE STOTTERS – 1ˢᵀ AUGUST, 1999

Held at the Morangie House Hotel.

The thirty-third annual match of the Stotters v Tain – and the last one of the Millennium – ended with a stunning, albeit a tad repetitive, 20 hole victory for the Stotters.

Captain Hamish Robertson Junior in the chair.

APOLOGIES

Received from R. Towart, H. MacIntyre and I. Walkington.

Captain Robertson thanked the team for leading the Stotters into a bright new era with such a comprehensive victory over Tain. The team thanked Captain Robertson for leading them into a fantastically drunken state, with such a comprehensive supply of whisky.

MINUTES OF THE PREVIOUS MEETING

These were read out by the Secretary, who was making his debut in this Department, and who quickly realised he might as well have been reading from the Book of Great Venezuelan Fly-Fishing Moments, for all the dozen or so drunken b's around the table cared.

CAPTAIN'S REMARKS

First to come round, Captain Robertson thanked the Secretary for his efforts and added that the Stotters had found a worthy successor to immediate Past Secretary Kemp.

He then asked the assembled gathering if there was any business arising from the Minutes.

MATTERS ARISING FROM MINUTES

Donald Sutherland thanked all for inviting him to the AGM as an Honorary Stotter, and thanked the Secretary for pointing out that this title allowed him to utter lots of the obligatory AGM bullshit, but carried no voting rights.

Frank Cougan kindly told the new recruit that he could ask as many questions as he liked during the meeting, as long as they did not stray from: 'what you having?'; 'what'll it be?'; and 'can I top up your glass, Mr Cougan?'

Wilson Kemp then told Donald not to bother buying a new yellow jersey, because he had one that did not fit him anymore. He refused to specify whether the said jumper had become too large or too small over the years.

D. Sutherland replied, informing the meeting that he could lay his hands on some short sleeved shirts, thanks to a guy called Del he knew down the market and, if you needed any dodgy microwaves or CD's he was 'your man'.

At this stage Frank Cougan was fined £1 for taking an unofficial piss break.

ELECTION OF OFFICE BEARERS

Captain Robertson proposed George Ross as his successor. This was seconded by George's father, Ken. It was a proud moment for Ken who loves getting a chance to 'second' things at meetings.

The motion was carried unanimously.

George then waxed lyrical about how proud he was to become the face of the new Millennium, before being told to shut up or he would have his title removed in record quick time.

Captain Ross proposed Forbie Urquhart as Vice-Captain; this was seconded by W. Kemp and carried unanimously.

S. Houston was proposed as Secretary by H. Robertson Junior which was seconded, not altogether surprisingly, by Wilson Kemp and carried unanimously.

J. Houston then made a smart remark about preferring Wilson, only to be told that Wilson – Titleist – Callaway – it mattered not – he was still shit at golf and would not qualify.

ANY OTHER COMPETENT BUSINESS

A minute's silence was held in the memory of Hammie Mitchell and Ken Greig who had died in the previous twelve months, Ken only days before Golf Week in fact.

The sad moment was quickly followed by some traditional Stotters' fiery debate for – unbeknown to them – Hammie and Ken had conveniently provided us with a subject for debate – Membership.

Indeed, one unfeeling b------ said it was the best contribution Ken Greig had made to an AGM in his sixteen years of attending.

Still, numbers were down by two and H. Robertson Junior pointed out that his father was no longer fit to continue as a playing member.

Wilson Kemp added to the confusion by reminding us that I. Ferguson had not attended since becoming a Stotter and was, to all intents and purposes, a 'washoot' in respect of Tain.

But, as possible new names were tossed in to the ring, F. Cougan warned against hasty appointments because in the past, potential new members were given a year or two to see if they enjoyed Golf Week, or would fit the bill.

Ken Ross agreed and stressed that we must continue to place great value on membership. However, it was agreed that perhaps the appointment of two appropriate 'Associates' would be acceptable, plus one promotion into the First Team for Simon Ross.

H. Robertson Junior argued that his brother Roddy had not been well and had not been able to come to Tain in recent times, but he was now back for his second year and had even driven his father round the course that morning.

He said it would mean a great deal to the family if Roddy could be considered for an Associate place.

Following another wildcat piss break, this time inspired by Forbie, Ken Ross took the floor. But fortunately he left behind the table and chairs so we could continue.

Ken warned against Ross, Houston and Robertson dynasties controlling the Stotters, before suggesting long-time Ross family friend and common-law brother Mike Lloyd as a potential Associate. He said Mike loved to come up to Tain and would be part and parcel of the Stotters.

H. Robertson then proposed that Roddy Robertson and Mike Lloyd should be invited to join as Associates. This was carried unanimously.

175

It was then proposed by Frank Cougan that Hamish Robertson Senior, who would now be a non-playing Stotter, become the 2ⁿᵈ Honorary President of the Stotters, the 1ˢᵗ having been Anne Chalk. Again carried unanimously.

The Meeting threatened to descend into chaos when the subject of the wording on the Stotters' Millennium gift to Tain Golf Club was raised.

After pissing around with umpteen different ways to say the same bloody thing, a final definitive set of words was agreed. Forbie, who was going to choose his own wording anyway, was then despatched to the Jewellers with our timeless inscription in his hands.

All that was left was a fine to be imposed on the absent H. MacIntyre who had tried to use the excuse of his wife's imminent child birth as reason enough for missing Golf Week. It was agreed that with the wonders of modern medicine, Mrs. MacIntyre could not only have accompanied her husband to Tain, but could probably have caddied for him against Tain. He was fined £1.

The Meeting was closed at 4.45 p.m.

The strange re-election of Roddy as an Associate Stotter is one of the many Stotters' mysteries. Given that he was elected as an Associate Stotter eight years earlier and had played in some of the matches, this probably demonstrates the illogicality or perhaps the corporate memory loss often involved at AGMs.

Roddy had however just recovered from his first major brain haemorrhage, and his comeback was welcome.

Mike Lloyd's election as an Associate Stotter this year was extremely appropriate.

His son Tom came to Tain in 1995 with Bridger, Ken and Simon Ross and entered the 1 Day Tournament. Mike was working in the printing industry in South Africa at the time. Tom proceeded to win the Stirling Cup that year, caddied for by Simon.

The following year, 1996, Mike, a low handicap player, whose home course is East Sussex National, decided to fly over from SA to join Tom for his week in Tain and to play in the tournament – in his shorts which were to become one of his trademarks.

In a lovely twist of fate (Mike says: "surprisingly enough"), he too won the Stirling Cup (caddied for by Tom) and so his association with Tain Golf Week began.

One of his favourite memories arose from when the Rosses and the Lloyds had rented one of the cottages in Portmahomack.

"We had had a great AGM, as usual, on the Sunday after our match with Tain. As usual, too much liquor was drunk and we found ourselves back at our house in the Port around 5 o'clock in the afternoon.

I sat down to watch some TV but fell asleep in my chair. Ken and Bridget apparently headed off to the Castle pub about 7pm.

I awoke around 8 o'clock and pulled the curtains to reveal a beautiful morning. The sun was up and I felt fresh and ready to go. The first round of the Tain Golf Week was ahead of me. It was Monday morning.

I made myself some cereal and banana, some toast and a cup of tea. Then I thought I would wake up Tom, who in my opinion, was playing great and stood a good chance of doing well this year. I went up to his room to find his bed not slept in and immediately had bad thoughts about him wasting his chance having obviously got very pissed and unable to get back from the AGM the night before.

Being a little annoyed and not teeing off until my mid-day tee time I decided to lie down on my bed and read a few pages of my book.

Anyway, I fell asleep and the next time I woke up it was 12 o'clock and it was dark.

I was very disorientated and found myself checking Tom's bedroom and to my horror – there he was – fast asleep. I really didn't know what was going on! I went downstairs to check on Bridget and Ken and found them snuggled up together in their luxury suite.

What was going on?

I think it took about 10 minutes for me to figure out that it was now actually 12 o'clock Sunday evening and I was so alert that the next 8 hours were the longest time I had ever spent in bed AWAKE!"

MINUTES OF THE 35ᵀᴴ ANNUAL GENERAL MEETING OF THE STOTTERS – SUNDAY, 30ᵀᴴ JULY, 2000

Held in the Royal Hotel, Tain.

The thirty-fourth annual match against Tain and the 1ˢᵗ of the new Millennium had ended in a surprise victory for the home team.

Captain George Ross in the chair.

CAPTAIN'S REMARKS

Captain Ross thanked his team for helping secure his place in Stotters' history as the man who had not only masterminded the 1ˢᵗ defeat of the new century, but also brought to an end a run of straight Stotters' victories dating back to 1992.

The young Captain had lost his own match by three down and apologised for being somewhat 'out of sorts' on the day, to which one of the more cantankerous members was heard to mutter under his breath 'never mind out of sorts, the wee bugger's barely out of nappies'.

MINUTES OF THE PREVIOUS MEETING

These were read by the Secretary and, as no dissenting voices could be heard above the snoring, they were adopted by the assembled gathering.

The Honorary President then congratulated the Secretary on his absolutely accurate account of the previous AGM. However, when he was reminded that it was not the Secretary's turn to get the drinks in he added: 'Oh, sorry in that case I have never heard so much shit in all my life'.

MATTERS ARISING FROM MINUTES

Somewhat concerned that the meeting had yet to swing fully into action, Forbie Urquhart asked if he could be Mother. He was quietly advised that his cross-dressing was none of our business but there was nothing to stop him pouring the whisky.

ELECTION OF OFFICE BEARERS

George Ross proposed Forbie Urquhart as Captain. The proposal was seconded by John Houston and carried unanimously.

The incoming Captain then complimented his predecessor on steering the Stotters into the new Millennium fantastically well and asked how he could possibly follow such a fine young stalwart.

John Houston replied, somewhat cruelly, that picking a winning team might be a start.

Captain Urquhart then proposed Hector MacIntyre for the role of Vice-Captain. This was seconded by George Ross and carried unanimously.

Vice-Captain MacIntyre, who was once advised by Boris Yeltsin to cut down on the binge drinking, then promised to treat his position with the respect it deserved and promptly ordered a round of whiskies.

Despite his best efforts to bore the AGM into submission, Simon Houston was once again elected unanimously, having been proposed and seconded by H. Robertson Junior and Wilson Kemp respectively.

ANY OTHER COMPETENT BUSINESS

Captain Urquhart quickly raised the matter of Mike Lloyd's remarkably hairy legs which were suddenly bothering him. Until this point he had thought they were a pair of dark trousers and, as reality is an illusion that occurs due to the lack of alcohol, he duly reached for the whisky bottle.

The subject of the number of holes played in the annual match was then raised. The Captain said he had been playing that morning with David Rutherford who had said he had no idea why the game had been reduced to ten holes.

Donald Sutherland then admitted that the idea had been his, as a method of ensuring that all the matches were in the clubhouse by noon, out of respect for the competitors in the One Day Open.

Wilson Kemp, who had been uncharacteristically quiet, insisted that ten holes at Tain were still better than 18 holes at Invergordon.

Ken Ross, who had spent the opening half hour clearing his throat in preparation for a long winded stroll down Verbosity Boulevard, decided it was time to take centre stage.

Like Peter Snow on election night, he revealed how the Stotters had been victorious in each of the previous eight encounters when the games were played over 15 holes but the swingometer had definitely swung back in Tain's favour since the introduction of the shorter course.

He feared that statistically we may have lost a winning formula.

Then, like a thoroughbred racehorse stretching his legs, he continued, adding that it makes no difference whether it be 10 or 15 holes because the noise usually comes from inside the clubhouse once the match is over.

He was cut off in his prime by Hamish Robertson Junior who suggested that some stewardship be introduced to stop noise from the 18th green reaching the 1st tee.

Mike Lloyd, still reeling from the hairy legs slur, commented that Tain Golf Club's relaxed attitude to the Stotters' match was very unusual in this day and age and that the club was to be admired for its extraordinary generosity. Moving on, Captain Urquhart said he would discuss the number of holes with the Committee and whilst we would certainly prefer 15, we were of course at the mercy of Tain Golf Club.

It was also agreed that to return to 15 might not be met with much opposition because there was not as great a problem surrounding the match as we perhaps perceived.

Captain Urquhart then stressed that for the sake of the matches' future it was important that the young members of Tain Golf Club be brought in.

Simon Ross said he could possibly help on that matter as he had a couple of friends from University who were from Tain and who would be keen to get involved. However, that remark was dismissed out of hand because the idea of Simon Ross having two friends of any description was simply too ridiculous to be taken seriously.

The booming tones of Robert Towart could then be heard muttering something about the Tain team needing to be regenerated, only for his comments to be met with the usual chorus of 'I can't understand a single word that f---er is saying' from one of the more evergreen corners of the room.

Undeterred however, he pressed on, raising the subject of tee off times for the 4-Day Open, and that the Stotters competing should all try to get times, if possible, between 10 and 11, rather than spreading ourselves out over the course of the day.

A piss break was declared.

When the meeting reconvened it was announced that the Royal Hotel would allow use of the Residents' Lounge for the presentation of Gilbert's Goblet the following night. It was then unanimously agreed that the return of the Royal as a focal point for the Stotters during Golf Week would be a very welcome move indeed.

With that the meeting was brought to a close at 3.45 p.m.

Appended is the then record of the Official Membership of the Stotters. There are one or two slight inaccuracies, but Appendices 9 and 11 contain the facts.

The Stotters - 2000

Official Membership List

H. Robertson Snr - Hon. Pres. and Founder Member
I. Walkington - Founder Member.
F. Cougan - 1971
W. Kemp - 1973
R. Towart - 1987
J. Houston - 1988
S. Houston - 1991
K. Ross - 1992
H. Robertson Jnr - 1994
H. McIntyre - 1997
G. Ross - 1997
S. Ross - 1999

THE ASSOCIATES
M. Lloyd, R. Robertson

HONORARY STOTTERS
F. Urquhart, A. Urquhart, D. Sutherland

DECEASED
WW. McKenzie (1971), R. Robertson (1973), G. Tocher (1979), T. Armstrong (19
J. Campbell (1991), J. Houston (1991), I. McColl (1992), W. Kerr (1993),
S. Ferguson (1994), J.L. McPherson (1994), T.S. Young (1994), R.F. McKenzie
(1997), H. Mitchelll (1999), K. Greig (1999)

In association with Tain Golf Club and Glenmorangie

MINUTES OF THE 36TH ANNUAL GENERAL MEETING OF THE STOTTERS – SUNDAY, 5TH AUGUST, 2001

Probably held at the Royal Hotel, Tain.

The thirty-fifth annual match of the Stotters v Tain was won comfortably by Tain.

Captain F. Urquhart in the chair.

Apologies were received from Hamish Robertson Senior, the President.

CAPTAIN'S REMARKS

Captain Urquhart said that he was sad at the absence of our President, who would prove quite a miss at the AGM, and that it did not seem the same without him sitting in the corner with pipe in one hand and whisky in the other – mouthing obscenities at whichever unfortunate soul had inadvertently rattled his cage.

He added that he was delighted to see Founder Member Sport Walkington at the meeting.

The Captain then expressed satisfaction for the Saturday meal at the Royal, which those present agreed had been a roaring success. He also welcomed the return of 15 holes in the match against Tain.

Captain Urquhart then asked those present if they were happy with their new jumpers.

All said they were, even though the bright canary yellow did not quite match the red faces on display after the comprehensive thumping by their hosts some hours earlier.

MINUTES OF THE PREVIOUS MEETING

These were read by the Secretary and as no dissenting voices could be tolerated, were adopted as correct. They were proposed by Captain Urquhart and seconded by Ken Ross.

MATTERS ARISING FROM MINUTES

Sport Walkington, clearly fascinated at the amount of time spent discussing Mike Lloyd's legs at the previous meeting, asked whether the hairs had grown longer during the last twelve months.

He replied "yes they had" and added "they would probably grow another couple of inches before the close of the meeting if Sport continued to interrupt with such inane shit".

ELECTION OF OFFICE BEARERS

Captain Urquhart thanked the meeting and said it had been a great honour to have served as Captain for a third time. He then proposed Hector MacIntyre for Captain. This was seconded by H. Robertson Junior. The proposal was carried unanimously.

Newly elected Captain MacIntyre was informed by the Secretary that it was now his turn to make a nomination. However, he proved that he had not quite grasped the required protocol when he nominated Frank Cougan to be the next to leave the Big Brother House.

Realising his mistake, he proposed Cougan for Vice-Captain. This was seconded by S. Houston. The new Captain then arranged a round of whiskies in time-honoured fashion.

S. Houston was proposed by F. Cougan and seconded by W. Kemp. His election was unopposed and carried unanimously.

The Secretary then banged his forehead against the table several times in an apparent display of delight.

ANY OTHER COMPETENT BUSINESS

A celebratory piss break was declared. Captain MacIntyre was last to return and as the assembled gathering became concerned for his safety, Vice-Captain Cougan suggested that he had either "f….. off for a piss, or pissed off for a f…".

The meeting agreed that he was in no fit state to perform either function and a search party was dispatched to bring him back to his seat.

Forbie Urquhart, on a sad note, reminded the AGM that Neilly Robertson had died during the year and that he had passed on our sympathies to his family. Frank recalled the first time Neilly and Ronnie Duncan had played together in the Annual Match many years ago and what a terrific show they put on.

I. Walkington then asked why the Stotters' flag was not flying outside the Clubhouse.

It emerged that the flag had been in the Professional's shop and appeared to have been lost in the upheaval when David Geekie sold the business. Despite being 200 miles away at the time, it was agreed that the Secretary should take the rap for the missing flag.

Ken Ross then asked if the Saturday night meal might be put back until a bit later because the One Day Open was taking five hours a round and the better golfers were missing out on the grub.

R. Towart took exception to that remark, and on behalf of the less gifted golfers, he rubbed his tummy, licked his lips, and said 'Mmm – yum yum – what a lovely buffet we had'.

As the exchanges became more heated, F. Cougan declared that the meal is for Stotters and their families and whilst it is great to see golfers representing Stotters in the One Day, we can't hold up the meal for just 4 people.

However, people not turning up because they are watching football would be unacceptable.

K. Ross said he was just glad to have created some dissension in the ranks.

H. Robertson Junior brought some much needed sanity to the proceedings with the radical proposal that the meal should be arranged for 7.30 for 8pm. This was seconded by I. Walkington, with the condition that provisions be made for those playing in the competition.

K. Ross, who had only used the meal issue to soften the meeting up in preparation for more serious matters, brought up the possibility of a Stotters' website, where visitors could look at the pictures of the Stotters through the years.

The idea of the movement taking its place on the electronic information super-highway proved more than a little bewildering for some of the older members. One was heard to ask if that meant he would have to go out and buy one of those bloody internets.

After much discussion of little significance, nothing was agreed and the meeting moved on.

F. Cougan remarked on how nice it was to see the association with the Royal Hotel rekindled and the children's concert the previous evening had brought back many fond memories.

S. Ross then brought up the old chestnut of Stotters' ties and asked why he did not have one.

R. Towart – whose loud booming voice and ferocious banging of the table could put the Reverend Iain Paisley to shame – suggested a Stotters' tattoo instead.

Mike Lloyd, sensing that nothing of any great importance was likely to be tackled by the dozen or so drunks present, decided to crank things up a little by suggesting that the AGM should perhaps be tempered by what the members of Tain Golf Club actually want from the Stotters, and that this could be put into context by Donald or Forbie.

W. Kemp said that he had spoken to two new members who had been delighted to take part in the match and would not miss it for the world.

F. Cougan asked if the match could be used to raise money for charity and mentioned The Keepers of the Green, in memory of Old Tom Morris – designer of the Tain Golf Course – which provides powered wheelchairs for children.

W. Kemp said 12 powered wheel chairs would be ideal to get the Stotters from the Club House to the Royal for the AGM.

Sport then proposed the setting up of a three-chap Sub Committee of local Stotters who could keep an eye out and advise on how best the Stotters could help Tain Golf Club. This was seconded by Roddy Robertson.

The question of new members was then raised and S. Ross proposed Tom Lloyd for Associate membership. This was seconded by W. Kemp.

I. Walkington then proposed that the old members be asked to die quicker, therefore allowing new blood to bolster the team. Younger members agreed that this would indeed be helpful.

In an historic moment Andrew Urquhart then made his maiden speech, despite being a Stotter since 1995.

He recalled how his father-in-law, the late Tommy Young, had thrown him a yellow jersey one Sunday morning and it brought a tear to his eye.

John Houston was then fined for taking an illegal piss break.

There then followed the usual aimless discussion about a possible Spring Meeting away from Tain which resulted in the inevitable false promises and lack of any recognisable conclusion.

With that the meeting was brought to a close at 5 p.m.

The discussion initiated by Ken about a website was ahead of its time but not by much as the Stotters, thanks to Geraldine Houston, took to Facebook in 2015, and to Twitter, thanks to Simon Houston, later that year. Deen also set up the very actively used Stotters' Wots App network.

Tom Lloyd, born in Cuckfield in Sussex in 1980, is Mike's son, who won the Stirling Cup in 1995 on his first Tain visit.

He remembers the following year: "I had to come back to defend my title and dad decided to come up to see what all the fuss was about.

I again qualified for the Stirling and played dad in the second round – a tricky situation for both of us!

However, dad played well and beat me 3&2 and then went on to win the Stirling himself, with me caddying for him in the final. I think this is the only time a father and son have won consecutive trophies in Golf Week, which we are very proud of".

A low handicap player, Tom has also reached the McVitie & Price first round twice and the semi-final once.

Now living in London, running a Facilities Services Company, he is married to Jelena and they have a son Oliver and a daughter, Isidora.

In a moment of agonised self-reflection, Tom confesses: "I know that I have a terrible record in Stotters' matches, probably due to me drinking too much. During the early years of my Stotters' career I remember caddying in the infamous match which culminated in one of the Tain team taking a dip in the burn on the 17th. This certainly taught me what the Stotters was all about!

I always look forward to the annual match and try to keep a good balance between drinking rusty nails, having fun and playing good golf. I have failed to find this balance as yet, and it's usually the good golf that goes out of the window...by the 2nd tee".

Tom comes back year after year to Tain to: "spend time with great friends and family, have a good laugh and to get the chance to play a bit of golf!"

MINUTES OF THE 37TH ANNUAL GENERAL MEETING OF THE STOTTERS – SUNDAY, 4TH AUGUST, 2002

Held in Morangie House Hotel, Tain.

The thirty-sixth annual match of Tain versus the Stotters was won by the Stotters.

Captain Hector MacIntyre in the chair.

APOLOGIES

Ian Walkington, Robert Towart and George Ross.

CAPTAIN'S REMARKS

Captain MacIntyre complimented his team on a great victory, before asking who had won the cup.

The Stotters' triumph had not been without controversy. While they won most matches, Tain had a greater hole-up aggregate.

After some debate in the Clubhouse, it was decided that the match be awarded to the visitors. The fact that the decision was taken by an All Stotters' Committee behind closed doors was neither here nor there.

Forbie Urquhart reassured the meeting that it was never a cause for debate because the outcome is always decided by matches, and the holes-up aggregate is only used in the event of a tie.

His words were met by shouts of 'Here! Here' and 'who bloody cares, get the bloody drinks in'.

Captain MacIntyre said both teams had played some great golf in typically trying conditions and asked if anyone had particularly reminiscences about their individual games that they wanted to share.

But given that most present could hardly remember sitting down five minutes earlier, the chances of a bountiful response were more than somewhat remote.

The meeting moved on.

MINUTES OF THE PREVIOUS MEETING

These were read by the Secretary and adopted as correct.

MATTERS ARISING FROM MINUTES

Ken Ross asked if journalists could be trusted.

The Secretary took great exception to the remark as he could prove that every word had been freshly prepared by Alistair Campbell the previous week.

Captain MacIntyre then asked the local members whether the match still enjoyed the support of Tain Golf Club and whether any issues pertaining to Stotters' Sunday had arisen during the year.

He was informed by Forbie, Donald and Andrew that all was well – unlike Captain MacIntyre, whose anxiety at chairing the meeting, combined with generous helpings of Glenmorangie – was slowly turning his face a rather impressive shade of grey.

ELECTION OF OFFICE BEARERS

Captain MacIntyre proposed Frank Cougan as his successor. Hamish Robertson Junior seconded this.

The election was met with cries of 'Here – here!' and 'There – there!' as Cougan was pointed towards the bar.

Incoming Captain Cougan said that before he proposed a Vice-Captain he wanted to thank Hector for being a first-class Captain, a first-class person, and a third-class golfer.

During the morning's match Captain MacIntyre had led from the front, allowing his partner – as ever – to come from behind.

Captain Cougan thought it only proper to explain why he had topped the tee shot at the 1st. It was in honour of the late, great, Gilbert Tocher who specialized in duffing and running.

The new Captain then brought up the subject of the previous night's meal at the Carnegie Lodge which everyone agreed was first class and suggested we asked them to pencil us in for the next year.

There was a problem, however, in that a lot of members were not wearing ties. He stressed that as much as you might not like wearing ties, you should at least turn up wearing them, as it is the only occasion – apart from funerals – that we get to wear them.

One dissenting voice was heard to ask that while the tie issue was indeed relevant wasn't it a bit early for AOCB?

In this case: Any Other Cougan Bullshit.

Before ending his State of the Nation address Captain Cougan brought a serious note to the proceedings by informing those present that he and Wilson Kemp had attended Ronnie Duncan's funeral during the year.

It was agreed that Ronnie, who had played in the match since its inception for Tain, would be sorely missed.

Glasses were raised to absent friends.

Captain Cougan proposed John Houston Junior as Vice-Captain. Wilson Kemp seconded this. Houston, much to the relief of the meeting, took it upon himself to say bugger all.

Ken Ross, no doubt still feeling some guilt over his earlier attack on the Secretary's professionalism, proposed Simon Houston as Secretary. Simon Houston seconded this.

ANY OTHER COMPETENT BUSINESS

The Vice-Captain suggested a Scott Ferguson memorial trophy for the first person to fall asleep at the meeting. He pointed out that he was not making reference to anyone in particular, although his words were barely audible above Donald Sutherland's snoring.

Captain Cougan issued a yellow card for Sutherland and warned him that if everyone else had to stay awake through this shit then it was only fair that he did as well.

The Captain then brought up the Hic-Cup.

He proposed that the pairings that win by the highest number of holes in the match v Tain are declared the winners of the Hic-cup. Such a system would mean that no strange names could appear on the trophy – only strange golfers. Kemp agreed that it would indeed make it a Stotters' only contest.

Simon Ross, however, was keen to keep the Competition for it at the Port, while Hector MacIntyre said he was keen to move it around. He was advised that his sexual preferences were all very interesting but we were

190

discussing the format of the Hic-Cup.

The Secretary asked why it would be so difficult away from Tain.

A long discussion ensued. After a series of complicated votes, and secret ballots that made the American primaries seem almost elementary by comparison Captain Cougan's proposal that it should go to the highest margin winners on Stotters' Sunday won through by 10 for and two against. It was therefore agreed that this year's trophy should go to John Houston and Simon Ross who won three up.

A piss break was declared and the Secretary collected money for the new polo shirts.

When the meeting re-convened Ken Ross brought up the question of ties.

If we are going to have them, he said, they would have to be ties that we actually wear. He added that he would be proud to wear his to work if it was nice. It would also be a pleasure at Eastbourne so that people can enquire as to its origins.

The Captain warned that new ties might be costly, whilst Hamish Robertson Junior said that social etiquette had moved on and that people don't always wear ties any more, plus there are people who are not Stotters who come to the Saturday night meal.

Simon Ross said it would be a shame to do away with an old tradition and Vice-Captain Houston supported him in this view. Wilson Kemp said he thought it commendable that the young ones wanted to keep up the tradition, especially as the older ones were having a great deal of difficulty keeping anything up these days.

Honorary President Robertson then intervened and stressed that while it is nice to keep up tradition there are more seasoned members who can't be bothered wearing ties. A younger voice was heard to mutter: 'That's the problem with the old ones these days, they have no sense of tradition. All they want is change, change, change, wasn't like that in our day ……'.

The debate went on, and on, and on. Mike Lloyd, whose hairy legs had escaped scrutiny for the second successive year, suggested a vote. Those in favour of a club tie won 9-3.

The subject of Country Membership of Tain came up. Ken Ross said he had been considering a Country Membership for four in order to put something back into the Club but it is cheaper nowadays just to pay the green fees instead. Wilson Kemp said he would happily become a member again if they lowered the cost.

A discussion ensued but with no immediate end in sight the Captain thought it best to leave this thorny issue for another day and brought the meeting to a close at 5.15p.m.

Captain Hector MacIntyre receives the Stotters' Trophy – 2002. L to R – Hector shields David Rutherford, Simon Houston, Tori Houston, with Pat Houston holding Rachel Robertson

MINUTES OF THE 38ᵀᴴ ANNUAL GENERAL MEETING OF THE STOTTERS – SUNDAY 3ᴿᴰ AUGUST, 2003

Held at the Carnegie Lodge Hotel, Tain.

The thirty-seventh annual match of Tain v the Stotters was won by Tain.

Captain Frank Cougan in the chair.

APOLOGIES

George Ross, Simon Ross, Tom Lloyd, Wilson Kemp, and Ian Walkington.

CAPTAIN'S REMARKS

Captain Cougan began by reminding the meeting that he had already spoken for ten minutes in the Club House so we were getting 15 whether we liked it or not. Accepting apologies, he said he looked forward to the return next year of Simon Ross and Tom Lloyd following their travels, but expressed some concern about Sport, who was letting his recently discovered talent for producing erotic literature get in the way of his golf.

However, on second thoughts, he suggested that a team reading of some of Walkington's more murky material might not be the worst preparation for next year's match, as Tain is a course clearly suited to a stiff shaft.

On the match itself, the Captain said he was dismayed at the defeat but at least we had tried our best and, with the exception of Ken Ross and Roddy Robertson, the remaining members can only improve.

He added that more should be made of the fact that Tain Golf Club has a lady Club Captain.

MINUTES OF THE PREVIOUS MEETING

These were adopted as correct by the President, and seconded by Mike Lloyd.

Ken Ross then proposed a vote of confidence, applauding the Secretary on a wonderful record. The Secretary's pride was tempered by the fact that Ken Ross also thought that 'Mandy' by Barry Manilow was a wonderful record ...

MATTERS ARISING FROM MINUTES

The previous night's meal at the Carnegie Lodge had been a roaring success. Despite being asked to deal with staggered sittings, not to mention staggering Stotters, all agreed that the staff had performed admirably.

The Captain said they had only charged £20.00 a head as a thank you for the custom. It was therefore agreed that the Carnegie be approached again about hosting the Saturday night meal and the AGM.

Members then expressed their delight that Tain had not only fielded a full team this year but two players extra, proving that the annual match continues to receive warm support from the local membership.

ELECTION OF OFFICE BEARERS

Captain Cougan said that it had been a great pleasure being Captain again. His term had been great fun. Everyone turned up when asked, and paid up when asked. If only they had shut up when asked!

Captain Cougan proposed John Houston as Captain. This was seconded by Robert Towart.

After taking his seat, the new Captain said he wanted to ask a true gentleman to serve as his Vice-Captain, but since that was not possible he would have to ask Mike Lloyd instead. This was seconded by Forbie Urquhart.

New Vice-Captain Lloyd, in a moment of nauseating sincerity, said that it was indeed a great honour to take up the post, as those present knew only too well how much he enjoyed coming up to Tain and being a part of it all.

Hamish Robertson Junior proposed Simon Houston to continue as Secretary. This was seconded by Roddy Robertson.

The President, always a stickler for the correct protocol, politely reminded Roddy Robertson (his son) to speak through the chair or shut the f... up.

ANY OTHER COMPETENT BUSINESS

This began in time-honoured fashion, with a scatter-gun burst of meaningless suggestions, empty promises, and not an insignificant helping of bullshit.

Ken Ross argued that despite his advancing years the President himself should be asked to play in the team once again, such was the sub-standard level of performance from the younger members that morning.

However, the words 'Not on your bloody Nellie' quickly quashed the idea.

Captain Houston, clearly taking his new responsibility seriously, offered perhaps his most profound utterance of the day, when he suggested that since Sport had taken to writing erotic poetry, should he not be renamed 'Spurt' – quite appropriate really, as most members saw that joke coming a mile off.

A debate about numbers ensued as the Stotters and Tain had both fielded 14 that morning.

Robert Towart, known to enjoy the occasional cliché, said that 'Once a Stotter, always a Stotter' and if too many squad members turned up in the future then it was up to the Captain and Vice-Captain to pick a team of 12.

There then followed a noisy discussion about whether the extra players should count in the overall score.

The relevance of this debate was called into question, however, when it was pointed out that this year's extra participants were probably still out on the course having despatched their caddies from the 10th green to the Clubhouse to collect more booze.

Moving on, the Captain said he was delighted to see a fine representation from the Robertson family.

The subject of families sparked Ken Ross into action. He stressed that it was important to look at recruitment as he has always been worried about family ties and the danger of bringing people in too quickly. After all we have a perfectly good body of people as it is.

In a counter argument Captain Houston said no-one would have thought that Wilson, for example, would not be here this year and it would not take much to be three or four bodies down. A 40 ouncer should do the trick, muttered one malcontent.

Undeterred, the Captain pressed on, explaining that in his opinion, we can't say to people that we don't want them to become an Associate but we might need them for the match on the Sunday.

Then, paying particular heed to Ken's concerns about too many family ties, he proposed that his brother-in-law Liam Hughes become an Associate. This was seconded by Robert Towart.

Vice-Captain Lloyd welcomed the appointment describing Liam as just the sort of person we should have in our ranks, fully committed and of questionable sanity.

Ken, having entertained the ranks during a piss break, with a joke about Doris having Parkinson disease, then raised the tie issue.

Simon Ross, he said, had been dealing with a company that produces ties and had come up with a couple of designs. These were sent to the Secretary, who had plainly forgotten to bring them North for perusal. The Secretary hoped that such a faux pas might lead to his immediate dismissal, but sadly that was not the case.

Robert Towart said that a decision on tie-wearing was required.

Vice-Captain Lloyd said that if we had a tie it should be worn, and he proposed that its annual airing should be on the Saturday night before the match. This was seconded by Roddy Robertson.

Chaos ensued and Hamish Robertson Junior bluntly told the assembled gathering that he would not wear a tie – 'Full Stop'. It was agreed that a decision be deferred until next year by which time the new ties will have hopefully materialised.

And on that note of customary indecision and infighting the meeting was brought to a close at 4.20p.m.

The reference to Ken and Roddy's play referred to their winning the Hic-Cup.

Ken Ross's joke about Doris and Parkinson disease has been a favourite (of his) for a very long time, and still endures today, as fresh audiences reinvigorate its telling.

Mrs PA Shearer was Tain's first (and so far, only) overall Lady Captain in 2003/4.

Liam Hughes here begins the Irish connection with both Tain and The Stotters.
Born in Magheraft in County Derry in 1967, he was raised in Armagh from the age of four.
Destined to continue to strengthen the Tain and Stotters' connection with alcohol, he was to comment in 2015: "After many years in the drinks Industry I have built the first Gin and Single Malt Whisky Distillery in Glasgow in over 112 years. We have

launched Makar Glasgow Gin which is Glasgow's first ever gin and are now laying down our new make spirit which will become the first single malt in Glasgow since 1903".

From the Glasgow Distillery, The Makar made its mark on the Stotters' match in 2016 and Liam presented miniatures to all who attended the 2016 celebratory dinner.

Married to Geraldine Houston, Liam first came to Tain in 1997.

"Having been in the drinks industry since University I can't imagine what attracted me to the Stotters! Over the years I have fallen in love with the whole area and made many friends and even built a house in Portmahomack".

One of Liam's good friends is Mike Sangster, a regular Tain opponent in the Stotters' matches, who used to give Liam golf lessons in the Royal's bar late at night with a candle for a pretend golf club.

He also, one year after a very late night, gave Hamish Junior and wife Shirley golf lessons in Tain High Street at some unearthly hour in the morning.

Liam and Deen's three children are Calum, Tara and Ronan.

He has been a member of Tain GC since 1998 and plays his Glasgow golf (off 8) at Hilton Park.

For the first few years, Liam actually played for Tain more than the Stotters as there were no places in the Stotters' team, but he plays with a degree of consistency in the 4-Day Open, having reached the semi-final of the Stirling Cup three times, each time losing to the eventual winner.

Liam's father, Dennis, a regular visitor during Golf Week with his wife Sheila, won the Teddy Brookes Trophy in 2010, aged 70.

Liam continues: "In 2014 there was very nearly a unique final when Denis and my son Calum were in opposite semi-finals of the Stirling but Calum aged 13 and off 11 was beaten like his dad by the eventual winner who then beat my dad in the final – if I was to take a guess, Calum has a better chance than me on emulating his Grandfather(s) and he is probably in a unique situation in that he has BOTH his grandfathers' names on the boards as winners in Golf Week. I expect the tradition will be safe for another generation at least on the Hughes / Houston front".

Liam loves Tain: "It is the only time of the year I get to spend a week with my own parents on or near a golf course which is very special. Tain has become as much a part of me as Ireland – I can think of no finer accolade".

MINUTES OF THE 39TH ANNUAL GENERAL MEETING OF THE STOTTERS – SUNDAY, 1ST AUGUST, 2004

Held in the Carnegie Lodge Hotel, Tain.

The thirty-eighth match of the Stotters v Tain played in the afternoon at 2p.m. No match result recorded in the Minutes *(The Stotters won)*.

Captain John Houston in the chair.

The meeting began without lights which came as some comfort to most members who said they were used to spending much of the AGM in the dark. By way of divine intervention, the lights came on around the same time as a phone call from Frank Cougan. He passed on his apologies and expressed his best wishes for the afternoon ahead.

CAPTAIN'S REMARKS

Captain Houston remarked on what a great evening the previous night had been and how it had been good to see so many up and shaking a leg on the dance floor. He thanked Forbie Urquhart for arranging the event and expressed thanks to the Carnegie Lodge for being such fine hosts.

MINUTES OF PREVIOUS MEETING

These were read by the Secretary and after being proposed by Hamish Robertson Junior and seconded by John Houston, were adopted as correct.

MATTERS ARISING FROM MINUTES

Hamish Robertson Junior said he had begun the previous evening wearing a Stotters' tie but was dismayed to see no-one else had done likewise. This caused some disquiet among the members who suggested that Robertson Junior's advancing years were clearly having an adverse effect on his eyesight, and, with all due respect, he was talking bollocks, because at least half a dozen others had also worn their ties.

Robertson quickly removed his observation amid a frenzy of blunt recommendations as regards his future conduct.

ELECTION OF OFFICE BEARERS

Captain John Houston proposed Vice-Captain Mike Lloyd as his successor. Ken Ross seconded the proposal.

Outgoing Captain Houston said he had enjoyed his brief tenure but remarked upon how unusual it was to be handing over the reins prior to the annual match. In a rare display of modesty, he said that while the absence of his natural leadership qualities on the field of play would undoubtedly put the team at a disadvantage he was certain that if everyone pulled together and put the disappointment behind them, victory was by no means impossible.

He was told to stop talking unless it was in the direction of the bar staff and normal order was restored.

Captain Lloyd proposed Simon Ross as Vice-Captain, seconded by Wilson Kemp. Young Ross was congratulated on the appointment and ordered to help Houston at the bar.

Captain Lloyd proposed Simon Houston as Secretary, seconded by Hamish Robertson Junior. The Secretary displayed his delight at yet another unchallenged appointment by slumping forward in his chair, placing his head in his hands and muttering his heartfelt thanks to everyone.

 Captain Lloyd then reminded the meeting that the 40th anniversary of the Stotters was only two years' away and he felt it important that there should be some kind of special appointment to concentrate solely on this matter.

Ken Ross welcomed this suggestion but urged those present to take some time discussing ideas for marking the milestone before actually elevating a member to the new position.

So 'Ken it is' said a number of voices in unison.

Before ordering more drink to toast the unusually swift pace at which the meeting was progressing, Ross could be heard faintly above the bedlam, stressing that if, for example, we were to choose a weekend in France, the appointee should be someone with an appropriate knowledge of France.

The Secretary was asked to check the availability of Jacques Chirac or at the very least Zinadine Zidane.

Hamish Robertson, clearly aiming his sights slightly lower suggested a family day at Tain Golf Club complete with bouncy castle. John Houston on the other hand thought a dinner dance during Golf Week would be welcomed.

Ken Ross, suddenly warming to the idea of a special envoy, insisted that a golf trip somewhere really nice was the only realistic option and, indeed, it should be up to the Special Envoy, whoever he may be, to investigate this possibility as a matter of urgency. He made a note to ask Bridget how the Air Miles were doing and to check out some decent hotels in the Pebble Beach area.

Hamish Robertson Junior proposed Ken Ross as the Special Envoy. This was seconded by Roddy Robertson.

It was agreed that as well as a one-off golf event we should look at the possibility of a 40th Anniversary Dance.

ANY OTHER COMPETENT BUSINESS

Mike Lloyd brought up the timing anomaly and asked whether in the future we should have a meeting after the match.

John Houston explained that a letter received from Tain Captain Trish Shearer had outlined the reasons for the game being moved to 2 p.m. The club asked that we try the new later tee time for a year to see whether it led to a larger entry in the Sunday One Day Open.

Andrew Urquhart informed the meeting that 81 players had entered this year compared to 42 the previous year and it was generally accepted locally that a later start for the Stotters' match should be a permanent one.

The Secretary said that he had also e-mailed members seeking views on the most suitable time for the AGM and the general consensus favoured an early AGM as holding it after the later match would be unfair on families.

On a point of clarification it was made clear that the outgoing Captain at the AGM would Captain the team for the forthcoming match against Tain. Wilson Kemp then tried to politely hurry matters along by suggesting that had John Houston Senior been alive today he would have said 'For f...'s sake can we bloody well get on with it?'

Members were then advised by John Houston Junior to keep the noise down on the early holes during the match and Forbie Urquhart stressed the importance of not walking onto the 18th green glass in hand. But as the chance of any whisky remaining undrunk by the 18th green was more than somewhat remote this advice was met with bewildered stares.

Ties were then handed out and a special vote of thanks was given to Simon Ross for taking the time and trouble to not only design the tie but also arrange for them to be produced.

On the subject of membership Hamish Robertson Junior said he would like to propose his brother Roddy for full Stotter status in what was a particularly sad year for the Robertson family, Hamish Senior having died in May.

Some debate followed on the subject of Stotters who for one reason or another had failed to appear for a number of years. It was doubtful, for example, whether Robert Towart would reappear and Forbie Urquhart said he thought it unlikely that Sport Walkington would be back. With that in mind the meeting felt it wise to add to the list of full members. Hamish Robertson Junior proposed Roddy Robertson, seconded by Simon Houston.

John Houston proposed Tom Lloyd seconded by Ken Ross.

Hamish Robertson Junior then took the opportunity to invite fellow Stotters and friends to a memorial service during which his father's ashes would be laid to rest in Tain's cemetery.

It was originally to be a private family affair but so many people had kindly asked for an opportunity to pay their own respects, the Robertsons had decided to invite those outside the family. Hamish and Roddy were warmly thanked for their very touching invitation.

And on that poignant note the meeting was brought to a close at 1.25 p.m.

This AGM was rather strange as it was held in the morning before the afternoon match against Tain, thus explaining the absence of much of the drunken hilarity permeating other Meetings.

A large number of Stotters and friends of Hamish Senior did indeed appear at the graveside in the St Duthus Old Cemetery where the Robertson/Ross family headstone is in the front row of stones facing the Golf Course. Hamish Junior said a few words paying tribute to his dad.

Later in the year, the family donated The Hamish Robertson Trophy to Tain GC for competition each May/June in a Texas Scramble open to all comers, and awarded to the best Tain team.

Later, Frank Cougan was to present a beautiful statue of Old Tom Morris as a trophy to be awarded to the best visitors' team in the Competition.

MINUTES OF THE 40ᵀᴴ ANNUAL GENERAL MEETING OF THE STOTTERS – SUNDAY, 31ˢᵀ JULY 2005

Held at the Carnegie Lodge Hotel, Tain.

The thirty-ninth annual match between Tain Golf Club and the Stotters played at 2 p.m. after the Meeting. No match result recorded in the Minutes *(Tain won)*.

Captain Mike Lloyd in the chair.

APOLOGIES

Hector MacIntyre, George Ross, Wilson Kemp and Robert Towart.

In a break with tradition the AGM was taking place again in the morning, ahead of an afternoon tee off.

However, the more hardened drinkers among the assembled gathering failed to allow the ungodly hour to alter their blueprint for a drunken day ahead, and breakfasted on freshly baked Glenmorangie with an assortment of chilled lager and a selection of grilled Guinness.

Some mere mortals, who asked that their identities be withheld, instead ordered coffee and were roundly booed and indeed probed about their sexuality.

The meeting was delayed by the later arrival of Messrs. Houston, Houston and Hughes.

The elder and less charismatic of the Houston brothers had insisted on taking a shower before leaving Portmahomack for the AGM, clearly a man who likes to precede one annual event with another.

Fines were duly suggested and ignored.

MINUTES OF THE PREVIOUS MEETING

These were read by the Secretary, during which time a phone call was received from Wilson Kemp. He passed on his apologies to Captain Lloyd and said he would be returning home from Hospital the following day. The meeting wished him well and he demanded an increase in the drinking levels and called for a sound thrashing of Tain in his absence.

The Minutes were adopted as correct by John Houston and seconded by Roddy Robertson.

MATTERS ARISING FROM MINUTES

Not for the first time, the issue of membership prompted some earthy debate and the age-old adage: 'Once a Stotter always a Stotter' was given its annual dust down and airing – this time by the sweet and melodic tones of Cougan.

While numbers appear to be healthy, he pointed out that it would be unlikely to expect Tain to produce a team of more than 12, and if we were oversubscribed for players on the Sunday, then the Associates would have to stand aside.

Ken Ross, somewhat unhelpfully, suggested a secret ballot on such an occasion and was told to be quiet and get the bloody coffees in.

Liam Hughes, who remarkably was not one of the coffee drinkers, burped and farted his way through an argument that, perhaps, a deadline be set after which repeated Golf Week absentees would become inactive.

'This is about as inactive as you get' muttered one tired and hungover voice, whose owner was slumped in an almost horizontal position on the settee. The Hughes' suggestion was warmly embraced by Cougan who went a step further by proposing a five year cut off point.

Ken Ross said he did not agree with this philosophy and warned against straying too far from 'O.A.S.A.A.S.' Indeed he reminded the meeting that he himself had not come for 8 years.

Frank, in his inimitable playground style then asked if that's why he started taking Viagra. A younger member was then heard to ask if that's what is meant by the term 'hardened drinker'.

Ken managed to keep his train of thought going long enough to make the following proposal: 'that an absentee can choose to self-elect at any time, but after five years would be removed from playing status to non-playing/sleeper'. This was seconded by Hamish Robertson Junior.

ELECTION OF OFFICE BEARERS

Captain Mike Lloyd proposed Simon Ross as his successor and thanked him for all the sterling work he had done during his year as Vice-Captain.

This was met with much laughter and hilarity – not least when an emotional S. Ross admitted that he did not realise that he had been Vice-Captain.

Outgoing Captain Mike Lloyd, somewhat cruelly, then proposed that in tribute to the new Captain, the golfing abbreviation 'NR' be changed to 'SR'.

The proposal for Captain was seconded by Tom Lloyd.

In one of the least nepotistic moments in Stotters' history, new Captain Ross said: 'I want to propose my Dad' as Vice-Captain. This was seconded by Bridget, who had sneaked into the meeting in a John Houston disguise.

Simon Houston was proposed as Secretary. This was seconded by Roddy Robertson.

ANY OTHER COMPETENT BUSINESS

Ken Ross chose this moment to give his special 40th Anniversary Special Envoy Report. Ken said he had visited a variety of clubs around the world with a view to inviting one of them to host a Stotters' Anniversary outing.

In discussion with the Past Captains, he came down to two ideas, one of which would be a formal dinner dance the evening before the match against Tain. This would provide an opportunity to invite and therefore thank members of Tain Golf Club who have become part and parcel of the event.

Two questions arose however – firstly, would the assembled gathering be prepared to pay for such an extravaganza?

And secondly would the assembled gathering be prepared to pay for the Special Envoy to shut up?

In all seriousness it was also agreed that a weekend long event should be staged away from Tain in somewhere like Eastbourne, as the East Sussex National has two premier courses and a brand new hotel in the process of being built.

While most thought such an idea was great in principle, it largely depended on the calendar, and therefore Ken and Mike would put their heads together before formally inviting Stotters and their families south.

Liam Hughes then stressed that it was important to reinvigorate interest in the match among Tain members as they had been struggling to get a team on the field in recent years and the 40th anniversary was an excellent opportunity to do just that.

Ken said: 'we perhaps need to court the better players from Tain in order to make more of a match of it.'

It was at this stage that the caffeine-fuelled proceedings threatened to descend into chaos.

Fortunately Simon Ross, always a stickler for tradition and ceremony, was on hand to restore some order and issued strict instructions that any players attending the Prize Giving should be dressed in yellow.

The Secretary then urged those present to elect a 40th Anniversary Working Party in order to maximise mutual benefits.

Liam Hughes, Donald Sutherland, Ken Ross and Mike Lloyd agreed to get together by phone and e-mail throughout the coming months on a regular basis and would collectively shoulder responsibility for anniversary events and celebrations. The Secretary relaxed in the knowledge that matters were in hand and he looked forward to watching such an energetic and imaginative team of professional brain stormers slip into gear.

Roddy Robertson, equally relaxed at the prospect, turned to the question of membership and proposed his son-in-law to be, Chris Rafferty, as an Associate Member, as he had now been attending Golf Week for a number of years and would make an excellent addition to the Society.

Frank Cougan applauded the idea and said he was certain Chris did indeed have the required credentials but perhaps Roddy could do the decent thing and actually introduce people to the Society prior to proposing them as it always helps to know what someone looks like when welcoming them into the fold. This was seconded by John Houston.

Frank then proposed Ian Walkington as President of the Stotters ahead of the 40th year and this was warmly welcomed by all present and formally seconded by Tom Lloyd.

And it was with a heavy heart that the Captain brought the meeting to a close at 1.20 p.m.

Fines being duly suggested and ignored mark the acknowledgment of change.

During all of the years up till 1999, fines were a big part of the Stotters' AGMs, often levied arbitrarily and with great good humour, and always paid, albeit sometimes reluctantly. However, with influxes of new Stotters, unused to this quirk of Stottership, they have since died, been buried and all but forgotten.

For the record, the last fines were levied in 1999 by Hamish Junior on Frank Cougan – for taking an unofficial piss break – and on Hector – fined in his absence for not coming to Golf Week because of Maggie's confinement.

Christopher Arthur Rafferty here makes his debut in Stotters' history.

As Roddy's future son-in-law, he was at the time engaged to Shona, Roddy and Alice's eldest child. They later married and have two sons – Matthew James and Dale. Chris reckons his debut at Tain was some form of wicked test devised by Roddy, regarding his intentions towards his daughter: "Needless to say I passed with flying colours being able to get a decent score in Tain and drink myself stupid at the AGM!"

He recalls: "the great welcome of David Rutherford to the course, game and Stotterdom".

Born in 1969 in Castlemilk, Chris and family now live in Rutherglen from where Chris works in the Hospitality Industry, "specialising in running organisations in trouble, on their last legs or shut. Perfect for a committee role in the Stotters".

He has variously worked with and rescued companies including The Bean Scene, Little Chef, Harry Ramsden and Riley's Snooker Halls and Bars.

His playing Handicap is 21, but as he has little time to play in competitions, reckons he should be off 17. He has played his golf as an itinerant at courses such as East Kilbride, Aberfoyle, Ross Priory (Strathclyde University) and is now a member of Tain itself.

As an experienced and well-seasoned club hockey player, a game he was forced to abandon due to "dodgy knees", he still has aspirations on the golf course.

He has qualified twice for the Teddy Brookes Tournament: "First time I survived a tsunami of a first round, with a gross 90 and the second round was cancelled. Straight in – result! Won my first game and was put out in the quarters by a retired police officer who played on average 720 rounds a year. Second time round (2009) I was expelled by a 16-year-old, son of the Captain, who went on to lift the trophy- no disgrace there". (This was Charlie Hudson).

Chris's first few rounds were: "as a willing caddy to my Stotters' hero, Roddy. Unsure as to the protocol, and still courting Shona, I took it easy on the drink up the first.

A can of cider and a triple rusty nail soon put my trepidation to rest.

Blazing drunk by the fifth.

This continued for my caddying career till I got the call and my first cap in 2006.

Bringing up the rear of the team usually meant playing the lesser talented golf- wise, but gifted drinkers of the Tain team. This provided ample opportunity to "get mad with the drink" on the course and enjoy some wonderful banter with many characters such as Murd, Sugar, David Rutherford and others from Tain. Wonderful memories of sun-kissed afternoons, blooming local flora and fauna and 12 shots out of a bunker to treasure.

As my stature has grown as a reliable, witty and able drunk, my golf has regressed exponentially to a resounding hammering in most games!"

Chris's trusty caddie, mother-in-law Alice, still hankers for that perfect round from him – four large Glenmorangies and beer chasers at the 6th!

Chris's top ten memories, in no particular order, are:

"Driving into the flower bed on the first in my captaincy year – poor.

Chas and Dave playing live at the 40th event at the Royal.

Threatened by locals at the Port for relieving myself out of bounds post-AGM.

Various rusty nails recipes over the years – might do a book on that.

Still thinking golf improves with drink.

Hospitality at Murd's Bed and Breakfast.

Feeling very unwell on the first – see previous point.

Started drinking whisky for the first time in Tain – Glenmorangie Port Cask.

The drive at the second – haunted me for years.

Birdie at the second – never happened".

Chris also remembers the AGM Minutes from Simon as a highlight of every trip: "mindless and futile ramblings confused as points of order; dear Bob Beveridge's ten metre dash and illegal tackle on Frank Cougan in the Royal board room (2009); various opinions on how to fix a destroyed antique Victorian dresser thanks to Bob's illegal tackle; and Hamish Robertson's continued quest to ban ties from Western Europe".

In his first match against Tain: "against anonymous opposition who, on the first, stated they were not interested in drinking whisky of any description in the game and would not entertain anything of the ilk on the course. Fearing a dry round and complete despondency, I walked up to the second tee to be greeted by a litre bottle of vodka! Game on".

MINUTES OF THE 41ST ANNUAL GENERAL MEETING OF THE STOTTERS – SUNDAY, 30TH JULY, 2006

Held at the Royal Hotel, Tain.

The thirty-ninth match of the Stotters versus Tain played in the afternoon at 2 p.m. following the Meeting. No match resulted recorded in the Minutes *(The Stotters won)*.

Captain Simon Ross in the chair.

CAPTAIN'S REMARKS

Captain Ross opened the proceedings by saying a word of thanks to all involved in organising the Stotters' 40th Anniversary Dinner Dance, which all agreed had been a roaring success.

The event had taken place the previous evening in the Clan Ross rooms and the Captain reserved a special word of thanks to President Walkington, who from the stage had stolen the show in his own inimitable style.

In response, the President thanked the Captain, the Secretary and the Special Envoy for helping to make the evening such a memorable occasion.

APOLOGIES

These were received from Wilson Kemp and George Ross.

Ken Ross explained that George had been called to Prague but that he would much rather be here.

Frank Cougan proposed that we open the meeting with a drink.

His timely if not altogether unexpected intervention was met with a chorus of approval. One voice was heard to mutter that this was not the first time Cougan had adopted such a cavalier approach to the bevy and if he was not mistaken, he had also called for a round of drams prior to the 1976 and 1984 AGM.s.

The Secretary was asked to check the authenticity of this claim.

MINUTES OF THE PREVIOUS MEETING

These were read by the Secretary. Mike Lloyd proposed that they be adopted as correct, seconded by Ken Ross and the proposal was carried unanimously.

MATTERS ARISING FROM MINUTES

Mike Lloyd congratulated the 40th Anniversary Working Party on a job well done, before asking who exactly was on the said Party because he had heard a nasty rumour that he himself might have been on it, but he was not sure. In any event, they should be toasted whoever they were.

Frank Cougan saw this as an ideal opportunity to tell a story about how he once flashed some unsuspecting French people on holiday, although the relevance was lost on the majority of members, except Liam Hughes, who gave Cougan a knowing wink.

It had been suggested in the previous meeting that the 40th Anniversary Celebrations would go a long way towards reinvigorating the annual match and this had certainly proved to be the case as the Tain team that afternoon would include gents who had not played against the Stotters for many years such as Murd, and Gordon McKie.

A vote of thanks was then proposed for Ken Ross for organising the Eastbourne trip. Those unable to make it south for what was a memorable weekend of fine hospitality were duly informed of the historic result which saw the Stotters defeat an East Sussex National team by 2½ matches to 1½.

Ken said that the feedback from members of East Sussex had been very favourable, given that they had not understood a damn word any of us had said for the entire weekend but they liked our yellow jerseys and bright red faces, and for reasons of colour scheme alone, we should be welcomed back.

And finally, Liam Hughes asked that the sterling effort put in by Donald and Morag Sutherland in preparing a fine collage of Stotters' photographs from throughout the years be minuted.

ELECTION OF OFFICE BEARERS

Keeping up a fine family tradition of unashamed nepotism, Captain Simon

Ross proposed his Dad, Ken Ross, as the new Captain. Seconded by Hector MacIntyre.

Captain Ken Ross then proposed Simon Houston as his Vice-Captain, seconded by Frank Cougan.

Simon Houston, despite repeated protestations, was proposed as Secretary by Liam Hughes. Seconded by President Ian Walkington.

ANY OTHER COMPETENT BUSINESS

President Walkington proposed Wilson Kemp and Frank Cougan as joint Vice-Presidents. This was seconded by John Houston and warmly welcomed by the assembled gathering.

Hamish Robertson noted how lovely it had been at the dinner dance to see Alice and her family in such great numbers and in memory of his late brother, Roddy.

Alice, with the support of the Robertson clan, had donated to Tain Golf Club a fine silver tray which would be used to serve drams to players, caddies, and supporters on the 1st tee prior to the annual match.

It was inscribed with the simple words 'Roddy's Round' and Hamish held the tray aloft for the assembled gathering to view.

It was a wonderful gesture, remarked Captain Ken Ross, and a fitting way for all to remember a great man and a fine Stotter. At that, spontaneous applause broke out in memory of Roddy, and another round of drinks was called for.

Roddy's passing had created a vacancy and Captain Ross proposed that Liam Hughes be promoted to full Stotter status. Seconded by Mike Lloyd.

On the issue of membership, Frank Cougan suggested that on this, our 40th year, it was important to recognise the efforts made by some of the longstanding members of the Tain Golfing community for the support they have given the Stotters over the years. Most notably, Bob Beveridge and Johnny Urquhart. Frank proposed that the aforementioned pair be given Honorary Stotter Status and this was seconded by Forbie Urquhart and carried unanimously.

With the issue of membership on the table, members agreed that the number of Associates was falling dangerously low and a fresh intake of new blood was required.

Consideration for such a position should boast a combination of strong golfing qualities, adequate social skills and a proven knowledge of how to get their hands in their pocket and buy a drink. However, in the absence of anyone fitting those criteria, Malcolm Fraser, Gary Toal and Chris Fraser were suggested by a number of members. Again, all three were believed to look good in yellow, played a bit of golf, and were partial to the occasional glass of dry sherry.

On the basis that we could work on the social skills, the trio were collectively proposed by Hamish Robertson and seconded by Frank Cougan and welcomed into the fold unanimously.

With the meeting now drifting aimlessly in no particular direction someone with a southern nancy-boy accent, possibly Mike Lloyd, suggested an overhaul of the club uniform.

He was becoming more than a little tired of the 'garish yellow' and wondered whether a replacement colour, perhaps midnight puce with a hint of summer-meadow lilac, might be more pleasing on the eye.

'Bollocks to that' was the dominant response. However, clothing was now on the agenda and after an hour or so of tiresome debate, false promises, and varying degrees of bullshit, Chris Rafferty kindly agreed to look into the possibility of acquiring new polo shirts, sweaters and half-sweaters.

The question of a return trip to Eastbourne was then raised and the general feeling was that such a prospect would be well supported but perhaps on a bi-annual rather than annual basis.

A two year gap would allow John Houston's sunburn from the first visit the chance to calm down sufficiently for another victory to be secured.

And on that blisteringly hot note the meeting was brought to a close at 12.50 p.m.

As well as donating the Roddy's Round salver, Alice and family gave all the Stotters a neat commemorative trio of golf balls, housed in a clip-on carry shell, and engraved "1966-2006" under the Stotters' Logo – to mark Roddy's passing and 40 years of the Stotters.

Appropriately, 2006 marked the biggest single influx of new and promoted Stotters since 1966, with Malcolm Fraser, Gary Toal and Chris Fraser joining the Associate ranks; Liam Hughes becoming a full Stotter; and Bob Beveridge and Johnny Urquhart being appointed as Honorary Stotters.

Malcolm John Fraser was born in Sept 1966 in Inverness.

He comments: "My dad built his house in Balloch (four miles East of Inverness) in 1960 where I grew up and I built mine in the field next door in 1996 and still live there. We have a stunning view of Ben Wyvis and the Moray Firth and I can't imagine living anywhere else".

A quiet slim-built Malcolm proudly says: "My family are butchers, fish merchants and game dealers and I run two shops in Inverness which also supply to the catering industry. We won Best in the North of Scotland 2016 at the Independent Retail Awards in Glasgow".

As a carer for his mother, who sadly passed away in July 2017, and always busy at work, Malcolm has had little chance to play his golf, but is noted for his magnificent slice off the tee.

He was a member of Tain GC for ten years but now just plays Torvean or Fairways in Inverness.

With a holiday home beside Liam and Deen in Portmahomack, Malcolm got to know the Stotters.

He says: "I played in five or six Stotters' matches, including once for Tain and have never lost or been on the losing team oddly enough – but that's more to do with my playing partner than me – and my prowess at pouring whisky!"

He loves the camaraderie of being a Stotter and adds: "who wouldn't want to walk Tain golf course playing or not?"

He fondly remembers Gary Toal falling into a bunker at the 18th, not a unique event.

Gary's election to Associate status broadens the Irish connection.

Born in Armagh in 1968, Gary, who was introduced to the Stotters by Liam Hughes in 2000, lives in Bridge of Weir and plays his golf, off 9, at Ranfurly Castle.

Married to Louisa, they have 3 sons – Conor, James and Michael.

Tall and slim, and with a truly wicked and constant sense of humour, Gary is a doctor and a big tribute-band fan, addicted to Golf Week performances by such luminaries as Robbie Williams and Neil Diamond (with Gary as chief US flag waver).

When he became a full Stotter, he has vague memories of "having a viscous prawn at the Castle at Portmahomack that night which slowed down my celebrations!"

He remembers his early years as challenging with six successive years of non-qualification for the final stages of Golf Week.

"Fearful of this turning into a country and western song, to match Hector, I screwed the nut and then qualified in year seven.

In 2011, I played Dennis Hughes in the final of the Brookes and was well spanked".

Of his Stotters v Tain matches, he comments: "I have variable recall and in particular no recall after the 6th in any match played with Alan Ross and Sugar".

Gary loves returning to Tain each year for "Laughter, golf the way it is supposed to be, good friends and the Highland hospitality".

Chris Fraser's election nicely extends the Houston franchise.

Born in Bellshill in 1965, Chris is married to Dr. John's eldest child, Anne, and they have two children – Simon and Eilidh.

He describes his choice of career: "My first job as a "yopper" was as a greenkeeper but I only lasted a week as I was found having a kip in a bunker at the ninth!

Then I started Medical School and worked part time in a kitchen as a dishwasher. After one day washing dishes I realised I had better stick in at Med School as I fell asleep on the bus home after my shift and realised real work was bloody hard so I'd better qualify as a doctor.

As a doctor, I've worked in various countries including Trinidad, Gibraltar and Australia. I am settled now as a GP in Govanhill in Glasgow which is an "interesting" part of the city!"

Chris plays his golf at Hilton Park, playing off 20. He started to come to Tain in 1999, and his key qualifications for Stottership are that he "enjoys drink and golf at the same time".

"I have never come anywhere near qualifying in the Open Week Tournament. Allying my standard of golf to a week-long hangover makes for a terrible combination".

However, he did actually come close one year: "On the cusp of qualifying (in my head) I reached the tenth tee and was playing five off the tee. Not happy – and then it began to rain. I hit my sixth into the rubbish, and after five minutes looking I had to declare it lost and run back to hit a seventh shot off the tee. On running back, the sole fell off my shoe. It was pissing rain now and I escaped with an 11 and all hope of qualifying gone".

He remembers one epic encounter as part of the Stotters' match –"Rhubarb rum is probably my maddest Stotter match. Gary Tonge from Tain brought along his home made potion, which was lethal. Fortunately we drank less than the Tain team and were able to manage two-syllable words in the clubhouse to their monosyllabic chat!"

Chris loves the Stotters' AGMs (!): "Ken talking, Liam shouting and swearing, everyone else laughing or getting drinks and some poor sod as the Captain trying to maintain order".

As the Minutes reflect, all the work put in by Donald and Morag Sutherland and by Forbie Urquhart in staging the 40th Anniversary celebrations in the Clan Ross Room in the Royal truly paid off.

Photos and memorabilia pinned on display boards made a focus point which all present enjoyed perusing.

Sport and Hugh Walkington brought Jess Mackenzie, widow of Willie as a guest, and many others from the matches through the years were there too.

The children had a separate table, speeches were made, maybe Chas and Dave did play-but maybe not – though there sure was dancing of a sort, and a good time was had by all.

SOMETHING ELSE HAPPENED IN 1966!

"In 1966 a group of golfers, who had been attending the Tain Tournament for a varying number of years, got together and decided, if the Tain Golf Club was willing, to play an annual match against the Captain's Select..."

THE REST IS HISTORY

INVITATION

YOU ARE CORDIALLY INVITED TO HELP *THE STOTTERS* CELEBRATE THEIR 40th ANNIVERSARY

SATURDAY 29 JULY
CLAN ROSS ROOMS, ROYAL HOTEL, TAIN.
BUFFET AND BAND
0PM TILL LATE
DRESS SMART/CASUAL (BUT THOSE NOT APPROPRIATELY DRESSED MAY BE FINED!)

PARTY PIECES WELCOME!

RSVP simonhouston@otrpress.com OR TELL DONALD AND MORAG SUTHERLAND!

Service of Thanksgiving

for the life of

Roderick Charles Robertson

(Roddy)

4th June 1950 - 17 May 2006

Remembered with love, gratitude and joy

Thursday 25th May 2006, 1.00pm

Roddy's Round – 2006.

MINUTES OF THE 42ND ANNUAL GENERAL MEETING – SUNDAY 5TH AUGUST, 2007

Held at the Royal Hotel, Tain.

The fortieth annual match of Tain versus the Stotters – Tain won the match.

Captain Ken Ross in the chair.

APOLOGIES

Ian Walkington, George Ross, Simon Ross, Tom Lloyd, Malcolm Fraser and Wilson Kemp.

CAPTAIN'S REMARKS

Captain Ken Ross promised to keep his remarks down to less than 90 minutes but was unable to provide a written guarantee.

The Annual Match had resulted in a defeat and Captain Ken Ross advised against any attempt to apportion any individual blame insisting that we win or lose as a team, but unless Hamish Robertson gets his finger out he will be carrying someone's bag next year.

He congratulated Tain and all agreed that the morning start had once again proved a success.

Frank Cougan said that he had spoken with Wilson Kemp who had kindly provided a bottle of whisky for the meeting but on hearing the result of the match was considering taking it back as we had clearly drunk enough.

MINUTES OF PREVIOUS MEETING

These were read by the Secretary. Hamish Robertson proposed that they be adopted as correct, seconded by Ken Ross and carried unanimously.

Before the Captain could move on, Bob Beveridge, making his AGM debut, deemed it appropriate at this juncture to take to his feet and request permission to regale the assembled gathering with a song. As musical interludes go, it wasn't quite Pavarotti at the Carnegie Hall, more mince and totties at the Carnegie Lodge.

However, he did create history by reducing the AGM to complete silence for the first time in 41 years.

Beveridge, not entirely sober it has to be said, was helped back to his seat before passing comment on events by way of an indistinguishable noise, which prompted five minutes of healthy debate as to its origins. A show of hands was called for and the majority agreed that it was probably not a burp.

ELECTION OF OFFICE BEARERS

Captain Ken Ross said he would like to propose an old friend who was ideally qualified to hold such a prestigious position. But as none were available he proposed Simon Houston for Captain instead. This was seconded by Liam Hughes.

John Houston thanked Ken Ross for an outstanding year at the helm.

Simon Houston proposed Hamish Robertson for Vice-Captain, seconded by Hector MacIntyre.

John Houston proposed that Simon Houston continue as Secretary and this was seconded by Hamish Robertson.

A comfort break was called for, after which Bob Beveridge decided enough was enough and left the meeting, ably assisted by a man under each shoulder. Someone suggested we contact the Guinness Book of World Records as Bob was surely the first man to be carried out of the Royal Hotel twice in the space of twenty-four hours.

An older member advised against wasting a call as he was sure that Gilbert Tocher had been carried out twice in twenty-four minutes.

ANY OTHER COMPETENT BUSINESS

Lengthy helpings of bullshit preceded a debate on team selection.

Mike Lloyd was concerned that not a lot of thought had gone into the pairings, whilst the rest of the meeting was concerned that not a lot of thought had gone into Mike's point.

Mike was unhappy that a strong partnership, Rafferty and Toal, had been playing at the back of the field. It was pointed out that whether they were out first, last, or middle order, their convincing victory constituted a point for the yellow jerseys regardless and Mike was therefore talking shit.

He was told to be quiet.

He obliged.

Further nonsensical debate ensured, much of it centring on reasons for the defeat. Did Tain refuse too many drinks? Did the Stotters refuse too many soft drinks? Were Tain cheating?

Several possibilities were examined before bedlam was restored when one member suggested that perhaps, just maybe, the Tain team had better golfers. Amid the chaos, horrified Stotters looked to the heavens for divine intervention.

Surely not.

Surely we were not beaten by the better team? Confusion was restored when Liam Hughes proposed that more thought go into team selection, a motion seconded by Mike Lloyd.

A counter proposal by Ken Ross that the status quo remain in place and that the Captain pick the team without unwelcome interference by meddling busybodies was seconded by John Houston and carried almost unanimously.

Like an angel from above, Cougan lightened the mood by suggesting that a Steward Stotter was required to make sure glasses were filled at all times.

Maybe the newest Stotter could fill the role as a kind of punkahwallah of sorts. Hamish Robertson quickly knocked that idea on the head, insisting that it would be demeaning as no punkahwallah worth his salt would be anywhere near Tain Golf Club on the first Sunday in August.

Second helpings of bullshit, lightly garnished with a moderate sprinkling of bollocks occupied the next ten minutes with Stotters' membership high on the agenda. It was agreed that all was well because if everyone entitled to wear the yellow jersey turned up we would have too many.

Chris Fraser apologised for failing to wear a tie to the dinner the night before but this was on account of the fact that he did not own one, and it was out of his control.

'Well, I've heard some lame excuses', scoffed Ken Ross, 'Let's fine the little prick anyway'. The proposal, whilst apparently un-seconded above the bedlam was carried unanimously regardless.

The age-old question of Sleepers then raised its head and, in particular, when does a playing Stotter relinquish his position in the team if he is a regular absentee from Golf Week?

Liam Hughes took control of the Minute Book and, proving that his new Night School class was working wonders, quoted from a recent AGM at which it was agreed that any Stotter who failed to make it to Golf Week for longer than five years could not expect to walk back into the team.

As the meeting drew to a close, some members spoke fondly to the meeting of Eastbourne in 2006 and the question as to whether such a weekend should be staged again in the near future was raised. A show of hands voted comfortably for a repeat sojourn in the coming years and on that positive note the AGM came to a close at 4.55 p.m.

Bob Beveridge's singing interlude was a definite Stotters' first, and a tradition which has done its best to carry on in subsequent years, outlasting Bob himself.

Bob's song — The Gay Caballero — and a nice tale — are reproduced in full at Appendix 3.

Frank fondly remembers Bob singing — and acting out — Goliath of Gath. David Rutherford also was noted for his rendition of the song.

It's supposed to be a New Zealand folksong, and it specifically advises lisping throughout, though it's not written that way:

[Tune] O Worship the King.

Thong to be thung with a lithp for full effect.

Goliath of Garth, with his helmet of brass,
One day he sat down, upon the green grass,
When up slipped young David, the servant of Saul,
Who said I will smite thee, although I am small.
Young David slipped down to the side of the brook,
And from its still waters six small stones he took,
He skilfully slung one, right high in the sky,
And struck poor Goliath right over the eye.
Goliath fell down, in a swoon on the sward.
Young David slipped up, and swiped his great sword.
He lifted his helmet, and swiped off his head.
And all Israel shouted "Goliath is dead".

Johnny Houston with the Munro Rose Bowl – 2007.

MINUTES OF THE 43RD ANNUAL GENERAL MEETING OF THE STOTTERS – SUNDAY, 3RD AUGUST, 2008

Held at the Royal Hotel, Tain.

The forty-first match of the Stotters v Tain Golf Club was won by Tain Golf Club

Captain Simon Houston in the chair.

CAPTAIN'S REMARKS

The Captain expressed his disappointment at the outcome of the Annual Match which had resulted in a 4-2 victory for the hosts.

Small consolation could be taken from an overall aggregate holes-up score line, that was helped in no small part by a brave and gutsy seven-up win for Ken Ross and Frank Cougan against arguably Tain's most dangerous pairing, namely Bob Beveridge and David Rutherford.

It had been no mean achievement as Beveridge, in particular, had been peppering the flag all morning, admittedly with droplets of red wine and saliva. The result earned Ross and Cougan the 2008 Hic-Cup.

Moving on, all agreed that the Saturday night meal once again in the Clan Ross rooms had been a tremendous success.

APOLOGIES

The meeting was held up for ten minutes whilst George Ross finished unfinished business elsewhere, before apologies were received from Simon Ross and Wilson Kemp.

MINUTES OF PREVIOUS MEETING

These were read by the Secretary and adopted as correct. One can only assume that this was the case as the identity of the Proposer and Seconder remains a mystery and indeed was far from apparent when the Secretary put pen to paper last night.

MATTERS ARISING

President Walkington, on a point of order, informed the Meeting that he needed to pee.

Bob Beveridge, sensing a vacuum which might require to be filled during the President's understandably lengthy piss break, seized the moment with a more than adequate rendition of the Gay Caballero. A freshly emptied President returned and order was restored.

Ken raised Eastbourne and the 2008 trip which had failed to materialise. He apologised and explained that events had overtaken him and Mike and by the time they got their fingers out it was too late.

Mike, in the finest tradition of collective responsibility, added that it had f… all to do with him.

It was agreed that we would discuss it again and Mike and Ken would come back with dates. That prompted sniggers from the younger members of the Ross and Lloyd clans who clearly found amusement in the idea of their decrepit old fathers coming back with a couple of dates.

ELECTION OF OFFICE BEARERS

Captain Simon Houston proposed Hamish Robertson, his less than able Vice, to be Captain for the coming year. This was seconded by Hector MacIntyre and carried unanimously.

The incoming Captain took a moment to thank his predecessor for his sterling efforts and noted that he had steered the Stotters to successive defeats as Vice-Captain and Captain.

He then proposed Tom Lloyd as Vice-Captain, citing the excellent service he had given the yellow jerseys over the years and stressed the importance of putting the immediate future of the Stotters in safe hands.

Bets were then taken as to whether Lloyd would bother his backside turning up next year. The proposal was seconded by Malcom Fraser and carried unanimously.

Captain Robertson then proposed Simon Houston as Secretary, seconded by John Houston and carried unanimously.

ANY OTHER COMPETENT BUSINESS

A debate then followed on the subject of red trousers. Simon Ross started the trend, Hamish Robertson followed suit, and now Ken Ross had joined the happy band. Ken Ross proposed that they should become official Stotters' uniform, seconded by Frank Cougan.

Mike Lloyd responded with a counter proposal banning Southern softies from wearing the offending garments. The meeting agreed and voted heavily in favour of such a ban.

On the issue of membership, the usual debate and the usual bollocks resulted in very little sense from anyone, so attention was then turned to the Tain team, which despite dishing out a sound thrashing earlier that day, was not getting any younger.

Donald Sutherland insisted that plenty of young thrusters were eager to get a game but the old farts were not dying off quickly enough. This was a situation we would do our best to rectify one way or another.

It was agreed that the Captain or Secretary, and let's face it that means the Secretary, should contact Tain ahead of Golf Week to see how many players they had available and Stotters in turn should also declare themselves fit and ready for action.

President Walkington, rapidly filling up again, said that he would write to thank Tain Captain Paul Thompson for his hospitality.

Some members then asked why the Stotters' flag was taken down before the match was finished. No obvious reason could be given.

Ken Ross, determined to press on with uniform changes, asked about the possibility of a short-sleeved sweater.

Members said that they were happy to spend, within reason, what might be required to keep the uniform updated.

Walkington asked if it might not be a good idea to have female Stotters. The randy old B was shouted down in double quick time.

Bob Beveridge stood up.

Bob Beveridge fell down again.

Chaos ensued.

Bob Beveridge sang an indistinguishable song.

Order was restored.

Gary Toal then raised the issue of a possible pandemic flu situation and demanded reassurance as to the organisation's state of preparedness in the event of such an outbreak.

He questioned our ability to adhere to good hygiene practice and as we were a high-risk group an emergency plan should be drawn up.

As such a pandemic reached a peak, members would receive a secret text ordering them to abandon wives and children and head for Tain golf course. They would go to a specific fairway with an allocated partner, pitch a tent and begin drinking heavily.

Drinking would continue and at intermittent periods members would launch a fairway rescue club to the neighbouring tent to check for movement/life.

All surviving members would meet two weeks later at 8 a.m. on the 1st tee. Funerals and body disposal could take place the following Monday evening instead of Gilbert's Goblet.

He said the plan was necessary to maintain playing numbers in the event of a catastrophic shift in the virus and its virulence.

Unaware of just how spookily relevant Toal's plan would become in the following twelve months, members told the pessimistic Toal to be quiet and get some drinks ordered and, on that note, the meeting was called to a halt at 4.26 p.m.

In 2009, the second of two pandemics involving influenza (the first of them being the 1918 flu pandemic), swept the country.

First described in April 2009, the virus was a new strain resulting from a previous triple mix of bird, swine and human flu viruses further combined with a Eurasian pig flu virus leading to the term "swine flu".

The Minutes do not actually record when Chris Rafferty became a full Stotter, but this was almost certainly in 2008, three years after being elected an Associate.

The Red Trousers – Ken and Hamish.

MINUTES OF THE 44TH ANNUAL GENERAL MEETING – SUNDAY 2ND AUGUST 2009

Held at the Royal Hotel, Tain.

The forty-second annual match of the Stotters v Tain – Tain won.

Captain Hamish Robertson in the chair.

CAPTAIN'S REMARKS

The Captain opened with the observation that we did shit today and asked all those ashamed of themselves to raise their hands.

We had suffered another defeat to Tain, but Chris Rafferty and Chris Fraser could hold their heads up high by winning their match by seven holes and therefore winning the Hic-Cup in the process.

Captain Robertson said that he had enjoyed a wonderful time in his role although he did not remember doing hellish much, but that was irrelevant.

A request was made to toast absent friends.

On a point of order, one member asked if that included Bob Beveridge who was physically present, but absent in every other way.

APOLOGIES

Received from Ken Ross, George Ross, Simon Ross, Diana Ross, Jonathan Ross, Luther van Ross, Ross Kemp, and Ross from 'Friends'.

Always one to embrace technology, Ken Ross had planned to join the meeting via the wonders of Skype.

Liam Hughes then admitted that Ken was probably trying to talk to his laptop which was, unfortunately, back in Portmahomack and switched off. The meeting agreed that most people switch off when Ken starts talking so Hughes escaped censure.

MINUTES OF PREVIOUS MEETING

The Secretary danced his way modestly through a literary masterpiece, often struggling to be heard over the deafening cacophony of laughter. Proposed by Mike Lloyd, and seconded by Liam Hughes, the Minutes were adopted as correct.

MATTERS ARISING FROM MINUTES

Gary Toal remained concerned that the organisation was still unprepared for a pandemic flu situation. He suggested once again that in such an event, members make their way to a pre-determined fairway on the Tain course, with a crate of Glenmorangie, until the danger had passed.

John Houston asked him to explain what a fairway was.

Forbie Urquhart took the opportunity to explain some history behind 'Mary's hole' on the 15th.

It seems that a kindly green keeper was the first person to frequent Mary's Hole on a regular basis and he often escorted her home of an evening.

It was agreed that, in tribute to him if nothing else, Mary's Hole should provide a flu pandemic sanctuary for the Stotters.

ELECTION OF OFFICE BEARERS

Captain Robertson proposed Tom Lloyd as his successor. This was seconded by Hector MacIntyre and carried unanimously. A glass was raised to the outgoing Captain who was thanked for his sterling efforts during a busy year. In a rare outbreak of seriousness, Captain Lloyd described becoming Captain of the Stotters as an enormous honour.

He had enjoyed coming to Tain for many years and this was a proud day

Mayhem was restored when he proposed Liam Hughes as Vice-Captain. This was seconded by Hamish Robertson and carried unanimously.

Mike Lloyd thought it might be amusing to propose replacing Simon Houston with Sport.

No-one else found this funny.

There was a stony silence and Lloyd spent a few awkward moments staring at his shoes and refusing to look up.

Captain Tom Lloyd proposed that Simon Houston remain in the secretarial role. This was seconded by John Houston and carried unanimously.

With the time at 3.51 p.m. Mr Robert Beveridge fell asleep. The relevance of this will become apparent later.

A customary piss break was declared.

ANY OTHER COMPETENT BUSINESS

Hamish Robertson attempted to deflect attention from his ridiculous red trousers by rounding on Chris Rafferty's hair-cut, which he described as reprehensible. In response, Rafferty said: 'If you win your game it doesn't matter if you wear a wig.'

'Tell that to George Raeside', shouted an older member.

On the tie issue, Mike Lloyd said that the Captain had let the side down by refusing to wear a tie at dinner the previous evening. He argued that if we do not have to wear one – fine – but there has to be some clarification and agreement on the matter.

Frank Cougan added that scruffily dressed members had let down the exquisitely dressed ladies and that standards had to improve.

Those without ties were assured the issue would be addressed in the coming months. The previous jacquard had been lost and John Houston suggested the replacement should be kept somewhere safe, such as Ken's wallet.

Frank suggested there could be a password to access it, such as Mary's Hole.

The Captain said that without exception he wanted to see everyone wearing a tie next year.

A solid twenty minutes of Hamish bashing followed with the general consensus being that it surely would not be too much to ask to wear a tie for one night of the year. It was also agreed that as a valued member of the Society we would rather that he turn out without a tie than not turn up at all.

John Houston said it was once again a delight to see President Walkington in Tain for Golf Week, prompting nods of approval and raised glasses all round. He added that Sport's presence was due in no small way to the fine efforts of his son Hugh who was, himself, becoming an integral part of the Stotters' family.

It was agreed that having played a blinder for many years, Hugh should be given Honorary Stotters' status without hesitation.

The meeting was informed that Hugh was downstairs in the bar.

A message was despatched requesting his presence in the Lounge, and Captain Lloyd insisted that his arrival be greeted by way of a standing ovation.

In the meantime Hamish Robertson asked whether members would support the reintroduction of the children's concert which had been a great success in the past. The idea was welcomed with widespread approval as it would give the golfers something to look forward to after the qualifying rounds.

In the words of Jack Bower, the following events occurred in real time.

As per the Captain's request all members took to their feet and welcomed Walkington Junior into the fold with a hearty ovation and applause, cheers and whistles.

Surprised and a little embarrassed by the hoo-ha, Walkington nodded his appreciation, and was about to take his seat when, put simply, all hell broke loose.

The bedlam had apparently achieved the impossible and woken Bob Beveridge from his slumber.

In seeing all around him on their feet, a somewhat dazed and confused Beveridge took it upon himself to do likewise and rose sharply to attention.

It is fair to say that if a tornado had ripped its way through the lounge at that very moment, it would have caused less damage than was caused by the flying Beveridge in the chaotic moments that ensued.

Never mind Cruise Missile, this was a Booze Missile.

A nuclear Bob.

It was like a scene from Armageddon.

Arms, legs and expensive pieces of wood appeared to fly in every direction. Yellow jerseys raced around the room in blind panic as startled Stotters attempted to make sense of the turmoil unfolding before their very eyes.

An inquisitive lot, some were heard to ask: 'What the f... happened there?' Those who had witnessed the event spoke of a rugby tackle, the likes of which Jeremy Guscott would have been proud as Beveridge launched himself head first across the room in the direction of an unsuspecting Frank Cougan.

The pair crashed against the wall and on to the floor, destroying an antique table and chair in the process.

Unsure whether his dear old friend was trying to kill him or shag him, an ashen faced Cougan sat speared against the wall, while Beveridge lay draped across him, arms outstretched around Cougan's tummy like he was cuddling his favourite teddy bear.

Several doctors in the room held an emergency meeting and quickly reached the conclusion that Beveridge was pissed.

The pair were helped to their feet and, after a short comfort break, the meeting continued.

Hugh Walkington, who, let's be honest, was to blame for the madness, was officially welcomed. John Houston unhelpfully suggested that from now on every new Stotter should have his mettle tested by way of a Bob Bev flying tackle and be speared against the wall in some kind of satanic ritual.

The meeting rumbled on aimlessly with the annual uniform and Eastbourne discussions.

Clearly aggrieved that he had been overlooked and that Bob had fondled Frank instead, Hamish Robertson stormed out of the meeting in a huff claiming it was dragging on too long. The assembled gathering noted its disappointment at the immediate Past Captain's hissy fit.

Captain Lloyd, who had pretty much lost control of the room, in what had been a baptism of fire, thought it best to draw matters to a conclusion before any more damage could be done and, on that note, the meeting was called to a halt at 4.43 p.m.

The Bob Beveridge Cruise Missile incident is the most fondly remembered AGM event in the entire history of The Stotters.

The scene was indeed like a battlefield, with Bob's cross-room stagger and collapse on to Frank Cougan putting paid to a table and chair (subsequently, of course, paid for by The Stotters).

Gary Toal remembers:

"In the famous Bob Bev versus Frank rumble I was called in to action with another Stotter medic, Chris Fraser, and trying to find Bob Bev's pulse was clinically challenging.

Chris at one point asked me: "what are you doing?", and was informed: 'I dunno, but it's important to look busy'.

Glad to say that Bob resuscitated himself which is more than can be said for the antique sideboard".

Bob was once again assisted home, none the worse for the ordeal.

Sport's son, Hugh, joins the Stotters' fold in real style.

"My first AGM was in 2009. Having been summoned by phone call to the Royal Hotel, I knocked and was invited to enter. All the Stotters leaped to their feet ... but Bob Bev appeared to throw himself at Frank Cougan, knocking him over and demolishing a small nest of tables in the process. I vividly remember thinking to myself: "They didn't tell Bob about making Hugh a member and the shock's killed him!"

One of the most memorable AGM moments, even though Frank probably doesn't remember it fondly, as it stopped him from playing in the tournament the following day".

Frank himself, in a 2017 e-mail, requesting that his Stotters' bench plaque, when ultimately it becomes necessary, be placed between that of his dear friend Forbie, and Bob, said: "Bev made many a tackle for West of Scotland but kept his best one for big Hugh's entry to his induction at the Royal Hotel. It's safer to have him by my side.

Hooker Cougan☺"

Born in Cheltenham in 1963, Hugh lives in Tavistock in Devon.

After a brief stint as a trainee banker, he became a French teacher in 1987, and after many happy years teaching, retired from the classroom as Deputy Head in 2014.

He now works as a private language tutor / consultant; is doing some play writing; and helps a friend with her ceramics business.

He plays golf in Tavistock, a Club founded in 1890, the same year as Tain, off a handicap of 18.

At 6ft 8 tall, Hugh is indeed the gentle giant of the Stotters.

Because of the family connections with Tain, he has been a regular visitor almost every year since birth.

He has so far not succeeded in qualifying for the final stages of Golf Week, perhaps due to the fact that he plays often in the Qualifying Rounds with Hamish Robertson and/or Chris Rafferty, themselves accomplished non-qualifiers, and this despite the valiant efforts of caddies Fiona (Hugh's sister), Shirley and Alice! He even admits to once having to let Ken Ross play through as he took seven off the ninth tee.

However, in the Stotters' Match, he well remembers partnering Captain Hector MacIntyre in 2012 and securing "an honourable half".

Hugh remembers once caddying for Scott Ferguson, "who by the 12th was in an extremely mellow condition. He carved his drive way out onto the beach.

Sotto voce, one of the Tain team murmured "Sand wedge, please!" "

A dedicated Facebook devotee, Hugh is also a staunch English Sports Team supporter, but "feels more at home in Tain and Easter Ross than anywhere else in the world".

He loves standing at the 12th tee with his annual declaration that "this is the finest view in world golf".

The Stotters' Ties – Frank and Hamish.

MINUTES OF THE 45ᵀᴴ ANNUAL GENERAL MEETING OF THE STOTTERS – SUNDAY, 1ˢᵀ AUGUST 2010

Held at the Royal Hotel, Tain.

Forty-third annual match Tain versus the Stotters – Tain won.

Captain Tom Lloyd in the chair.

CAPTAIN'S REMARKS

Captain Lloyd welcomed all to the 2010 Stotters' AGM and began by raising a glass to the late Wilson Kemp, a true legend of the yellow jersey.

The Captain expressed his disappointment at yet another defeat in the annual match against Tain and noted that the overall score was now 23-21 in favour of the Stotters, and something should be done urgently to reverse this disturbing trend.

He asked for suggestions from the floor as to how best this could be achieved. An awkward few moments of uneasy silence followed as members shuffled uncomfortably in their seats and stared self-consciously at their shoes.

Some stared out of the window for fear of making eye contact with others. Some scratched their chins, others looked blankly at the Captain as though he was speaking Swahili.

Finally, a voice from the back of the room spoke up: 'We could maybe learn to play golf?'

Captain Lloyd confirmed that the winners of the Hic-Cup were Mike Lloyd and Hector MacIntyre.

APOLOGIES

These were received from George Ross and Andrew Urquhart.

MINUTES FROM THE PREVIOUS MEETING

These were read by the Secretary. This took longer than usual as they included a first-hand account of an attempted assassination by the flying Beveridge.

The Secretary then proposed that they be adopted as correct and this was seconded by the Secretary, who gave himself a well-deserved pat on the back and poured himself a dram and shook his head in disbelief that he was still getting away with this shit after all these years.

MATTERS ARISING FROM THE MINUTES

Ken Ross asked how Bob Bev managed to get so pissed. Had someone spiked his drink?

Mike Lloyd insisted he had not used the word Eastbourne whilst referring to his home golf club, but had instead referred to it as East Sussex because Eastbourne is for old people.

This prompted Ken to tell the meeting the joke about the railway porter who calls: 'Dover for the Continent, Eastbourne for the Incontinent' – a gag which is older than the combined age of the Eastbourne Bowling Club life members.

President Walkington, growing visibly irritated by these blatantly ageist jibes, urged the Captain to move things along because he desperately needed to pee.

ELECTION OF OFFICE BEARERS

The outgoing Captain Tom Lloyd proposed his Vice-Captain Liam Hughes and this was seconded by Hamish Robertson.

Incoming Captain Hughes said it was a tremendous honour and pleasure to take on one of the most coveted positions in International Amateur Golf and very much looked forward to ripping up 44 years of history and doing it his way.

He said it was also a delight to go back full circle and propose the oldest playing Stotter, Frank Cougan, as his Vice-Captain. This was also seconded by Hamish Robertson.

ANY OTHER COMPETENT BUSINESS

President Walkington noted that the annual match between the Stotters and Tain does not appear in the Tain Golf Club fixture diary and promised to take the matter up with the appropriate authority.

Captain Hughes said he had inside information that more than £1,000 had been spent in the bar after the match, reaffirming the importance of the occasion to the finances of the club.

It was unclear how he knew this, not having actually made a trip to the bar himself.

It was also agreed that Captain Hudson's post-match remarks had been extremely positive, particularly when he commented that the Stotters had been a Golf Week fixture long before the mixed foursomes, for example.

This had been an especially appropriate observation as at least half of the members present had played like a bunch of lassies that morning – and some were sporting an ample set of jugs, to boot.

Mike Lloyd expressed concern that some Tain Committee members still associate us with getting drunk and nothing else.

'What damn cheek!' snarled one disgruntled member as he reached for the bottle of Glenmorangie in front of him.

There followed five minutes of largely incoherent debate which produced little to trouble the Secretary's pen.

Captain Hughes did his best to stem the aggressive tide of weary listlessness and jaded indifference by demanding suggestions as how best to reclaim MacPhearson from the Tain Team.

Ken Ross helpfully suggested a warm-weather training camp. This was met with roars of approval and the refreshing sound of glasses being filled.

In a rare moment of thoughtfulness, the members took the opportunity to propose a vote of thanks to Frank Cougan and Forbie Urquhart for donating a tremendous set of Old Tom Morris hickory shafted clubs to Tain.

President Walkington then proposed a vote of thanks to Bob Beveridge for staying awake.

Bev responded with his now customary chorus of The Gay Caballero.

This was followed by the now customary and ultimately fruitless discussion about shirts, pullovers and ties, during which all eyes turned to Chris Rafferty who gave his now customary nod and wink and promised to do pretty much f… all about it during the forthcoming twelve months.

The Secretary made a mental note that the term 'Simon Ross had the jacquard' might make a good title for a book about the history of the Stotters.

The annual Eastbourne false promises then followed and talk of a men-only trip in May seemed to capture the imagination briefly before flagging apathy was restored.

As the meeting drew to a close, the newest member – Hugh Walkington – sought clarification as to his status and was reminded that he was an Associate as opposed to an Honorary.

Donald Sutherland then asked what kind of a Stotter he was: 'A wee fat, baldy one' was the general consensus.

On that cruel note, the meeting came to a close at 4.19 p.m.

Hugh was actually elected as an Honorary Stotter in 2009, rather than an Associate Stotter, though the distinction may be largely academic.

Similarly, as the years have passed Donald has invisibly morphed from an Honorary to an Associate Stotter, at least as far as voting rights are concerned.

Wilson Kemp's funeral had a huge turnout including a strong presence of Stotters and families.

Simon Houston delivered a very personal and moving eulogy, and his concluding words were:

"When I close my eyes and think of Wilson Kemp, I see him sitting in his caravan, the waves of the Dornoch firth rolling on to the beach behind him.

His favourite cigar in one hand, a large dram in the other.

His eyes smiling with laughter and that unmistakably cheery grin across his face.

Take care Wiz – I'll see you at the 19th".

MINUTES OF THE 46TH ANNUAL GENERAL MEETING OF THE STOTTERS – SUNDAY 31ST JULY, 2011

Held at the Royal Hotel, Tain.

The forty-fourth annual match of Tain v the Stotters – the Stotters won.

Captain Liam Hughes in the chair.

CAPTAIN'S REMARKS

The meeting began in jubilant mood as cries of "welcome home MacPhearson!" filled the air.

Captain Hughes congratulated his players on winning back the trophy and in the usual understated manner, said we had managed to beat the best Tain team ever.

He admitted that the right royal humping he and John Houston had suffered in the opening match might not have set the right tone but fortunately the more able golfers in the rest of the team were able to repair the substantial damage.

President Walkington prompted further cheers of approval when he produced a bottle of Glenmorangie, courtesy of Rita Kemp.

The bottle was duly opened and the Captain asked passengers to fasten their seat belts for take-off and the Tain crew switched the doors to automatic.

Ken Ross and Simon Houston were then congratulated on winning the Hic-Cup with the largest ever holes up victory against the best Tain pairing.

APOLOGIES

These were received from George Ross, Simon Ross and Bob Beveridge. Andrew Urquhart then offered an apology for missing the match and the AGM for the last two years but promised to be back next year.

Forbie Urquhart then thought it was reasonable to produce a bottle of Glenmorangie of his own, much to the delight of the assembled gathering, which had been working its way through Rita's bottle with thirsty enthusiasm.

Urquhart said his offering was by way of an apology for being unable to play. His words were met by confused stares by many of those present, who had always assumed that being unable to play was a prerequisite for wearing a yellow jersey in the first place.

MINUTES OF THE PREVIOUS MEETING

These were read by the Secretary.

Liam Hughes proposed that the Minutes be adopted as correct and this was seconded by Mike Lloyd.

ELECTION OF OFFICE BEARERS

Outgoing Captain Hughes proposed his Vice-Captain Frank Cougan as Captain and this was seconded by Hector MacIntyre.

Captain Cougan accepted the role to warm applause and began his tenure by congratulating the immediate Past Captain on his victory.

The meeting was then interrupted by the late, yet extremely welcome, arrival of one Robert Beveridge Esq.

Glasses were keenly charged in excited anticipation of the carnage which would surely now ensue.

Captain Cougan suggested a fine for the late appearance and then insisted that under new health and safety rules, Beveridge would have to sit at least three seats away from him, in case he felt the urge to carry out another assassination attempt.

Order was restored and Captain Cougan informed the meeting that he was now taking on the captaincy for the fourth time and he felt incredibly honoured to be doing so and it was something he treasured greatly.

This was greeted by hearty applause and much hurried pouring of whisky.

Captain Cougan proposed Hector MacIntyre as Vice-Captain and this popular choice was seconded by Simon Houston and carried unanimously.

Captain Cougan said he wanted to propose Simon Houston as Secretary because he used to kiss him as a wee boy. This somewhat bizarre admission caused the Secretary to blush somewhat and prompted a battery of semi-coherent paedophile jokes from John Houston who, let's face it, was probably jealous that he hadn't been the subject of Uncle Frank's questionable advances all those years ago.

The proposal was probably seconded, although the Secretary was too shell-shocked to notice and it was carried unanimously.

ANY OTHER COMPETENT BUSINESS

In time-honoured fashion the meeting entered the phase usually reserved for discussing ideas which sound good in theory but, in reality, will never happen. The Eastbourne trip is usually top of the agenda and this year's meeting didn't disappoint.

Mike Lloyd asked if the position of Special Envoy was up for grabs because his tan was starting to fade and he fancied spending a few more months of the year in a warmer climate at the Stotters' expense.

Failing that, he said it was high time the Stotters visited Eastbourne again as five years had elapsed since the last get together.

He said a group of friends from South Africa were coming to England the following spring and it would be great if a Stotters' visit could coincide with that.

Ken Ross, who had been unusually quiet to this point, agreed with Mike and they agreed to get their heads together to formulate a plan.

Members nodded excitedly at each other in anticipation.

We all love a good Eastbourne plan.

There followed a lengthy, often heated and untypically serious debate on the question of team selection.

Simon Houston said he felt it wholly unfair that Hugh Walkington was 13th man and therefore unable to play in the match that morning, given the commitment he displays year in year out in bringing himself and his father North from the very Southwest tip of England.

Not only did he stay for the entire week but he also played in the 4-day Open and, as the entire Stotters' movement was all about supporting Golf Week, then it was only fair that such a huge effort be recognised.

A discussion on membership numbers, status and team selection raged on for a full half hour although apparently at no point did the Secretary bother his backside by writing any of it down.

Bob Beveridge suggested lightening the mood with the Gay Caballero but he was politely told to shut the f… up while we dealt with the matter in hand.

Houston was very keen that some form of rule change be introduced to avoid a similarly unfair omission in the future because he was determined that Walkington would be given a game next year, adding that: 'If I can't have Hugh, I don't want nobody, baby'.

The general consensus was that those members who show the greatest commitment to supporting Golf Week should indeed be given some form of preferential treatment on occasions where a surplus of players are available to play on the Sunday morning.

The Secretary proposed that a Captain's pick be introduced, allowing the Captain and Vice-Captain to select which Associates should play in the event of too many players being available. This was seconded by Hector MacIntyre.

On a lighter note Hamish Robertson reminded the meeting that in five years the Stotters would be celebrating the 50th anniversary and proposed a special Sub-Committee be formed to concentrate on coming up with ideas to mark the milestone. This was seconded by the President.

MacIntyre then proposed a Stotters' outing to his home island of Benbecula, which was seconded by Chris Fraser and met with murmurs of varying degrees of apathy and disinterest.

Chris Rafferty said he was putting his foot down and was not going anywhere until he had heard the Gay Caballero. Bob duly obliged and much merriment followed.

As the meeting drew to a close, Mike Lloyd called for a group hug and told us never to forget how much we bring to Tain Golf Week every year.

His timely remarks were met with cheers of approval and the clinking of freshly charged glasses.

On that upbeat note, the meeting was brought to a halt at 4.45p.m.

MacPhearson's welcome return was close to not happening as Donald Sutherland recounts: "Carole and Morag were cleaning the cups ready for Golf Week and had laid the Stotters' Cup on the window sill with MacPhearson in his usual place in the cup. Unusually the sun was shining (only joking, it always shines up here) and the rays of the sun were concentrated on MacPhearson somehow. After a wee while Carole and Morag got this burning smell but couldn't figure out where it was coming from until they saw smoke coming from MacPhearson. He was burning but they got the fire out quickly and no real damage was done apart from a few singe marks!"

Liam Hughes' proudest moment as a Stotter was the 2011 match under his captaincy: "After an abysmal run of defeats to Tain, we eventually stopped the rot with a very narrow victory despite the fact the top match of myself and Johnny lost. This had been my banker as we were both playing really well at the time. The better ball on the day was under par which showed the quality of the golf was very very high – and given the drink consumed was no mean feat – in fact miraculous would be closer".

Simon's passionate intervention during the AGM in favour of Hugh Walkington fairly reflects Hugh's years of involvement.

Every year, Hugh set off with father Sport several days in advance of Golf Week and devised a fun way of splitting up the long journey.

Each morning he gave Sport a sealed envelope inside which was a riddle which Sport had to decode – the answer to the riddle revealed that night's destination.

Hugh gives a few examples from over the years:

"Church where what the cow chews is not dim?" – Kirkcudbright.

"Saw an elk so must be confused" – Kelso.

"Human card ran in a confused manner" – Ardnamurchan.

"What a U Boat did to the Lusitania?" – Sanquhar.

"Under intense gaze starts to reveal name" – Uig.

"Wretched keep staying in this place" – Ballycastle (Northern Ireland!).

MINUTES OF THE 47TH ANNUAL GENERAL MEETING OF THE STOTTERS – SUNDAY, 5TH AUGUST 2012

Held at the Castle Hotel Portmahomack.

Forty-fifth annual match – Tain versus the Stotters – The Stotters won.

Captain Frank Cougan in the chair.

Prior to commencement, Hugh Walkington informed the meeting that his late father Ian Walkington was under the table, not for the first time at an AGM.

With that, he produced the President, resplendent in his urn and displaying his usual air of calm authority and placed him on the table, with a bottle of Glenmorangie.

The President's late arrival was met with much cheering and charging of glasses.

APOLOGIES

These were received on behalf of Tom Lloyd, George Ross, Simon Ross, Andrew Urquhart, and Bob Beveridge.

CAPTAIN'S REMARKS

On the event of the 46th AGM, Captain Cougan said he was delighted and honoured to be Captain for the fourth time, which was indeed a record.

He suggested that, being no spring chicken, it would probably be his last captaincy.

Members shook their heads and told Cougan that was nonsense, in a particularly patronising way.

Hugh then told him to hurry up as he could sense his father was already getting bored.

The Captain said his team had all done very well to win the match because at the halfway stage things were not looking good, but he had brought all the players a much-needed whisky laced with Speed and that appeared to do the trick.

He then thanked his more than able Vice-Captain Hector MacIntyre for some sterling help and support.

Then, recalling two giants of The Stotters' movement who had passed on during the previous 12 months, Frank said that Sport Walkington and Pat Houston would always be with us.

It was great, he said, that all the children who come to Tain in increasing numbers, could look at all the names on The Stotters' bench and learn about the legend.

Addressing younger members, he said that the future is in your hands, and with a third generation establishing itself, the future appeared to be in very safe hands.

The Captain's suggestion that perhaps an annual competition involving The Stotters' children be organised was warmly welcomed.

All present then agreed that Hugh Walkington's words about his father on the first tee, prior to the match, were fantastic and very moving.

MINUTES OF THE PREVIOUS MEETING

These were read by the Secretary.

Mike Lloyd disputed the reference to a visit to England by friends of his from South Africa, which could perhaps coincide with a Stotters' trip to East Sussex.

This couldn't be the case because for one thing, he didn't have any friends.

There is no official note of the Minutes being adopted as correct, but the Secretary is certain Sport Walkington offered a nod of approval.

And never being one to let the facts stand in the way of a good story, he has duly signed them off anyway.

And if you don't like it, you can take it up with Lord Justice Leveson, or some other bugger.

ELECTION OF OFFICE BEARERS

Captain Cougan proposed Vice-Captain MacIntyre as his successor and this was seconded by Hugh Walkington and carried unanimously.

The new Captain thanked his predecessor and congratulated him on steering the team to victory.

Captain MacIntyre proposed Chris Rafferty as his Vice-Captain, which was seconded by Ken Ross, and carried unanimously.

The Captain then proposed Frank Cougan for the role of President. This was jointly seconded by all present.

New President Cougan said he was delighted to accept and it was an honour to be following in the footsteps of his dear old friend Sport.

He added that he loved The Stotters as much now as he did four decades ago and it's what made him come back every year.

Word then filtered through from the bar that Andy Murray was nearing match point in his Olympic Final against Roger Federer. A collective cry of "f... this – we're on our way through!" filled the air and the room was temporarily vacated.

One Olympic gold and piss break later, the question of Secretary was addressed.

Captain MacIntyre proposed Simon Houston, seconded by Hamish Robertson and carried unanimously.

John Houston asked that, as the Secretary was now working for The Sun, did it mean that the Minutes would be full of lots of tits and bums?

The Secretary said there were enough tits and bums present as it was, and there was no real urgency for any more.

ANY OTHER COMPETENT BUSINESS

Liam Hughes brought up the question of the venue for dinner the previous evening, which had not met with everyone's approval.

The Clubhouse at Tarbat GC, it was felt, was not an adequate venue as too many people had been squeezed into too small a space.

There had also been a question mark over the quality of the food provided at the barbeque.

Hughes however, felt that much of the criticism had been unfair and that the catering team should have been applauded for doing their best to accommodate so many people as best they could at relatively short notice, after it became apparent that The Royal Hotel was not an option.

He said that Geraldine had gone to great efforts to organise the night and if anyone else thought they could do better, they were welcome to try.

With the dummy well and truly out of the pram, a heated debate followed.

Most agreed that Tarbat Golf Club had not worked, but being condemned to the Clan Ross Rooms at The Royal was not ideal either, so what next?

Ken Ross said Tain, and in particular, The Royal Hotel, was the spiritual home of the Stotters, and had been our original base, so efforts should be made to re-establish a connection.

Ross added that the barbecue was fine, but if it had rained, it would have been a disaster. It was, he stressed, all about The Royal.

Twenty or so minutes of largely incoherent pish followed. Everyone present threw in their tuppence worth.

Past President Walkington struggled to make himself heard over the rabble, and instead chose to maintain a dignified silence.

Varying degrees of verbal abuse and insults flew back and forth across the table as Captain MacIntyre tried to restore order, with limited success.

His ancestors would have dealt with such lawlessness and insubordination by despatching the offenders to the Russian Front, but this was Portmahomack 2012 and such measures were frowned upon.

Instead he looked at the Secretary and muttered: "What should I do, Simon?"

Vice-Captain Rafferty intervened and asked that special thanks to Geraldine be minuted, and added that the general mood supported a return to The Royal, so he and Captain MacIntyre would approach the Hotel to discuss it.

The issue of membership was raised and Chris Fraser said he would like to propose Alan Gordon for Associate status as he had become a welcome addition to Golf Week in recent years, and with his wit, golfing prowess and drinking ability, he would make a right good Stotter. This was seconded by John Houston, who in turn gave a long tribute to the Ghost, stressing that he epitomises everything that's important about the organisation.

The proposal was carried unanimously and Gordon was invited to join the meeting. In his usual shy and retiring manner, he announced his arrival with a 20-minute speech and a dirty joke.

The passing of President Walkington had created an opening for full Stotter status.

Chris Fraser and Gary Toal were jointly next in line and even the most limited mathematician knows that two into one doesn't go.

Some drink fuelled idiot suggested the pair should be asked to leave the room while the issue was discussed.

And in a display of breathtaking incompetence, this was agreed, and they departed to the bar – quite enthusiastically as it turned out – while their fate was discussed.

A long and heated discussion failed to trouble the scorer and in the end common sense prevailed when it was agreed that it was unfair to split them up and both should be granted full Stotter status.

The gents were invited back into the room and congratulated on their promotion.

Cheers filled the air, glasses were charged, and much merriment, fun and hilarity ensued.

The meeting was brought to a close at 5.45pm – a record?

Whilst the starting time of the meeting was never recorded, it is likely that it began at 2pm or shortly afterwards, so an AGM of almost 4 hours was indeed a Stotters' record.

It was a very stormy meeting which Simon's Minutes fortunately gloss over, with lots of angry remarks and insults bandied about, particularly over the question of who should graduate to full Stotter status, with Malcolm Fraser narrowly missing out, and the number of full Stotters now extended to 14.

Sport, who died on the 12th January 2012, had his ashes subsequently scattered at Tarbat Ness. Hugh had faithfully strapped the urn containing his ashes in to his passenger seat and driven him from Tavistock to make his unique urn appearance.

The sad demise of Pat Houston ended another long-term association with the very early days of the Stotters.

Dr. John's widow had been omnipresent during Golf Week for decades, supporting, cajoling and decrying in equal measure all those in the yellow jersey.

With a deliciously acerbic wit, she often sat in the Clubhouse doing her crosswords awaiting her family finishing their rounds of golf with a wry smile for poor rounds and a proud and emphatic nod of approval for good ones.

She had been a huge pillar of support for Hamish Senior when his wife Helen became ill and died in 1994, emphasising the strong ties between the Houstons and the Robertsons.

Simon's reference to Lord Justice Leveson was timeous in that he led a judicial public inquiry into the culture, practices and ethics of the British press following the News International phone hacking scandal.

A series of public hearings were held throughout 2011 and 2012. The Inquiry published the Leveson Report in November 2012, making recommendations for a new independent body to replace the existing Press Complaints Commission, which would have to be recognised by the state through new laws.

Prime Minister David Cameron, under whose direction the inquiry had been established, said that he welcomed many of the findings, but nevertheless declined to enact the requisite legislation.

Alan Gordon, alias Ghost, now joins as an Associate. With a brilliant sense of humour, superb drinking skills and playing off 8, Ghost is a potentially great asset.

From Kilbarchan in Renfrewshire, he is married to Anne and they have three sons and three grandchildren. He is Regional Sales Manager for a kitchen appliance distribution company and travels extensively.

Having recently achieved golf Senior status (much to his own disgust), he is Captain of Ranfurly Castle.

He first came to Tain in 2009.

He remembers: "I am a long-standing friend of the Houston family and they talked about it all the time but I always felt it was too far away, and the weather might be a bit suspect (!).

We finally made the trip – combined with a bit of business – and absolutely loved it. I wish I had come years ago but now I wouldn't miss it".

He has qualified three times for the knockout stages of Golf Week and was part of what he describes as: "the great non-qualification debacle of 2009" with Simon Houston.

"I actually think I might have a 100% record, but couldn't swear to it as I was pissed!"

He extends Chris Fraser's rhubarb rum memory: "I remember Gary (Tonge) falling over on the 17th tee – Rhubarb rum was involved – and Gary may have been unable to continue!"

MINUTES OF THE 48TH ANNUAL GENERAL MEETING OF THE STOTTERS – SUNDAY AUGUST 4TH 2013.

Held at the Royal Hotel, Tain.

The 46th Annual Match between Tain and the Stotters – Tain won.

Captain Hector MacIntyre in the chair.

Drink had been taken, so the assembled members strapped themselves in for a bumpy ride.

CAPTAIN'S REMARKS

The highlights of a great year included a trip to East Sussex and a Stotters' victory.

A fine weekend was only slightly marred by an alleged sexual assault by Ken Ross on youngest son Simon. Unclear about who he was sharing a bed with, Ken woke up and planted a loving kiss on his startled offspring's shoulder and muttered "Morning, darling".

Moving on, the annual match v Tain ended in a 3-3 draw, but because Captain MacIntyre and Vice-Captain Rafferty were slaughtered by five holes, Tain won the cup on aggregate.

The Captain admitted that to lose in such a manner was hard to take after what had been a tremendous year in office.

Vice-Captain Rafferty added that while many of the Stotters were in East Sussex, a home guard battalion were simultaneously performing heroics at the Hamish Robertson Memorial Texas Scramble in Tain.

APOLOGIES

Bob Beveridge asked Mike to pass them on.

MINUTES OF PREVIOUS MEETING

These were read by the Secretary.

Hamish Robertson proposed they be adopted as correct, seconded by Chris Fraser and carried unanimously.

However the Secretary picked up on his own mistake.

The previous year's meeting had been adjourned for the closing stages of Andy Murray's Olympic singles win over Djokovic and not Federer as stated. He apologised and insisted that his resignation be accepted. It sadly fell on deaf ears.

It was noted that Donald Sutherland had fallen asleep less than ten minutes into the meeting. This was a new personal best and smashed the late Scott Ferguson's long-held record by a good three or four minutes.

Sutherland's sterling effort – or lack of it as the case may be – was met with nods of approval and glasses were filled and raised in a toast of appreciation.

ELECTION OF OFFICE BEARERS

Captain MacIntyre proposed Vice- Captain Rafferty as his successor and this was seconded by Hamish Robertson and carried unanimously.

The outgoing Captain said he hoped his replacement would lead the team to victory which he had failed to do.

Immersed in pain, MacIntyre said he was half German and therefore not used to losing – momentarily forgetting about two World Wars, several World Cups, the Eurovision song contest and various fashion awards.

The appointment was warmly greeted with applause and more drink all round.

Captain Rafferty then proposed George Ross as his Vice-Captain.

"You remember George?" he asked the gathering. They did indeed and this was seconded by Ken Ross and carried unanimously.

Frank Cougan and Tom Lloyd both remarked on a fine captaincy by Hector MacIntyre, Lloyd describing his spreadsheet for the dinner orders as a work of art.

Hamish Robertson proposed that Simon Houston continue as Secretary, seconded by Hugh Walkington.

Hector MacIntyre then attempted a surprise but not entirely unwelcome coup d'état, to have the Secretary removed and replaced by Alan 'The Ghost' Gordon, a recognised wordsmith and raconteur.

The rebellion was swiftly crushed by Captain Rafferty who insisted Houston 'will not be ousted on my watch!'

The Secretary then asked MacIntyre for his fiver back and reprimanded him for making a rip-roaring mess of their secret plan.

The meeting was adjourned for the customary five minute piss break.

ANY OTHER COMPETENT BUSINESS

The meeting was given an update from Ivan that the Royal would be available again for the Saturday night meal, but bookings couldn't be taken until the New Year.

Ken Ross however argued for a return to the Morangie as it served us very well the night before. It had been a great night and moves should be made to book it again and perhaps sound them out about the AGM.

A long debate on possible venues for the AGM followed – none of which the Secretary saw fit to minute in any great detail.

Gary Toal then raised the issue of the 2016 captaincy and suggested some kind of Papal conclave where a college of Stotter cardinals would eat, sleep and more importantly, drink, until white smoke – or Fumata Bianca – signalled that a worthy incumbent has been elected.

A discussion on procedure ensued and it was largely agreed that given the importance of 2016, it would be fitting to elect a fitting Captain for the occasion rather than simply choose the next in line on the usual rotational basis. It was agreed that a vote would take place sometime in 2014 and the format could be fine-tuned nearer the time.

More untypically coherent debate followed, much of it steered manfully by Hamish Robertson, and it was agreed that a 2016 sub-committee be formed to look specifically at matters pertaining to the 50th Anniversary celebrations.

Mike Lloyd suggested that one such inclusion could be a children's supporters' shirt.

Other ideas included a specially made glass engraved with the words: 'I survived the Stotters' being presented to each of the opposing Tain team in 2016.

Captain Rafferty suggested we build an Anniversary war chest and appoint a Treasurer.

Hugh Walkington said the important thing would be to get the Sub-Committee up and running and focus on solid ideas.

One confused member reached for a freshly opened bottle of Glenmorangie and asked Walkington if he could run that 'solids' thing past him again.

Frank Cougan added that 2015 saw the 125th anniversary of Tain Golf Club and perhaps something could be done to mark the occasion, perhaps an Old Tom Morris tribute act, which he could supply. It was agreed that the Sub-Committee could look at this. Ken Ross asked for an update on the whereabouts of the Stotters' flag. It was explained that the flag was still in the shop but the Pro had buggered off to France and the girls in the shop had no idea where it was. Another East Sussex tour was mentioned but Hamish Robertson asked that it didn't clash with the Texas Scramble. George Ross then set the proverbial cat among the pigeons by wondering, out loud, whether we might look at introducing ladies into the annual match in 2016.

A tumbleweed rolled through the meeting room before the silence was broken by the sound of Stotters falling off their chairs. In an attempt to explain himself, Ross argued that it might be nice to throw something back at the ladies in recognition of their efforts throughout Golf Week.

John Houston suggested throwing them some dirty dishes.

Ross conceded that his proposal was more than a little controversial, but he would be back in five years with another one.

A brief outbreak of sanity punctuated the dying embers of the meeting when Captain Rafferty stressed that a Treasurer should be appointed as a matter of priority.

All agreed this was a fine idea and sensing that the conversation might continue unless the bull was taken by the horns, the assembled gathering rose in unison to bring matters to a melodious conclusion with a rousing rendition of the Gay Caballero. The meeting was closed at 4.01 pm.

Despite Simon's admission to making a mistake about the Olympic Tennis Final, it WAS Federer and not Djokovic whom Murray beat 6–2, 6–1, 6–4.

MINUTES OF THE 49TH ANNUAL GENERAL MEETING OF THE STOTTERS – SUNDAY AUGUST 3RD 2014

Held at the Royal Hotel, Tain.

The 47th Annual Match between Tain and the Stotters – Tain won.

Captain Chris Rafferty in the chair.

APOLOGIES

Received from Tom Lloyd.

MINUTES OF THE PREVIOUS MEETING

These were read and proposed as correct by Chris Fraser and seconded by Mike Lloyd.

As there were no matters arising from the Minutes, the meeting moved swiftly on.

ELECTION OF OFFICE BEARERS

Chris Rafferty proposed George Ross for Captain – this was seconded by Liam Hughes and carried unanimously.

The issue of Vice-Captain triggered a long and at times coherent discussion on the ceremonial procedure for the 50th Anniversary celebrations of 2016.

It was agreed that as George Ross's number two would be Captain for the historic event, the matter would be put on hold until such times as a fitting selection process be determined.

A round of eeny, meeny, miney, mo; scissors, paper and stone; and who could down a bottle of Glenmorangie the fastest were all briefly considered but dismissed as a too frivolous.

Instead the matter was deferred to the 2016 Sub-Committee (Sub of course standing for Sober Until Bedtime) to unearth a more business-like strategy.

One member helpfully pointed out that as the incumbent would be an ambassador during the society's most important year since inception and would be following in the footsteps of fine upstanding Stotters such as Gilbert Tocher, Hammy Mitchell and Ian MacPherson, it wouldn't do to have any old booze-bag in the chair.

A similar amount of anticipation surrounded the position of Secretary.

But in an unexpected turn of events, Simon Houston emerged as a surprise candidate for the post. This was proposed by Chris Rafferty, seconded by Mike Lloyd and quickly carried before Houston could get all needy and uppity, as was his wont at this time of the meeting.

Chris Rafferty proposed Hugh Walkington as Treasurer – this was seconded by Alan Gordon and carried unanimously.

Captain Ross then congratulated the outgoing Captain on his fine stint at the helm and thanked the continuing office bearers for their sterling efforts over the preceding 12 months.

At this stage a piss break was probably declared although the Secretary has no clear documentary evidence to back this up.

ANY OTHER COMPETENT BUSINESS

Captain Ross said this was his second year back after a long, unenforced absence and yet again he had thoroughly enjoyed the match against Tain.

The whole experience had been a great deal of fun and he had really enjoyed seeing everyone again. He was looking forward to the next year with huge enthusiasm.

The Treasurer then gave a brief financial report. A discussion followed on the membership direct debit into the central pot for 2016 with a view to raising enough money to fund a series of events.

Gary Toal wondered whether a more sensible fiscal policy might include placing an annual bet on the winner of Golf Week.

On the question of communication, Frank Cougan said his old e-mail address had been seized by the FBI as part of Operation Nocturnal Keyboard and he had a new one, which he asked be added to the distribution list.

Chris Rafferty suggested we start a new user group. This was met by cheers and nods of agreement. Hector MacIntyre was halfway to the bar when it was pointed out that Rafferty had said user group, not boozer group.

A ten-minute recess followed during which a mouth-watering buffet of crisps arrived.

The meeting recommenced with a brief discussion on future trips to East Sussex National and it was agreed that any future weekends away would not clash with the annual Hamish Robertson Texas Scramble at Tain and that it would be a boys' weekend, rather than a girly one.

More cheers followed and this time MacIntyre made it all the way to the bar.

Ken Ross then asked Sub-Committee stalwart Hamish Robertson to give the meeting an update on preparations for the 50th anniversary.

Robertson gave a clear and crisp report, bringing a rare moment of welcome lucidity to proceedings.

He said preparations were progressing well and included plans for, among other things, hickory clubs for the annual match, a memento for the Tain team, and commemorative whisky glasses for those taking part.

Further debate ensued, much of which centred on a possible marquee at the golf club for the Saturday night meal and the prohibitive costs of such a venture. This prompted much discussion on venues which went round in circles for what seemed like an eternity and clearly outlasted the Secretary's attention span or indeed will to live.

He did however look up and nod approvingly at Hugh Walkington's use of the word 'gravitas' before staring back into the abyss.

The arguments swung between getting a quote for a marquee and approaching the Town Hall, with the general consensus being that the Sub-Committee would sort it out and we should move on to other matters.

Mike Lloyd suggested that a giant awning with the words Mike is Cool emblazoned on the side in giant letters might not be the worst idea.

Frank Cougan brought up the logo which he felt no longer symbolised the Stotters.

Some members murmured their disquiet at this sacrilegious talk and clutched their whisky glasses even tighter than normal in defiance. It was defeated without further discussion.

Much more chat about 2016 followed, some of it threatening to make sense, with lots of noteworthy ideas and suggestions floated around the table.

A vote then took place on a suitable venue for Gilbert's Goblet and it was agreed that 8pm on the Monday night at the Castle Hotel in Portmahomack would best serve the occasion.

Donald Sutherland then suggested a Sub-Committee meeting during the year to discuss uniforms for both teams.

It was also agreed that the question of extra matches at the end of the 2016 game against Tain to accommodate the Associates should be looked at.

Liam Hughes proposed a vote of thanks to the Sub-Committee for making so much happen in such a short space of time. The Sub-Committee in turn congratulated Hughes for making so much happen in such a short pair of trousers.

As the meeting threatened to draw to a close, Alan Gordon and George Ross both helpfully raised the issue of voting procedure to elect the 2016 captain.

After a lengthy debate it was agreed that an e-mail vote would take place with the Sub-Committee ironing out the finer details in the forthcoming months.

The meeting closed at 5.17pm.

Bob Beveridge died in May 2014, a sad loss to his family, to Tain and to the Stotters. He had enriched the annual golf matches, was a great friend, and created huge hilarity at AGMs.

As a footnote to his passing, Hamish was checking the date of Bob's death, and saw that the last mention of Bob was in the Minutes of 2013.

He scribbled a note to remind himself. "Bob Bev dies after 2013 Minutes". Only the next day did he see the irony in that footnote!

MINUTES OF THE 50TH ANNUAL GENERAL MEETING OF THE STOTTERS – SUNDAY 2ND AUGUST, 2015

Held ringside, Madison Square Gardens – AKA the Royal Hotel, Tain.

The 49th annual match between Tain and the Stotters was won by Tain.

Captain George Ross in the chair

APOLOGIES

Donald Sutherland apologised for turning up. This was duly noted and he was warned not to do it again.

CAPTAINS REMARKS

Captain Ross, who was still just about in control of the meeting at this stage, said he was quite frankly disappointed in his team. He had dragged the McVitie and Price champion to victory in their own game, but we had lost the cup.

This meant that the Stotters were only one victory ahead overall, going into the 50th anniversary match – an observation which was met with murmurs of discontent.

Even at this early stage, the Captain sensed that maintaining even the vaguest semblance of decorum was probably beyond his modest skillset, and declared: "I've driven 14 hours to be here, so please shut up and listen".

Failing to heed this instruction, Secretary Houston pointed at Frank Cougan and gasped: "My God hasn't Bono aged?" (a reference to the President's swanky new sunglasses).

Captain Ross pressed ahead and made a lovely speech about how much fanny he enjoyed. Sorry that should read how much his family enjoyed coming north each year and it had become a firm fixture in their annual calendar.

Cheers and applause echoed around the room as the Captain took his seat.

MINUTES OF THE PREVIOUS MEETING

These were read by the Secretary. Hamish Robertson proposed they be adopted as correct. This was seconded by Hugh Walkington.

MATTERS ARISING FROM MINUTES

There were no matters arising, apart from the bit about Hector going to the bar. The meeting agreed this was clearly a case of the Secretary's over-fertile imagination playing tricks on him.

A piss break was declared.

ELECTION OF OFFICE BEARERS

Captain Ross proposed John Houston for Captain in 2016. This was seconded by all present and carried unanimously.

The Captain-elect said his memories of the previous night were slightly hazy but it was a good thing he had prepared a speech in advance in anticipation of his election.

He spoke very highly of rival contenders Simon Houston and Ken Ross, but in recognition of the magnificent work he had carried out in preparation for the 50th celebrations, he proposed Hamish Robertson Junior as his Vice-Captain. This was again seconded and carried unanimously.

The Secretary made it clear he no longer wanted to be considered for the post but added that it had been an honour and a pleasure to serve for around 15 years. However it was time for someone else to take up the reins.

Ken Ross proposed a vote of thanks for the outgoing Secretary and offered some very kind words about his tenure.

He then proposed Hugh Walkington as Secretary and this was seconded and carried unanimously.

A lengthy discussion followed during which many of the assembled gathering offered more words of praise for the outgoing Sec. Some said it was only right and proper that he should never again have to put his hand in his pocket during Golf Week, while others offered to taxi him around, allowing him to drink as much as he wanted without having to worry about getting behind the wheel for the foreseeable future.

Houston reluctantly agreed but duly noted these promises in black and white because everyone was so pissed they would probably forget making them.

The Captain-elect proposed Hugh Walkington also continue as Treasurer. This was seconded by Mike Lloyd and carried unanimously.

ANY OTHER COMPETENT BUSINESS

Ken was first to speak up, much to the surprise of those around him.

He asked if there was an appetite for another East Sussex trip to mark the 50th. It was agreed that he would liaise with Hector MacIntyre.

MacIntyre wondered if we should invite the Junior Stotters too. There was an awkward silence during which tumbleweed meandered through the room. Eventually someone said: "F… that".

And the discussion was promptly knocked on the head.

George Ross invited Hamish to give the meeting an update on plans for 2016.

Hamish then delivered a full and detailed report into where we were regarding the forthcoming Anniversary celebrations, all of which was terribly interesting but clearly not interesting enough to capture the outgoing Secretary's attention because he failed to write any of it down.

Suffice to say it was a comprehensive report into who was doing what and stuff like that.

There then followed a lengthy and at times coherent discussion into the dress code for the 2016 dinner dance. Would it be smart or smart casual and would kilts be in order?

It was agreed that this could be discussed nearer the time.

The Treasurer then provided an excellent financial report, the crux of which was that we would have £5,000 in the bank account by August 2016.

What followed next tested the Secretary's shorthand skills like never before. But it's best summed up thus:

Cutlery and the cost of said, dominated discussions for a good ten minutes as the overall price of the Saturday night Anniversary meal was examined in fine detail.

Ken Ross attempted to defuse the incendiary atmosphere by suggesting that it be left to the Sub-Committee to organise in the sober light of day.

Things were going well until Captain Ross kind of, well, lost it, and launched into a tirade about how we were all useless at answering e-mails and we needed to sort it out because too much was being done by too few.

Chaos and bedlam ensued.

Alan Gordon said it was ridiculous that we were paying £5 a head to hire cutlery.

Hamish said he'd had enough of this bollocks and threw his clipboard at Alan, inviting him to organise it himself.

The Ghost responded by calling Hamish a 'bawbag' – indisputably a Stotters' AGM first – and threw a bottle cork back across the table.

Forbie Urquhart, famous for downing most of a thirty ouncer before reaching the third green and putting exploding balls on his opponents' tee peg when they weren't looking, said he was not used to such outrageous behaviour and left the meeting, followed by Malcolm Fraser, who returned briefly to tell the remaining members they were a bunch of b......s and he would be resigning forthwith. Captain Ross warned Fraser to sit back down or face the consequences. Fraser told him to f... off and marched out.

Stunned silence filled the room before the word: "Result", was heard (said in a London accent, just to narrow things down).

Unprecedented scenes of bedlam ensued, during which Hector MacIntyre very nearly bought a drink and Liam Hughes very nearly woke up.

Ken Ross didn't exactly help the departing Captain's fragile frame of mind by pointing out that: 'This is all going rather well, George.'

Sanity finally prevailed and a sensible discussion on which Tain dignitaries should be invited to the Anniversary dinner dance took place.

All agreed that we should trust the Sub-Committee to press on with anniversary plans,

And at 5.26 PM the meeting was called to a close.

Well then!

This was by far the most tempestuous AGM since records began. Tempers ran even higher than the alcohol level, and many plots were lost, but from the shambles of a meeting emerged a new concord.

Hamish and Ghost hugged and made up; Forbie eventually came back into the fold; and Malcolm and Ruth were willing and most welcome attendees at the 2016 dinner.

And it is believed that George and father Ken remained father and son.

George ruefully remembers: "trying to keep order. I stood up after the enth person interrupted and asked everyone to speak through the chair, which I'd been saying pretty repeatedly for two hours.

Simon Houston stood up, grabbed a chair and started talking through the gap in the back of it. I knew at that stage it was pointless to continue trying".

The election of Captain for 2016 was done by secret e-mail ballot, coordinated by George Ross, and the subsequent election of Johnny Houston was strikingly appropriate, given that father, Dr. John, had been the first Captain of the Stotters in 1966.

The election of Hamish as Vice-Captain was also appropriate given the family connection; and completing the Office Bearers for 2016 with Hugh Walkington as Secretary and Treasurer meant that all three Office Bearers for the 50th year of the Stotters were sons of original Stotters – synchronicity indeed.

Roll on 2016!

2016

2016 marked 50 years of the Stotters, an incredible journey of camaraderie and golf, sprinkled with the gold dust of humour and alcohol, often mixed together but sometimes not.

A huge amount of effort went into this celebratory year.

The special Sub-Committee responsible for pulling it all together, with Hamish Robertson coordinating the activity, were Hugh Walkington, George and Simon Ross, Geraldine Houston and Anne (Fraser) Houston, Donald Sutherland, Chris Rafferty, and Simon and Johnny Houston.

Hugh, who managed the Stotters' monthly contributions, nagged the non-payers into submission, and most ably and promptly paid all the various bills.

Deen coordinated the organisation of the specially designed clothing for Stotters' supporters and children. Yellow hoodies and polo shirts with Stotters' 1966-2016 logos and Stotters' caps were liberally supplied and worn throughout Golf Week.

She organised and manages the Stotters' Facebook pages which have been an invaluable tool for promoting the Stotters and displaying an amazing collection of photographs and articles from over the years.

She also painstakingly pulled together from the Stotters, their families and friends, an incredible number of photographs from though the years, supplied in a mix of hard copy and electronic versions.

Simon Ross then worked his producer's magic on these photos to produce a stunning montage which played throughout Golf Week in the Clubhouse. This montage included cine film from the 60s and early 70s which was originally taken by Hamish (Senior) and wife Helen. Hamish (Junior) provided the appropriate clips.

During Golf Week, there was often a small group watching the montage play, and amongst some poignant moments were George and Simon Ross seeing, for the first time, their Grandfather, Ken, on film, having only ever previously seen photographs.

The Clubhouse also acted as the display base for Claire Cougan's scrupulously researched and elegantly presented Stotters' Family Tree showing the connections, relationships and friendships developed through 50 years.

Chris Rafferty, with great support from Tain Professional, Stuart Morrison, ensured that the Stotters were kitted out in new yellow tops emblazoned with the logo carefully and professionally updated by Simon Ross, bearing the legend in green on the left breast:

STOTTERS
1966-2016

On the left sleeve was the Tain Golf Club coat of arms.

Chris also organised new stone coloured caps.

Donald Sutherland ensured that the Tain team wore their own new tops, in green, with their logo on the left breast and The Stotters' logo with dates on the left sleeve.

Forbie and Margaret Urquhart, with help latterly from Donald, asked Glenmorangie to make commemorative tumblers with the Stotters' logo 1966-2016, and these were provided to all those playing in the annual match and also to all the Stotters' guests who attended the celebratory dinner in the Duthac Centre in Shandwick Street.

The dinner was a terrific affair, organised by Chris Rafferty with Red Poppy catering, and the Golf Club provided the bar.

Hamish and Shirley Robertson put together the table plan and name cards, many carrying little messages for the guests (like "Don't drink too much tonight"; "You're looking lovely tonight"; "Your turn to buy a drink"; and many more). The top table's name card remarks included the following: Johnny Houston: "Now – no tears tonight – no swearing – no dirty jokes – and definitely no "Dad" dancing!"; Ewan Forrest: "Johnny will try to get you drunk, so bite the bullet and get hammered anyway!").

Together, Red Poppy and the Golf Club looked after 70 Stotters, family and friends (including eight children), and 41 guests, which included the Tain team for the Sunday match and their partners, and Tain GC notables including those having a long association with the match.

Many a kilt was in evidence.

The top table was graced with the presence of the two Presidents, Forbie (and Margaret) and Frank (with daughters Claire and Catherine); David

Rutherford, mine host of yesteryear; Tain Captain Ewan Forrest and his wife, Alison; and Stotters' Captain Johnny Houston.

Ewan and Johnny both made upliftingly pithy speeches, fondly recognising the Stotters/Tain association, and friendship, and wishing for their own team's success the following day.

Forbie, who had only that morning returned from a holiday cruise, set up on the Hall stage a brilliant Stotters' display which was subsequently moved to the Clubhouse.

Hamish Robertson spoke about the Stotters' history in a near factual manner, but with the decency to apply some humour to keep everyone awake.

There were a few toasts!

Ken Ross then said some words, but nobody was very sure what they conveyed given that food and drink had been taken.

All the Stotters received a copy of Tony Watson's book – "Tain – a Golfing History of People, Places and Past Times", signed by himself and Ewan.

Johnny Houston presented Hamish with an elegant whisky-still decanter, suitably engraved as a thank you for his organisation.

There were many reunions, many new associations, many funny stories and many memorable moments, all washed down with an appropriate modicum of alcohol.

A cheerful disco played out the last hour or so until carriages arrived at midnight.

The carriages included buses conveying most of The Stotters and families to their Portmahomack base, and also a minibus taking a large Robertson contingent to Pitcalzean House where 29 Robertsons, Rafferties and MacDonalds were staying for the week – a huge family gathering organised specially to coincide with the celebrations.

Six special "out and back" buses were organised by Hamish for the dinner, the Sunday morning match, and for the Children's Concert – to ensure no difficulties with drink driving.

On Monday night in the Clubhouse, Anne Fraser (Houston), herself a legendary participant in Children's Concerts during the early days, organised a great evening's entertainment with acts young and old, separately described in the Children's Concerts Chapter.

And so to:

THE MATCH!
SUNDAY 31ST JULY 2016

It's 7.20am, and a very pleasant morning in Tain.

The sky has that faint blue-grey tinge that characterises days not quite sure what weather to bring, but at least promising some golf to be played.

The Tain Golf Club car park is almost deserted, with only four cars in it, two of them parked by the Clubhouse and two left the previous night by golfers persuaded to abandon them in the interests of licence preservation.

Into the still silence comes the throaty roar of a heavy-duty vehicle, the noise echoing against the walls of the adjoining St Duthus Cemetery.

Through the entrance into the driveway of the Club, and under the watchful gaze of Old Tom Morris, beautifully carved from one of four cut-down fir trees bordering the first tee, comes a minibus which carefully circles the car park and disgorges the first of the Stotters and their supporters to arrive.

Vice-Captain Hamish Robertson and Chris Rafferty appear, both still slightly alcoholically challenged from the successful Duthac Centre Dinner the night before.

With them the travelling support consists of Hamish's wife Shirley, his eldest son Dale, wife Julie, and two sons Chris and Adam, whilst Chris Rafferty is supported by mother-in-law Alice.

The car which follows unloads Hamish's second son, Scott, wife Jenny, and two sons, Corey and Nathan, with that teenage dragged-from-bed look.

They are greeted by Honorary Stotter and Tain Team organiser Donald Sutherland, his bearded face cheerfully lit up by an insanely large grin.

Hugs and handshakes are exchanged and the car park begins quickly to fill up with an assortment of cars, four-wheel drives and a large McLeod's bus from Portmahomack which carries the bulk of the Stotters' team and families – 14 Stotters and 22 family and friends, led by a lean and slightly lopsided Captain, Johnny Houston.

The cars spill out more and more people, including the Tain team, clad in their specially designed green polo tops.

The Stotters' team wear mirror image tops, in their trademark bright yellow, also sporting the new stone coloured caps.

Hugh Walkington, at 6ft8, has the best view of proceedings as the crowd mass round the Professional's Shop and the first tee, a complete riot of green and yellow, with most of the Stotters' support wearing yellow hoodies, tops and caps.

There are now close to 100 people joking, laughing, chatting, and reuniting friendships and relationships formed over the many years the two teams have played against each other.

Golf bags, backpacks and even the occasional cool bags bulge with an amazing array of whisky and Drambuie bottles, rusty nail hip flasks, cans and bottles of lager and beer, and an odd soft drink or bottle of water for the youngsters and those who will need rehydration later in the round to come.

Donald sets the tone by beginning the annual and rather pleasant ritual of Roddy's Round, more whisky than normal being required.

The Stotters' bench outside the pro shop is surrounded by the press of whisky-drinking golfers and support.

Captain Johnny proposes the toast to absent friends and Tain Captain Ewan Forrest welcomes the visitors in his inimically whimsical way hoping for a resounding victory for his Team.

They pose for photographs and form a rugby team-like huddle on the first tee muttering victory mantras and erupting in a victory cheer.

More sedately, the Stotters assemble on the tee for photos and recreate the pose of the early Stotters, front row kneeling and back row standing, with Honorary President Frank Cougan in the centre.

The summer smell of freshly-cut grass permeates the air as Frank appears with one of his hickory clubs to perform the ceremonial Presidential tee-off.

Unfortunately, he narrowly misses the ball with a majestically supple swing.

At the second time of asking however, the ball soars down the fairway and the stage is set.

The teams have been expanded this year to ensure that all the Stotters, and Associates play, so there are eight matches instead of the usual six.

Since 1966, the Stotters have won the Stotters' Cup 25 times and Tain have won it 24 times.

Ewan wants to tie the contest up at 25 all, and his tee shot displays his determination – 220 yards straight up the middle to gasps of amazement all round, not least from himself.

Vice-Captain Graeme Ross hits his drive nearly as far as Ewan but off centre.

To a massive cheer up steps Johnny Houston playing off 8, and his drive bounces ten yards past Ewan's and rests at the top of the slope a hundred yards from the 365-yard first hole's green.

Hamish's drive is not one of his best, landing in the left rough, but it doesn't matter as the format is Greensomes, with each duo playing alternate shots.

Hamish's and Graeme's balls are picked up and the match is off!

There are about a dozen caddies and supporters accompanying this group of four, including Hamish's faithful caddying wife, Shirley, plus sons and grandsons; and an astonishing caddying appearance from Murd driving his customary buggy and allegedly caddying for Ewan.

Despite Johnny and Hamish's best efforts, Ewan and Graeme never look like losing. Even valiant attempts by Johnny to drown Ewan in a cocktail of whisky and lager, fail dismally.

Donald Sutherland has organised hickory clubs for the short par three 16th, and Hugh Walkington has put up an impressive pewter tankard bearing the legend: "A Bit of Sport", to be awarded to whoever comes closest to the pin.

George Ross remembers: "I'm still agonising over the 16th. Having been the first person to hit the green with a hickory club (into the wind to about 10ft, yes I was pleased), Sangster-the-Gangster knocked the same club to about 8ft. Worse still, and my memory is rather selective at this stage, I think I may have three putted whilst he made a two – pretty much summed up the round on both accounts, and how I feel about Mike!"

Hugh himself comments: "Yours truly put his ball agonisingly about two feet off the putting surface and really quite close to the pin, so perhaps I ought to carry on with hickory clubs!"

Mike Sangster, needless to say, won the tankard.

Hector MacIntyre, who partnered Ken Ross, is rather vague on the subject of who he played against: "I think we won two up, and as a left-hander I certainly struggled with the right-handed hickory club at the 16th".

Ken however remembers: "From my recall Hector and I won two and one against Michael Sutherland and Gary Tonge".

Hugh remembers partnering Chris Rafferty:

"Our match was somewhat dominated by the play of young Iain Moffat. He played with a massive slice, normally aiming approximately 40 degrees left of the fairway. The whisky started to catch up with him pretty quickly – with the result that he started to hit the ball dead straight!

Unfortunately for him (and his long-suffering partner ex-Captain Robin Nairn), he continued to aim 40 degrees left, with inevitably disastrous consequences. The final indignity for the Tain pairing came down the 18th fairway when he took an enormous swing at the ball, missed and fell over".

Chris reckons that he and Hugh were the tallest pairing ever (at 6ft 8 and 6ft 4) to represent the Stotters: "We certainly towered over the opposition, and won the Hiccup for the biggest margin of victory on the day".

Sugar remembers: "I was playing again with Alan Ross – maybe that's why my memory is a bit woozy on this one. I am pretty sure we lost our tie but won the drinking competition".

Nobody remembers the detail of the match result, and Donald Sutherland best sums this up: "As for results, I haven't a clue. I know Gordon and I came a very comfortable second. I asked Morag, but her memories of that day are very poor as well".

A huge crowd greets the incoming golfers at the 18th, and most of the matches finish with the same golfers who started, with the notable exception of Tain's Frankie Sutherland who was overcome by emotion (or possibly alcohol) at around the 6th hole, with Donald's wife Morag ably taking his place!

There are delirious scenes in the Clubhouse as the Trophy is presented by Ewan to Johnny, who receives it with pride and a sideswipe jibe about Tain's valiant efforts.

After some refreshment and lunch, one large bus takes families and friends back to Portmahomack via Pitcalzean House, whilst the Stotters wind their way up the hill to The Royal for the 2016 AGM.

The story of this event will have to wait until another day for the telling, as the Minutes are never written till the week before the following year's AGM, and they should be fun as they mark the debut of Hugh Walkington as Secretary.

The Stotters' Team 2016 – Back Row – L to R – Hamish Robertson (Vice-Captain), Hugh Walkington (Secretary/Treasurer), Tom Lloyd, Simon Houston, Alan Gordon (shielded by Frank Cougan – President), Gary Toal, George Ross, Ken Ross, Johnny Houston (Captain), Simon Ross. Front Row – L to R – Chris Fraser, Liam Hughes, Malcolm Fraser, Mike Lloyd, Hector MacIntyre, Chris Rafferty.

The Tain Team – 2016 – Back Row – L to R – Donald Sutherland, Mike Sangster, Gerry Revie, Alan Ross, Johnny Neil, Ian Moffat, Graeme Ross (Vice-Captain), Craig Moffat, Frankie Sutherland, Ewan Forrest (Captain). Front Row – L to R – Michael Sutherland, Alastair (Sugar) Kennedy, David Ross, Gary Tonge, Gordon Bannerman, Robin Nairn.

The Stotters' Ballwasher, courtesy of Sean Sullivan.

The Stotters' Commemorative Flag – the 11th (Alps).

THE MANY MEN OF TAIN

Over the 50 years of the Stotters v Tain match, Tain have been represented by a vast array of talent, including Club Champions, Club Captains, and Trophy winners galore, and like Glenmorangie, the world famous distillery 1.8 miles away, and marketed for many years under the slogan: "The 16 Men of Tain", it is very appropriate to celebrate the many men of Tain who have played in this amazing match: 77 men and two women, heroes all – and apologies to any missed out.

Ian Anderson, Gordon Bannerman, Bob Beveridge, Teddy Brookes, Davie Buchanan, Jim Byars, Ross Campbell, Willie Clyne, Bertie Clyne , Andrew Duncan, Ronnie Duncan, Munro Ferries, Alistair Fleming, Ewan Forrest, Andrew Gardiner, Sandy Gordon, Dr Robin Graham, Rob Hudson, Iain Innes, Tom Johnstone, Alastair Kennedy, Bob Lindsay, Hughie Macdonald, Ian MacDougal, John MacDougal, Ian MacGregor, Dods McKay, Tommy Mackay (pro), Derek Mackenzie, Duncan Mackenzie, Hugh Mackenzie, Roy Mackenzie, Gordon McKie, Roddy MacLennan, Iain Macleod, Steve Martin, Bob Meikle, Craig Moffat, Iain Moffat, Stewart Morrison (pro), Hugh Munro, Willie Munro, Robin Nairn, Johnny Neil, Hamish Patterson, Davie Pearson, Gerry Revie, Neil Robertson, Alan Ross, David Ross, Graeme Ross, Ian H. Ross, Ian 'Murd' Ross, Jimmy Ross, Willie Rostock, Willie Russell, David Rutherford, Martyn Ryan, Mike Sangster, Trish Shearer, Ross Shearer, Jack Slaughter, David Sutherland, Donald Sutherland, Frankie Sutherland, Michael Sutherland, Morag Sutherland, Neil Sutherland, George Thompson, Paul Thompson , Stuart Thompson, Albert Tonge, Gary Tonge, Andrew Urquhart, Forbie Urquhart, Johnnie Urquhart, Craig Watson, Tony Watson, and Wayne Wilcox.

Honourable mention also to several non-Tain based Stotters, including Chris and Malcolm Fraser and Liam Hughes who also have played for Tain in their lean years.

In 2016's match, the Tain team, superbly organised by Donald Sutherland, was:

Ewan Forrest (Captain)
Graeme Ross (Vice-Captain)

Robin Nairn
Ian Moffat

Michael Sutherland
Craig Moffat

Donald Sutherland
Gordon Bannerman

David Ross
Gerry Revie

Sugar Kennedy
Alan Ross

Gary Tonge
Frankie Sutherland

Mike Sangster
Johnny Neil

Whilst this was the team, Donald comments that it may, or may not, have represented the order of play!

Donald, who has featured in the annual match for well over 30 years, says that: "The Stotters Matches are my favourite games of golf: If it wasn't for them I would probably give up golf. I often wonder why I keep punishing myself but then I remind myself of the Stotters. It's a great privilege to play in these matches and meet up each year with everybody associated with the Stotters – a great bunch of people".

He remembers wife Morag stepping in to help Tain out when he was Captain. "George Thompson from Glenmorangie Distillery was her partner that day. George wasn't the best player in the world and Morag really had her work cut out – I don't think they used any of George's drives!

They were playing the 15th and once again George was hitting the second shot and somehow managed to hit the ball backwards and Morag had to play their third shot from further away from the hole than the second shot.

George was a wonderful character – I remember him playing once with his son Stuart in a Distillery Match, during which he asked Stuart which club he should use for his shot.

Stuart told him to use any club he wanted just as long as he missed the ball!"

Donald remembers one former Captain of Tain having his clubs removed from his trolley so that he could take their place to get back to the clubhouse!

Some of the other key Tain players over the years include:

Ewan Forrest, Tain's hugely enthusiastic Captain in 2016, who was born in Peter Pan country – Kirriemuir – in 1956, and lives in Fearn.

Married with two daughters (all school teachers, hence: "Little wonder why I play golf") and two grandchildren: "who love to visit Grandad's Golf Pub".

A Self-Employed Financial Adviser, Ewan plays off 16 (up from 12 before he became Tain Captain).

He is proud that he has been involved on Finals day of Golf Week for the last four years, but when pressed admits: "not because of my golf but refereeing finals. I am going to peak for Golf Week one of these years – not sure which one yet".

He continues: "Obviously I can't remember much about the matches although they have all been very enjoyable at the time".

He distinctly remembers himself, together with brothers Donald and Michael Sutherland giving Johnny Houston a golf lesson on the Thursday before Golf Week: "The year he won the McVitie and Price – never thought we received the proper credit for his win!"

He also recalls that on his first stint on the committee there had been a complaint from a lady horse rider about drunken people on the Golf Course one Sunday morning, which was discussed for about ten seconds and brushed under the table.

Ian Ross, known popularly as Murd, because, as a youngster, he was one of a number of Ian Rosses in and around Tain, so was called after his father – Murdo – in whose butcher's shop he started to work at the age of 15.

At that time, in the mid-1950s, Tain had five butchers' shops, and Murd worked in his fathers' shop till it was finally sold in 1975.

Married to Ray, who was Ladies' Captain of Tain in 1990/1, they bought the beautifully positioned former Manse which sits above Tain and gives a splendid elevated view of many of the holes on the course.

They lovingly restored the Manse to its former glory by, amongst other things, removing the ugly pebble-dash and revealing the splendid stonework beneath.

This became Golf View Guest House, which was later to become the Golf Week home of many of the Stotters, including Hugh and father Sport who – he claims – could smell a bottle of whisky being opened at 400 metres.

Murd and Ray were kind enough to host the Stotters' AGMs for a number of years, at the back of Golf View, with Murd remembering: "the wives having to come to collect everybody".

He also remembers Hamish Senior: "coming downstairs with his 'medicine' case at 6pm for 'serious' business, telling lots of stories of his upbringing in Tain".

He and Ray have two daughters, one of whom lives in New Zealand, four grandchildren and two great grandchildren, and they still keep their B & B hats on, running the lovely Ross Villa B & B which they built before selling the adjoining Golf View.

Murd's lowest handicap was seven, and he won the Teddy Brookes Trophy in 1990 – though the Notice Board unfortunately calls him JA Ross.

Murd no longer plays golf but made a most welcome return to the Stotters' matches by driving a buggy to caddy for Ewan Forrest in 2016.

When he played, he drove a customised quad bike specially adapted for his artificial lower leg. The Stotters' children used to clamour for a ride on this unique vehicle and cling on for dear life as he steered down the seldom-hit fairway.

Derek Wynne, who runs Carnegie Lodge Hotel with his wife Heather, and who had Ewan as his best man, remembers his father John organising a clay pigeon shooting day at Gleneagles. The party had a splendidly alcoholic lunch, after which photos were taken at the hotel entrance.

For some reason, perhaps unbeknown even to Murd himself, he unscrewed his artificial leg and held it up beside Rory Stone's head (Rory runs the Highland Fine Cheese Company in Tain).

Rory promptly seized the leg, ran off with it and hurled it into the leafy branches of a tree, with Murd, uttering obscenities, hopping in vain after him!

The leg stuck in the tree and a rescue party with ladder was needed to restore the leg to its rightful owner.

The Japanese tourists watching didn't quite know what was going on!

Murd's wife Ray simply says: "Mad lot!"

Willie Russell, Magi Vass's late father, was born in November 1926 and brought up and worked on the family farm outside Glasgow, playing his golf at Balmore Golf Club. He married Jean in 1956 and moved to Kincraig (no golf there), then moved to a dairy farm at Fearn in 1960. He and Jean had four children – Mary, Anne, Jimmy and Magi.

Jean says: "He didn't play much golf till his first Golf Week around 1968 when he came home with lots of prizes – and was hooked! He was very fit because he did the milking at 5.30 every morning.

Whilst he thoroughly enjoyed being involved with the Stotters, I was always at home with the cows and family".

Jean remembers his always being involved in Golf Club matters – progressing through the Committee to become Captain in 1982/3. His lowest handicap was 9, and he was noted for hitting a low trajectory ball and for being a good putter.

Jean continues: "He took on the Secretary's role when we stopped the dairy farm and did it for three years until September 1991".

He died the following April, aged 65.

Willie was extremely hard working, and golf was his main pursuit.

Magi remembers: "At home he was pretty quiet really but at the Golf Club he was very outgoing and fun and liked being in the middle of everything, thoroughly enjoying the social (Stotters) side of Golf Week. He liked a drink when socialising at the Golf Club or when Johnny Pud – the previous Secretary of the Club – and his wife, Joyce – came to the house for very competitive games of cards".

Murd remembers him as "a lovely man – a real gent of the course".

Donald Sutherland remembers Willie testing out one of the early remotely controlled caddy cars, concealing the control from view and puzzling everyone by moving the caddy car around invisibly!

Gerry Revie can't remember when he was first invited to play in a Stotters' match, but knows it's over 30 years ago, and he has only missed a couple of the matches.

A Glaswegian, born in 1947, he moved with his family to Fort William aged 14, then serving an apprenticeship at a local garage.

Married to Fiona ("a living saint!"), for 50 years, they have two sons, a daughter and eight grandchildren.

Gerry followed his father-in-law and joined the police, serving for 30 years (not a day more) in the Highlands and Islands, over the years covering Inverness, Fort William, Benbecula, Stornoway and finally Tain.

He recalls when joining Tain Golf Club in 1984 that: "Prospective members were subjected to an interview with the Captain (Stuart Anderson) and Secretary (Johnny Pud).

Johnny, unaware of my occupation, was going on about the bar opening times and stressing that it didn't really matter if I came off the course and into the clubhouse before "normal" bar opening times as the bar would probably be open anyway(!).

No amount of Stuart saying that "that never ever happened" made Johnny back-pedal!"

Gerry's handicap has remained static at eighteen since the last century (!) and vaguely remembers many excellent Stotters' games "which involved great company, much liquid refreshment and the occasional good golf on my part".

Fittingly, Gerry considers the long association between Tain GC and the Stotters an integral element of the past, present and future of the club. "An association to be justly proud of. Long may it last".

Graeme Ross, Tain's 2016 Vice-Captain and 2017's Captain, first became aware of the Stotters as a youngster, when his uncle, Stotter Andrew

Urquhart, became a regular player, as Andrew's father-in-law Tommy Young, one of the originals, had been.

"However it wasn't until I started playing golf around the age of 10 or 11 that I began to realise how significant an institution the Stotters actually are.

Every year around Golf Week I would start to see those distinctive yellow jerseys appear around the Club and course.

For me, they had an almost mysterious allure, like a secret club within a club – at that point I had no idea that 30 years later I would actually be involved.

Fast forward those 30 years, and I find myself as Vice-Captain of our great club, and it was then when fellow Committee member Donald Sutherland asked me if I would play in the Stotters' match. He didn't need to ask twice!

To be honest I was a bit gobsmacked but absolutely jumped at the chance. For me it was a huge honour to be asked and become one of that elite group of players to be involved in this special match".

Graeme has now played in the match for the past three years and struggles with remembering much of the detail of the actual games due to a certain degree of alcoholic imbibement.

He gives some sage advice to anyone asked to play the match: "At some point during your round, you will inevitably see three golf balls where normally there should be just one. Don't worry, this is perfectly normal – hit the one in the middle!"

Graeme affectionately concludes: "I can honestly say that I have never in my life met a group of more friendly and approachable individuals. It would be very difficult to quantify the impact that the Stotters have made to Tain Golf Club over the past fifty years.

The club has benefited from our special relationship in so many ways and I am very grateful to be part of that going forward in my first year as Captain of Tain Golf Club".

Graeme has been working hard at reinvigorating the Golf Club and he and his partner Eilidh Mackenzie and daughter Tayler are frequent habitués of the Clubhouse.

Ewan Forrest's predecessor as Captain, Robin V. Nairn, was, like Gerry, born in Glasgow – in 1958, and lives with his wife Philippa in

Invergordon. A CA, Robin is Chief Operating Officer of the Albyn Housing Society.

Playing (he claims) one good round a year, he is off 15, and has played for the last seven years in the Stotters' match.

Astonishingly, he remembers winning as captain of Tain in 2013 and 2014: "Great conversation and not TOO much alcohol!"

In 2015, he claims: "to have won the last four holes to win my match on my own as my team mate (not to be named) missed every shot – he blamed his eye sight and nothing to do with alcohol".

Other fond memories include (apparently) Hamish's red trousers, Hector's golf, and the sun being blocked out by Hugh Walkington".

He was also delighted to present the McVitie & Price trophy in 2014 to Johnny Houston.

Alastair Kennedy (always known as Sugar – a nickname given to him by his older brother when he was five years old as he took five spoonfuls of sugar in his tea), was born in Inverness in 1953: "A leap over the back fence and into Kingsmills Park, the ground belonging to Inverness Thistle FC.

Little did I know at that time how significant this was, as I ended up signing for them at age 15, the first ever schoolboy to sign a youth form in Scotland".

Married to Anne, they have four children (a girl and three boys) and seven grandchildren. Sugar is very proud that his oldest grandson Rhys signed for Caley Thistle in 2016 at the age of 10.

A very busy businessman, he is Communications Director for the Global Energy Group, the biggest private employer in the Highlands with over 4,000 employees worldwide; and is Chairman of Nigg Skills Academy which addresses skills shortages across the energy industries.

His CV also includes directorship of the SHIRLIE project which assists less fortunate people to get back into work; acting as an Ambassador for MacMillan Cancer Support; and he has been a director of Ross County Football Club for over 20 years, 10 of which were as their full time CEO.

Playing off 14, Sugar has been a fixture of the Tain team for over 20 years.

He doesn't often get the time to play in Golf Week, but remembers: "My one and only attempt came on the back of a resounding victory Alan Ross and I had against a Stotters' pairing whereby I thought my form would carry me a long way into Golf Week.

I managed to get a late entry and turned up for a 10.10 tee time with a bit of a hangover, and my first drive went 150 yards out of bounds on the right.

I went three off the tee, hit my second shot into the bushes on the left of the first green and had to declare the ball lost.

My card was ripped up on the second; I walked back in after four holes and went to bed!"

His own personal tradition is to take a bottle of malt whisky out on the course, and if it is not in the bin by the 18th tee, he reckons to have failed.

It should be stressed that Sugar is generous to a fault and always gets a good deal of support in meeting his traditional objective.

"Liam Hughes and I have had some battles on the course where our rivalry is taken seriously for about five holes and then the "gimmies" seem to get a bit more generous.

Donald (Sutherland) likes to pair me with Alan Ross, a man we all know can talk for Scotland – and that's without a drink!

Alan and I have had more successes than failures in our matches which seem to please Captain Donald.

Obviously, without giving too much away I have had to develop our match tactics of having to be at least two up as we go to the 14th tee as I know Alan will be posted missing (physically and literally) from almost this point onward.

Over the years I have also understood that TGC must be doing quite well in our matches if Geraldine (Houston) appears on the scene and encourages us to charge our glasses at every opportunity".

In 2013, Sugar and teetotal Hamish Patterson were playing against Hamish Robertson and Simon Ross, and at the 10th Hamish put Sugar into the left-hand bunker.

Not just in the bunker, but buried right into the ribbed face so that the ball was about two and a half feet above the sand. It was an impossible shot to play, and logic should have determined that Sugar take a penalty drop. However, he elected to play the ball as it lay, and not just try to play it out but actually blast it through the face of the bunker and at least two feet of turf!

Hamish and the entourage following the game, which included a curious Forbie, out to check up on the state of the match, were convulsed with laughter at Sugar, crouched on one knee leaning over the shot and of course burying it even deeper into the face of the bunker.

Needless to say, Tain lost the 10th hole!

An effusive Sugar congratulates the Stotters: "on what has been an amazing journey of support they have provided to Tain Golf Club over their 50 years of coming north to support the Club and Golf Week. I am just so pleased the Club acknowledges this, and thank the Stotters for their support. It has been an absolute pleasure and honour to know so many nice people and to have been part of this wonderful tradition".

Alan Ross is well known for his friendliness out on the course and needs to be reminded each year of the names of the many Stotters' children (some now adults) that he spoke to the year before.

He fondly remembers his first game for Tain against the Stotters, when he was a little unsure of the format or etiquette. He made a conscious decision to pop both his hip flasks into his bag and was pleased to see he had made the right decision as Sugar took his bottle of malt whisky from its box on the second tee.

Alan confirms what Sugar says in that he has been known to miss out a couple of holes due to venturing into "too much course conversation!"

At the 2016 celebratory dinner, Hamish's two sons Dale and Scott, both massive Hibs fans were delighted to learn that Alan is an even bigger Hibees stalwart!

He also had an elderly (20-year-old) cat, as did Hamish and Shirley until early 2017.

Mike Sangster has been a Tain stalwart for a very long time (!).

He remembers: "About forty years ago, I first noticed some good-looking young girls up for Golf Week".

They were Anne and Geraldine Houston, and, through them, Mike got to know Dr. John.

Subsequently, when Mike was working in Bridge of Weir, he stayed with John and Pat, and played golf with John at Old Ranfurly ("I didn't beat him very often").

Mike is still a firm friend of the Houstons and loves the challenge of hosting the Stotters on a Sunday morning in August. He and Johnny are great rivals, and as low handicappers, some of the matches feature some surprisingly good golf. Mike does incredible coaching work with the youngsters of Tain – boys and girls – and he teaches them not just how to play, but how to conduct themselves on the golf course, a characteristic often sadly lacking in younger golfers.

He was nominated for a Highlands & Islands Regional Coaches and Volunteers Award in 2016 and won the Young Persons Coach of the Year category.

Mike won the Stirling Challenge Cup in 1979, and is the 2016 Seniors Champion of Tain.

Gary Tonge hails originally from Tain, and claims to "have been lucky enough to play in several Stotters' matches".

He moved away in 2000 when he joined the Royal Signals in the British Army, returning to Tain in 2009, "An amazing wife, Jo, and three children for the better".

As Gary works offshore, he cannot guarantee playing every year due to his rota. The first thing he checks on this rota each year is: "Am I home for Golf Week?" He remembers as a young teenager: "Two young lads coming to Tain when their father played in Golf Week. I hung about with them for the whole week. They were George and Simon Ross.

It was only when I became older – maybe 18 or 19 – that I knew the significance of their visit each year. I remember being in the clubhouse several times on a Sunday watching my uncles Donald and Michael Sutherland falling off the golf course and into the clubhouse, laughing and joking. It looked to me like the best game of golf in the world.

Eventually, at the age of 20, Donald asked if I would like to play. I didn't need to think about the answer. Now unbeknown to me were the unofficial rules of the game: "Don't drink as much as your opponents".

Being young and just delighted to play in such a prestigious match I didn't want to offend anyone by refusing a drink".

Gary now reveals his side of the story fondly remembered by others:

"The 15 holes we played are a complete blank in my memory other than one hole – or rather one shot.

I have no idea where my drive went on the 17th tee – nor anyone else's for that matter – but we were obviously playing my playing partner's ball as my memory begins from our 2nd shot – which I had to play.

The ball was perched on the bank of the 2nd river crossing on the green side of the hole. I was perched on the bank with a reasonable uphill lie considering how close to the river I was.

I remember actually "fancying" the shot and thought I could get it pretty close to the flag. I took my stance and lined up for my practice swing – nothing hard about that.

Then it happened – full blooded practice swing – body unable to control the momentum of the swing – feet needing to move to assist with balance – splash!

I am submerged in the river after falling backwards off the bank. Everyone is in hysterics, including myself. I was now a little refreshed to say the least so after climbing out of the water I took my stance again – no practice swing this time – just hit the thing.

I fell backwards and into the river again! I have no idea where my ball went but I did manage to hit it!"

Gary sums up his feelings about the Stotters' match: "When I do play it is always a privilege to meet, laugh, drink and be merry with such an amazing group of people".

Whilst the Stotters are well known for the quality of their caddies, Tain are noted for not having many, although they do have a hardy few regulars: Carole, Marie and Fiona (who has been caddying for Donald almost as long as he has played in the match).

And particular mention must be made here of Morag Sutherland, who has caddied on numerous occasions and has now played in the match twice. Over the period of the match she usually enjoys an occasional dram with her fellow companions – so much so that one year she was seen disappearing over a hedge, and when she woke up the next morning, she had no idea where all the scratches and cuts on her legs had come from!

The atmosphere of the annual match is nicely summed up by the classic goodbye in the morning from Gordon Bannerman to his wife Jennifer as she drops him off at 07.30 hours prompt on the Sunday morning for the annual match. The passenger window opens, and Gordon shouts a loving farewell to Jennifer: "Good night darling!"

Sport with Mike Sangster and Murd.

Frank, Bob Beveridge, David Rutherford and Ken Ross.

Sugar in the Bunker

Donald Sutherland.

SUPPORT FROM THE CLUB

It's a pretty obvious statement to make that the Stotters would not have lasted for 50 years without considerable support from the Golf Club.

In the early years, this was taken for granted, but as Tain began to hold Competitions on the Sunday of Golf Week, the Stotters fell out of favour with the Club, mainly because the various matches made more noise than would normally be expected on a Sunday morning!

In 1980, the Tain Golf Club Committee decided that because of the huge entry for the Sunday One Day Open, it was impossible to continue the match against the Stotters. It was decided instead that the game should be played at Invergordon Golf Club, and from 1980 to 1984, they most hospitably hosted the annual match over their verdant nine holes.

A small band of friends from Tain Golf Club forsook the Sunday Open so that the challenge match could be kept alive.

After these years, economic reality returned to Tain, and with August's bar takings considerably reduced, the Stotters were invited back and resumed their place in the schedule for Golf Week, teeing off after a dram at 8am and ultimately playing the now standard 15-hole Greensomes format.

Successive Captains have fallen under the spell of the annual match, and the 2016 team featured several former Captains, either playing or spectating.

During 2016, all the greens flew special commemorative flags celebrating the Stotters' 50 years – white for the front nine and yellow for the back nine. After the golf season, these flags were bought by various Stotters with a small donation going to the Club for their generosity in providing them.

In recent years, Tain Golf Club's support for and friendship with the Stotters has intensified under the stewardship of Magi Vass, with support from Dorothy Melville.

Born in Dingwall, now living in Tain, and coming from a family "full of golfers", Magi has been employed at the club since 2005 and been a member for more than 40 years. She started as a part-time administrative assistant and graduated to the post of Secretary in 2011. She is a former Under-18 & Under 22 Scottish International Golfer, and represented Great Britain in the De Beers Junior International Match against the USA in 1981, unfortunately ending up on the losing side.

Magi's family have an amazing record at Tain, with Magi, her sisters Anne and Mary and mother Jean having all been Lady Captains, and her father Willie, Men's Captain and Club Secretary.

Her brother Jimmy has won the McVitie and Price Cup twice and the Munro Rose Bowl three times, whilst husband David has twice been Club Champion and has won both the McVitie and Price Cup and the Munro Rose Bowl.

Magi won the Ladies Club Championships an incredible 12 times between 1979 and 1992 (older sister Anne has won it nine times; oldest sister Mary seven times; and daughter Sammy three times!).

Magi has always been a close friend of the Stotters, and each year when a marketing brochure for Tain Golf Week was produced, it ran a feature with photograph about the Stotters and the annual match.

She used to play off Scratch – now crept up to 8 – and says that if she ever got the chance to play now she would be off 36!

Magi's dad was W. W. (Willie) Russell, himself Club Captain in 1982/3, whose water fountain at the 11th hole is always a welcome feature for diluting the odd glass of whisky.

She remembers her dad playing regularly in the Stotters' match: "As soon as I could drive I would take dad home, dropping his mates off along the way – standing them up against their front door, ringing the door bell and running back to the car!

Whenever my dad was ill he refused to go see a Doctor and stated that he would see John Houston in Golf Week – no matter what time of year it was – he'd rather keep the pain till then. When he spoke to John he got given a dram with milk in it, stirred with a pencil from behind Dr John's ear...and all was good again".

Grateful for the Stotters' support, she says: "The fun they bring to the week is infectious and although it's so sad when the older ones pass away it's been amazing that new generations keep coming back".

Tain's PGA professional Stuart Morrison is also a weal kent face to the Stotters since 2007, dispensing golf balls, tees and other replacement items plus snacks and drinks (soft!) to the often needy Stotters. Stuart has always accommodated the Stotters and the Robertson family teams in June, though finds little time to play himself.

Hamish enjoyed playing with Stuart's father, another Roddy, in the Qualifying stages of Golf Week one year.

The course during Golf Week is always prepared to a standard which many of the Stotters struggle to play on their Sunday match. This is thanks to the hard work put in by Course Manager Iain Macleod and his small team.

Iain has seen The Stotters chew up his fairways for 40 years, and in 2016 was President of the British and International Golf Greenkeepers' Association.

Iain was the architect of the 18 flags which flapped on 18 greens, during 2016 displaying the Stotters' 50-year connection with Tain.

One of his American colleagues and friends, Sean Sullivan, from Butte in Montana, who gives up his time to develop amazing logo ball washers with much attention to detail, all in his own time and expense, provided a bright Stotters-yellow ball washer which now sits proudly at the 6th tee.

Iain was born in Southampton, and comments: "My father was working in Nigeria, and I was due to be born in Nairn in early 1957, but the long boat trip back to the UK set Mum off and I was born early in Southampton nursing home".

He is a self-confessed sports-mad individual, and plays off 7. He was invited to play in the match, "many years ago, and played twice. Unfortunately, can't really play nowadays, due to pressure of work".

He won the Teddy Brookes Cup in 1982, and has been a beaten finalist in the Munro Trophy Competition.

He remembers Forbie Urquhart having a broken leg which meant that he couldn't play one year: "His son drove him out on to the course in their estate car, laden with drink for the players – we had one at the 11th tee, the 13th tee and the 16th tees. Tain player, Davy Buchanan, was tending the pin at the 16th when he lifted it out of the hole and fell over – apparently the pin was what was holding him upright!

My Deputy, Gordon McKie, played one year and came straight to work after it. I had to send him home, as he could barely walk, let alone work on machinery.

I can also remember seeing participants crawling over bridges, too scared to walk over them, in case they fell into the river!"

Clubhouse host Richard Green, intriguingly began his career in golf as Assistant Professional at Royal Dornoch in the early 80s, but subsequently changed his vocation and turned to Club Stewarding, becoming Head Steward at Golspie GC before moving to Invergordon Royal British Legion, and to Tain via Royal Dornoch (as Clubhouse Manager) and Alness (as Clubhouse Manager and General Manager).

Richard and his team dispense an amazing volume of alcohol with great speed and accuracy during Golf Week, always with a smile and a comment.

The close ties with the Club are hugely appreciated by the Stotters, and it's true to say it's a mutually beneficial – and fun – relationship.

The Tain Golf Club Team, on and around the Stotters' Bench and complete with Stotters' Flag – Back row – L to R – Richard Green, Stuart Morrison and Iain Macleod. Front Row – Dorothy Melville and Magi Vass.

THE CHILDREN'S CONCERTS

As the Stotters' children, dominated numerically by the Houstons, began to grow and become an active part of Golf Week at the Royal Hotel, the Children's Concerts began, usually held on a Wednesday evening after dinner.

However, the precursor to these concerts is remembered by Frank Cougan:

"When the Stotters arrived in Tain, we all met on Saturday night and had dinner together. The children were fed by Florrie at five or six o'clock and went off to bed or played round the hotel to their hearts' delight.

The adults dressed up and went down to the Dining Room for dinner and from there moved to the Clan Ross rooms when they were built.

Sometimes we had a few visitors like Forbie Urquhart, Johnny Urquhart and Hugh Munro. We used to sit at a long table down one side of the Clan Ross room – between 24 and 30 of us – and started to do party pieces. Someone would sing and someone tell a story – Pat (Houston) and Rita (Kemp) would sing a song they had written, and which poked irreverent fun at various Stotters. Favourite songs of theirs were: 'A You're Adorable' and 'You're a Pink Toothbrush I'm a Blue Toothbrush' – both classics of their time.

Then, one night, Roddy Mackenzie's wife – Helen – got up.

She was a very polite and very clear speaker and she stood there with the face of an angel and started her recital:

"As I awoke this morning,
When all things sweet are born,
A robin perched upon my sill
To hail a happy morn.
He looked so young and fragile,
So sweetly did he sing,
That thoughts of joy and happiness

Into my heart did spring.
I smiled discreetly to myself
As I paused beside my bed,
Then quickly brought the window down,
And smashed his little head!"

This brought the house down!

Another epic was "My Baby Has Gone Down the Plughole" – featuring Claire Cougan as the mother and Simon Houston as the baby. In order to go down the plughole, Simon was unceremoniously dumped over the back of a couch if I recall correctly – wearing a towel as a nappy!"

Johnny Houston remembers – in the Plughole song – Simon crawling and hiding in his blue and white stripy underpants (he seemed to have the same ones on every year) as Claire shrieked "Oh where is my baby!"

Frank continues: "Other favourites were – "The Jeely Piece Song" (Johnny confesses this was his party piece, "belted out annually") and some well-known ditties like "High Hopes" and "Consider Yourself".

I also remember doing the Ugly Duckling (can't remember who morphed into the swan though) with costumes lovingly made by Janis Kemp. Hugh Walkington always provided a bit more 'cultyur' with some highbrow piano concertos.

One memorable character was Uncle Roddy – you just loved this guy – his theme song was: "I don't care if it snows or freezes, I am safe in the arms of Jesus. I am Jesus' little lamb, yes thank Christ I am".

He did that version with Claire and Geraldine at a concert one night – Claire remembers them singing – Roddy with his red hair and big smile. He was the Highland Gentleman".

Johnny remembers: "sneaking off one year with Ian Ferguson for a game round Tain in the evening and missing the concert. I was given hell for that one from my folks – although I suspect dad was probably secretly pleased that I had opted for the gowf".

Pat Houston and Dorothy Cougan put huge effort into organising these hilarious concerts, which Forbie remembered thus:

"On Wednesdays, in the Stotters' early days, round about 4 to 5 pm, before dinner, the children of the Stotter families staying at the hotel

294

would put on a show – song, dance, poetry and piano playing – which was always one of the highlights of the week.

Those occasions ended with "Uncle" Frank's auction of shirts, all the way from his factory in Belfast in Northern Ireland. This was also great fun with prices ranging from ten shillings to £5 per shirt but not always sold to the highest bidder – perhaps to one with blue eyes or the biggest handicap, big feet or whatever tickled his fancy.

Frank was usually the auctioneer, except on one occasion when he had a late tee-off time and I had to do the auction. The money raised went to a local charity – cubs, brownies or scouts. One year, Frank asked me who to give the money to, and I suggested the British Legion as they did a good job at Christmas. The British Legion Secretary, Bobby Sellar, came along with his camera and submitted a nice photo and a lovely write-up to the Ross-shire Journal".

On Monday 1st August 2016, Anne Fraser (Houston) superbly masterminded a full-scale Children's Concert, a terrific night for all concerned, in a packed Golf Clubhouse.

Her programme was:

Shut up and Dance with Me – featuring wee Eilidh
Rafferty boys – Ye Cannae Shove Your Granny off a Bus
Anna/Eilidh and Eilidh Grace – Hello
Grace – Edelweiss
Emily-Anna – Riptide and Your Song
Adam Robertson (Saxophone)
Jack Watson – Cello
Sam – Oasis
Houston Sisters – A You're Adorable
Hugh (piano)
Finale – History

Anna and Eilidh Houston's singing was beautiful and emotionally received by a hugely appreciative audience.

Chris and Shona Rafferty's sons, Matthew (age six) and Dale (four) sang a brilliant version of: "You Canny Shove Yer Grannie Aff A Bus" in redheaded Jimmy wigs (bearing in mind that Grannie was watching!); Sam Houston, comfortably seated on a stool with his guitar, sang two songs – Paolo Nutini's "Jenny Don't Be Hasty" and Oasis' "The Importance of Being Idle"; Hugh Walkington delivered a sterling keyboard performance of "The Entertainer" by Scott Joplin – exactly the same piece that he had played at a previous Stotters' concert some 40 years previously; Adam Robertson played two haunting tunes on saxophone – 'In The Mood' and 'Danny Boy' ; George and Sandra Ross's daughter, Emily-Anna sang "Your Song" and "Riptide" beautifully; and Grace Corrigan sang a sweet version of "Edelweiss".

The brilliant finale consisted of a group of Stotters' children, some 20 strong, singing an evocative and superbly composed (by Amanda, Eilidh, Tara and Julia) song remembering the Stotters' history, to the tune of One Direction's "History" (the words for which are at Appendix 4).

Frank Cougan, Johnny Houston, Alan Gordon, and Ken Ross related some poignant and funny (mainly true!) Stotters' anecdotes, and many a tear was shed – but many more laughs were heard from a hugely appreciative audience of Stotters, families, and friends from Tain and elsewhere.

Emily – Anna Ross.

Matthew and Dale Rafferty.

Geraldine Houston, Claire Cougan, Tricia Robertson (Houston), Catherine Harrison (Cougan) and Anne Fraser (Houston) shielding Eilidh Mackenzie and Graeme Ross

Geraldine leads the History Choir.

THE RACE FOR SPACE

Given the large numbers of Stotters, families and friends who make their way to Tain each year, it is no wonder that there is pressure to find places to stay.

Whilst the Royal Hotel was the original home for most of the Stotters, this has changed over the years, with the majority of Stotters now staying in Portmahomack, a slightly more family-friendly base than Tain itself.

Anne Fraser/Houston sums it up nicely:

"The Royal was clearly the Golf Week hub for many years and I remember being banished on many occasions with coke and crisps to our bedroom when activities in the bar became too riotous.

As children, we always enjoyed the tales of the night before – or even better, guessing what had happened the night before!

The Sunday morning early breakfast and rush down to the tee for the Stotters' match was always a riot.

Saturday evenings were a fabulous event and it's great that they have continued although not quite as crazy.

Over time however, Portmahomack seemed to draw many of the Stotters – partly due to changing management and the increasing cost of taking a family to the Royal Hotel for a week, and also the purchase of caravans in Portmahomack by the Houston and Kemp families.

Many happy times were had at the Portmahomack Free Church caravan site in the 'Stot In' – the Kemp's caravan – or the Houston's overflowing caravan and patio which hosted a few informal events.

The growing number of Stotters' children and grandchildren led to the gravitation towards the seaside where the children could be entertained on the beach.

The Castle Hotel became the Stotters' 'local' with one or two staying there over the years, and it hosting the regular Stotters' quiz and Gilbert's Goblet events.

Dolphin View holiday cottages have also hosted many Stotters over the years.

Getting accommodation in the Port became increasingly difficult as there are a finite number of self-catering cottages.

There is usually a scramble immediately after Golf Week to book somewhere for the following year – with tales of outbidding and skulduggery!

The Fraser and Hughes families eventually gave in and purchased holiday houses in Portmahomack – both of which are variously used for events during Golf Week, but often for the more informal coffee/morning after the night before discussions between various Stotters!

The Frasers, Hughes, Raffertys, Rosses, Lloyds, Cougans, Houstons, MacIntyres, and Toals all now tend to base themselves in and around Portmahomack, which has become a hive of activity during Golf Week. I'm not sure what the locals make of the invasion of yellow jumpers one week a year but they certainly seem to embrace it!"

Through the years though, resourceful Stotters have landed in all sorts of places – the Golf Club car park historically having hosted a good number of people, Frank Cougan and his then best man beginning the trend in the 60s in a caravan.

Geraldine Houston remembers, perhaps a trifle reluctantly: "HMMMM – I was 17 and my friend Sharon and I camped during Golf Week behind the car park. We had been inter-railing and brought some duty-free gin back with us which we left in our tent.

In those days, I hadn't really begun my magical relationship with the bevvy!

On ceilidh night, we arranged to meet up with some of the local lads for a wee few pre-ceilidh drinks in the local hostelries.

When we got to the ceilidh, an unfamiliar fuzzy and confusing sensation overtook us, and during the Gay Gordon, Sharon and I simultaneously had to run to the loo, and were promptly sick, then conked out in the cubicles.

Some kind lady members managed, much later on, to get us back to our tent, where we slumbered the rest of the night.

The next day we were a wee tad embarrassed and hungover (my first!) but very perplexed as people kept saying, "didn't know you were such a big Celtic fan", and "where was my invite to your tent party?"

After a day of this, we found out that wee brother Johnny, his friend Keith, and various other boys, had stolen into our tent, knocked back our duty-free, and proceeded to have a party, belting out Celtic/rebel songs, while we were unconscious in the ladies' loo!"

Ken Ross also remembers camping in the Golf Club car park – more of which later.

Johnny Houston's main memory is as a kid staying in the "Gods" at the Royal (the attic accommodation normally used by staff).

"I just loved it there. Every morning to get us up dear Florrie would sing a song through the intercom at some outrageously early time, and wouldn't stop until we were awake and had acknowledged her. I also remember being jealous of the older weans, i.e., Anne, Tricia and Catherine Cougan, being allowed to stay up that wee bit later while me, Deen, Simon and Claire Cougan (and for a few years my pal Keith) went to bed earlier".

When Johnny and Keith were 15, they persuaded the barmen at the Royal (one of whom was Mike Sangster's brother Colin, though he may not have been on duty at the time) to serve them Merrydown Cider. However, the duo: "got absolutely trolleyed, poor Keith threw up on the first tee the next day and had to withdraw from the competition!"

Johnny continues his youthful frolics: "On more than one occasion when arriving in Tain on the Friday night I would go out with Jamie Scott (the lad who introduced Hector to the Stotters) and hit the Underground disco below the Railway Hotel. We would have a late one and end up crashing at Jamie's dad's house, sleep in and miss our tee off times for the One Day Open on the Saturday. This prompted frantic calls to the club to try and squeeze us in at the tail end of the field. Unsurprisingly we never troubled the Prizegiving!"

In earlier years, Hamish and Helen Robertson, who often stayed in Balnagown Estate, also had weeks and weekends in the courtyard cottages belonging to Carbisdale Castle –through Hamish's friendship with Galloway's the Butchers.

Hamish (Junior) and Shirley now prefer to stay in Tain during Golf Week, but Hamish has stayed in Portmahomack, Alness, Evanton, Fearn, Balintore, Hilton, and Nigg over the years.

One year, Hamish and family, together with Roddy and Alice and family, had adjacent caravans in the Port, and the brothers made a last-minute decision to compete in the Dornoch Highland Gathering. Off they set to discover the Games were professional in the days when amateurs were not able to compete for money.

Undaunted, they adopted assumed names, and Hamish proceeded to win the Long Jump by around two feet, and the Triple Jump (called hop, step and jump) by more than four feet, wearing borrowed gym shoes and gaudily striped beach shorts.

His opponents were extremely worried about Hamish joining the Highland Games circuit and robbing them of potential prize money.

Roddy meanwhile finished second in the 100 yards, but was beaten into fourth place in the 220 by a fast-finishing young girl (!).

One of the amusing episodes from the day came when the massed pipe bands were about to enter the grounds. The stadium announcer, oblivious to their arrival, was thanking the volunteer staff over the tannoy system for their help in organising the Games.

A strong wind was blowing, however, and as he said: "We are extremely sad to note the passing of Mrs McLeod who has made such beautiful spreads over the years-----", this was greeted with a huge cheer from half the crowd who were upwind of the announcer and who were cheering the arrival of the pipe bands!

The brothers earned enough prize money to pay for the family fish suppers that night.

In subsequent years, Alice and Roddy often rented a farm cottage at Tarlogie where Roddy was known to silently commune with the local herd of cows.

The caravan site at Portmahomack has played host to a good number of Stotters and families, including all the Robertsons, most of the Houstons, the Cougans and Wilson and Rita Kemp.

In or close to the Port, Dolphin View and Tarrel Farm Cottages are popular rentals, as are Bay View, Bluebell and Killearn Cottages.

Alan Gordon says that he and Anne "have scurried about various B & B's in Tain, including Gulf View, but for the last 4 years we have made ourselves very comfortable in the Oystercatcher in the Port. The only downside for me is that, due to the Stotters' match on Sunday, the hangover on Monday, and the early start to match play on Wednesday I don't get to enjoy many of the gourmet breakfasts they're famous for".

Fortunately for Alan, as he says himself, he tends to make up for this on Thursday, as despite a decent qualifying record, he usually runs in to one of the locals who has no problem quickly dispatching him.

Hugh Walkington fondly remembers: "As a child and until my aunt's death in 2004, Tain was synonymous with Alderbrae, the beautiful house overlooking the old churchyard of St Duthac from its position just a stone's throw from the middle of Tain. Bought by my grandparents when they married in 1912, it remained in the family until my aunt's death, when (with great reluctance) we felt we had to sell it, as it was impractical as a holiday home.

Because there were six of us Walkingtons, staying with my aunt Rosemary and my grandmother, it often fell to me as the youngest to sleep in the rickety conservatory, or greenhouse as it was called.

Heady with the smell of ripening tomatoes, and surrounded by slug pellets, geraniums and other gardening paraphernalia, it was a magical place to sleep, never more so than when heavy rain drummed on the glass roof overhead.

In later years after the sale of Alderbrae, the Castle Hotel in Portmahomack became the accommodation of choice – however dubious that choice seemed to be on occasion.

In the great days when it was owned by the Urquhart family (no relation of Forbie), it was renowned as a brilliant place to drink and stay, albeit the standards were rather variable, due to frequent changes of ownership.

Staying in the Castle puts you at the eye of the Stotters' storm, and Sport loved it for that reason.

One memorable morning I remember us staggering down for breakfast to be met by the son of the owner looking even more bleary-eyed than we did. He apologised, and said that he needed to nip down to the village shop to get in bacon and bread to make our breakfast!"

Ken Ross remembers his first experience of staying in Tain – at the Royal Hotel when he was eleven years old.

"In those days Cecil Phillip was the proprietor and the bar seemed to be always open. It was the focal point of Golf Week where many future Stotters also stayed. On the Thursday night of Golf Week the annual golf dance was held in the two large rooms on the first floor and I can remember creeping down the stairs from my attic bedroom to see the spectacle, with everyone dressed in their finery and many of the men wearing kilts".

For several years, Ken and his father stayed at The Royal but also later stayed at The Mansfield and once at the St. Duthac.

303

"On that occasion, my father and I were locked out by the manageress (!), but on dad's instruction, I was encouraged to climb up a drainpipe, and through a window to get us in.

Alan (Shake) and Winnie hosted us also on several occasions at Graham Villa (beside the Station) and there were lengthy nightcaps of Glenmorangie".

Ian Murd Ross also remembers this era as a youngster when he and Alan's son David (the Stotters' erstwhile Hon Pharmaceutical Advisor) sat outside the downstairs toilet at Graham Villa where there was a strategically placed table.

As the various Stotters went to the toilet, they left their glasses on the table – Murd and David duly helped themselves to quick swigs of the Glenmorangie!

In 1972, Richard Jukes, a fellow medical student, and Ken had a camping golf holiday, pitching their tent at the back of the present caddy shed close to the putting green.

"Each morning alternately, one cooked breakfast on the primus stove whilst the other hit practice shots up the 18th. We discovered how good a bottle of McEwan's tasted as an appetiser before scrambled eggs – fortunately not a lasting habit".

Despite severely interrupted sleep the night before Ken was to play in the final of the Munro Rose Bowl Competition – due to his friend's attempts at an amorous adventure after a Clubhouse dance – Ken prevailed to win the trophy.

The following year he and Bridget, newly married, camped in the same place and were fortunate not to be soaked one night when the burn overflowed.

"Each morning we woke to find fresh eggs and mushrooms outside the tent, left there by Hunter Dunoon, a local farmer and Tain member, who took pity on the newly-wed bride whose cheapskate husband would not provide her with more fitting accommodation!"

Murd adds to this that Bridget often had to hastily cover up when Donald appeared!

After the arrival of George and Simon: "Cousin Ross lent us his cottage for about three years at Balnabruich, beside Portmahomack caravan site. The children could safely play on the beach whilst we could join Stotters and their friends for sundowners in the caravans".

Following the sale of the cottage, Ken and Bridget returned to Tain and stayed at The Morangie hotel, then owned by John Wynne, an excellent proprietor.

When Murd and Ray opened Golf View House, Ken reckons the long-dead minister must have turned in his grave.

Golf View became home to many of the Stotters, including Hamish and Helen Robertson, Walter Kerr, Frank Cougan, Ken, Bridget, George and Simon Ross, Mike and Tom Lloyd, Roddy, Alice, Hamish and Shirley Robertson.

Ken continues: "Every year was a house party, often ending with Murd and me drinking and playing backgammon into the late hours. In the morning, we could never quite remember who owed what to whom.

One year in a surfeit of efficiency Ray put a blackboard in the hallway on which guests were requested to write their breakfast orders. I immediately commandeered the board turning it into the Tain Golf Week Chronicle, including such gems as: "Stotters report sighting of Loch Ness Monster off Portmahomack".

A golden era of B & B came to an end with the sale of Golf View, subsequent to which the Ross family en masse returned to 'the Port' renting various houses and frequenting with other Stotters in the Castle Hotel.

Ross Robertson is well used to last-minute phone calls from the Ross family in desperate need of a bed or beds for a night or three during Golf Week, to avoid a potential return to camping in the car park.

With neat synchronicity, Johnny Houston tells of staying many years ago – with brother Simon and friend Keith: "With a very nice local couple who put us up for the week. It was only last year (2016) that I discovered that they were the parents of Tain's very own current Captain Graeme Ross!"

The Stotters in the Port.

BALNAGOWN CASTLE AND ESTATE

Behind the pink-harled walls of the fairy-tale castle, Balnagown – home to a succession of Lairds, heroes and Ross Clan Chiefs since the 15th Century – has seen its fortunes change and façade alter dramatically since the original building was constructed in 1490.

From the embellishments of the nobility who inherited the castle down the centuries through to the dark days of near dilapidation and bankruptcy in the 1960s, Balnagown's turbulent history underwent an uplift in fortune when Mohamed Al Fayed acquired the estate in 1972.

Mohamed's connection with Balnagown began as a boyhood fascination after a tutor taught him that the Egyptians discovered Scotland (!)

From that moment forward he was entranced by the myths and legends of Scotland and was determined that one day he would visit the Highlands.

When a business trip took him to Scotland in the early 1970s, he chanced upon the dilapidated façade of the Balnagown Estate. Despite its appearance, he was besotted and a short while later learned that it was up for sale. He immediately capitalised on this serendipitous intervention of fate, made an offer and within a week the Estate was his.

Helen Robertson saw in a newspaper that Mohamed al Fayed had bought Balnagown Estate, and promptly wrote to him at Harrods asking if she and Hamish could stay in one of the cottages.

She got a hand-written reply from Mohamed, saying he would be delighted for them to stay – as his guests.

They stayed in Grieve's Cottage, loved the tranquillity and splendour of the grounds and Castle, and asked to stay again – and again – and again – in both Grieve's and Gardener's Cottage.

During this time, Mohamed began the painstaking restoration of both the Castle and the Estate.

In a bid to preserve not only the buildings and lands but also the heritage of Balnagown, he commissioned research to determine the original Ross tartan, which he then subtly altered, creating a weave which celebrates the melding of Egyptian and Scottish history.

His unremitting passion for Balnagown has recreated a beautiful estate and castle, and in a nice touch of serendipity Hugh Walkington's brother, Alexander (Sandy) – M.A. (Cantab) of Gray's Inn, and a Barrister – co-wrote, with Elaine Henderson, J.P., a short history of Balnagown Castle and Estate, helped and encouraged by his aunt Rosemary – Tain Ladies' Captain and Champion.

The colourful booklet charts the turbulent history of the castle and estate and describes the interior and grounds in rich detail.

THE FUTURE STOTTERS

Because Tain Golf Week has always been a destination for family holidays, there has been a great deal of continuity through the years and accompanying generations, and it is precisely this closeness which will ensure the Stotters continue to thrive.

In no particular order, the future may – or may not – be represented by the sons and perhaps daughters, of:

Chris Fraser, who says: "Of my lot, the sporting one is Simon. Plays football, tennis and runs cross-country. He has won Scottish team titles in both football and cross-country, and now coaches tennis and is a qualified football referee.

In terms of golf it's very much a social sport for him which he really enjoys but not particularly competitively.

He tends to find golf hard to fit in around his other stuff, however he loves Golf Week and I would definitely class him as a future Stotter. He has a handicap of 21 currently and although I say he doesn't play competitively, the highlight of his golfing career so far was winning the Portmahomack Open Golf Tournament in 2015 aged 16, so he is probably showing some promise".

Chris Rafferty, who says: "Matthew (aged seven) and Dale (aged five) are swinging hockey sticks – not much golfing getting done, but you never know!"

He sees Matthew: "As a future GB hockey International, and Dale as a front row Scottish Rugby Internationalist – he'll probably get a game soon".

Alice, Roddy's widow, has seven grandchildren and therefore plenty of potential future Stotters under her wing.

Of the Glasgow Robertsons/Raffertys/McDonalds, Chris says: "Between Matthew, Dale, Louis, Blake, Harry and Roddy we may have a golfing star".

Roddy and Blake are the young sons of Scott and Gail McDonald – Gail being Roddy's second daughter, while Harry and Louis are sons to Katie and Michael Robertson, Mike being Roddy's son.

Chris adds: "Could Nina (Katie and Michael's daughter) break the mould?"

Liam Hughes, who says: "Calum at age 15 plays off 12 (should be lower) and has already made the cut a few times and got to the semi of the Stirling aged 13 – almost had that epic Grandad v Grandson final in 2014.

Ronan at age 11 should be playing off much less than he is and I expect a big handicap reduction over the next three years.

Tara is a typical teenage girl who loves her golf but has no one her own age to play with, so who knows?"

Gary Toal, who says: "Conor has already shown form at Tain having qualified at age 13 and been a top qualifier since. He has played off scratch aged 15 and could go the distance one year but we will need to get him to bed early (!).

James is showing promise having played very little to date and will be wearing a sombrero over the next few years if he starts to play a bit more. Michael is already used to golf in the Highlands having played every summer at Boat of Garten for the last few years. He is raring to go and can't wait to get the chance to play in the 4-Day in years to come".

Alan Gordon, who says: "the great white hope is our grandson Harry – although only six at the moment and probably preferring to kick the ball rather than swing at it, there is no doubt he is going to be a sportsman of some repute".

Simon Ross, who says: "I can't think of much worse than little Isabella being involved with the Stotters around Golf Week, but alas she will have little choice in the matter! Nonetheless, I assume she'll be a scratch golfer by her early teens, and as such might be qualified enough to caddy for me on Stotters' Sunday.

In the meantime, I'd like to think us "younger Stotters" will have a few competitive rounds left in us when the next generation comes through and hits their peak!"

Tom Lloyd, who says: "I would dearly love my son Oliver to take up golf and follow me into the Stotters. It's a little early for him just now, but I've bought some plastic clubs for him to practise with me in the garden. The first step is to stop him hitting his little sister with them!

I know that Isidora will love caddying in the match and if it ever becomes a mixed event, I'm sure she'll also want to play".

Hamish Robertson, who says: "With three sons, and four grandsons, all of whom can play golf, plus a non-playing grand-daughter who may yet pick up a club (she has threatened!) anyone would think there's a ready-made line of Stotters' succession.

However, none of them has a handicap and whilst all are keen to play, and indeed all have played the course on several occasions, nobody has yet been a regular enough Tain returnee to make a direct claim to become a future Stotter. Perhaps if they keep playing in the Hamish Robertson Texas Scramble Competition in early June each year, someone will be encouraged to make that leap of faith (and holiday time)".

George Ross, who says: "Of our spread, Oliver (12) has shown the most interest in golf. He doesn't yet have a handicap, but has spent a fair few hours "down the range" with the old man. In fact, only the other day he cracked his three-wood to about 175 yards, so his timing is just starting to flow nicely. More than I can say for his father.

Whilst Zachary (three) is too young to have swung a golf club in anger, he has swung a baseball bat in the back garden at his brother and sister and the sight was quite formidable.

Emily-Anna (ten) prefers to practice putting, though she does have a very good swing".

Simon Houston's son Sam, winner of the Stirling Challenge Cup in 2015, and Hector MacIntyre's son Greg, who very successfully debuted in the Stotters' match in 2017, are however clearly in pole position if their enthusiasm for Tain continues.

George Ross neatly sums up the mood of many of the Stotters when thinking of the future: "I hope they all continue to enjoy our annual pilgrimage as much as I have over the years, and build some wonderful memories to cherish".

The Future Stotters – Calum, Ronan and Tara Hughes

APPENDIX 1 – MY BROTHER SYLVESTE

Without The Wolfe Tones (and perhaps Scott Ferguson and Wilson Kemp!), this song would hardly be known, and it has variously been recorded by The Blaggards, The Jolly Beggarmen, The Masterless Men, Darby O'Gill and Patsy Watchorn from The Dubliners.

It is also known as "Big Strong Man".

Have you heard?
Have you heard?
Have you heard?
Have you heard?

Have you heard about the big strong man?
He lived in a caravan.
Have you heard about the Jeffrey Johnson fight?
Oh lord what a hell of a fight.
You can take all the heavyweights you got ('cause you got!).
You got a lad that can beat the whole lot (whole lot!).
He used to play all the bells in the belfry,
Now he's going to fight Jack Dempsey.

Chorus

That's my brother Sylveste (what's he got?).
He's got a row of forty medals on his chest (big chest!).
He killed fifty capmen in the West,
He knows no rest, kind of the man, hellfire.
Don't push, don't shove, plenty of room for you and me.
He's got an arm like a leg,

And a fist that would sink a battle ship (big ship!).
Takes all the Army and the Navy
To put the wind up Sylveste.
He thought he'd take a trip to Italy,
He thought that he'd go by sea,
He dived off the harbour at New York,
And he swam like a man from Cork.
He saw the Lusitania in distress (what did he do?).
Put the big ship Lusitania on his chest (big chest!).
He drank all the water in the sea
And he walked all the way to Italy.

Repeat Chorus

He thought he'd take a trip to old Japan.
They brought out the whole brass band.
He played every instrument they got.
What a lad he played the whole lot.
The old church bell will ring (will ring).
The old Church choir did sing (will sing).
They all turned out to wish him best,
My big brother, Sylveste.

Repeat Chorus

Yeah, that's my brother Sylveste.
He's got a row of forty medals on his chest (big chest!).
He killed fifty capmen in the West,
He knows no rest, kind of the man, hellfire.
Don't push, don't shove, plenty of room for you and me.

APPENDIX 2 – A POEM TO THE LADIES

This poem emerges in the early days of The Stotters – its authorship is not definitively known, but it was probably penned by Sport.

You may recall at last year's do
When each of us was unco fu'
Poetry by a clever pen
Described each of the "Stotters" men.

At the end of the poem, we were not amused
To be depicted as a "shower that boozed"
And so, by way of relaxation
Sit back and listen to the ladies' citation.

Let's start then with a word on Pat
Whom, when first I met was growing fat
Not for the love of a jelly scone
But more I fear for the love of John.

Tommy, a name exclusive to men
Describes a lady who can give you the gen
On things as different as chalk & cheese
And even on golf she has great expertise.

Helen, who graces the Royal's portals
Moves serenely among us lesser mortals
A woman of charm she can surely lay claim
To captain again the "Ladies of Tain".

Ian McColl has a wife named Chris
Tall, cool & composed, she's never amiss
She follow's Ian's progress from tee to hole
Man, that's more than even a wife should thole.

There's Helen, married to Roderick M.
We all agree she's an absolute gem
She wills her Rod to better his score
But alas he keeps taking more & more.

The doctor's wife from near Arbroath
Has I fear unpledged her troth
For two gents, not the least wary
Keep singing "I'm going to bed with Mary".

Shelagh, who is a native of Tain
You'd have thought she'd marry one of her ain
But she's wed to a big RAF moustache
Stuck on the lip of a Sassenach.

One there is of the MacPherson clan
Who is known by the name of Nan
The bandit in the clubhouse creaks and sighs
As she vainly tries to win the jackpot prize.

Dorothy, surname Cougan
Is often heard muttering "Who can
Get Frank away from the bar
I really do need the keys for the car".

Rita the spouse of muscles
Has plenty of red blood corpuscles
When she was incised by the scalpel blade
The surgeon got drunk on rum and lemonade.

For those whom I have failed to mention
It was done with no rude intention
Unlike my golf which bogies mar
My literary gifts are well below par.

So those I've missed sit back
But don't cheer
I may say something about you
Next year.

It is clear who many of the ladies are, but, for clarity, Pat is Pat Houston; the first Helen mentioned is Helen Robertson; Tommy is Chryss Robertson, Raeburn's wife; Mary is Gilbert's wife; Shelagh is Sport's wife; and Rita is Wilson's wife.

APPENDIX 3 – BOB BEVERIDGE AND THE GAY CABALLERO

Bob enlivened several AGMs with his rendition of The Gay Caballero, and this song's history is somewhat mysterious, its authorship and provenance shrouded in antiquity.

Someone with the initials BW said he learned the song from a phonograph record circa 1929 while going to Alaska on a ship carrying a crew to a salmon cannery in Chignik Bay on the Aleutian Peninsula.

He then met a man in a piano bar in San Francisco, who apparently improvised the tune, after BW hummed a few bars.

The song has several versions, all of which have a high degree of innuendo, some more so than others.

One version of the basic tune is as follows:

After the Sunday match in 2015, the Stotters *en masse* walked from the Golf Course to the St Duthus New Cemetery where Bob is buried with his wife, Nan

Donald Sutherland brought a bottle of red wine and plastic glasses, and Chris Rafferty brought the version of the song which follows, lovingly sourced and copied.

20 Stotters then stood in resplendent yellow at the foot of Bob's grave, with its then temporary wooden cross, and in the sunshine, glasses of red wine in hand, lustily sang Bob's song.

An emotional farewell was paid to Bob as the Stotters watered his grave with the red wine he had loved.

In the midst of these proceedings, and into an otherwise deserted cemetery came a lady in a powered wheelchair accompanied by her husband.

As the Stotters watched, they wheeled round the cemetery to the grave near to Bob's to pay their own tributes to a relative, and quietly withdrew.

Fortunately, they too had known Bob, otherwise these proceedings would have seemed extremely odd!

THE GAY CABALLERO

Oh, I am a gay caballero
Going to Rio Janeiro,
With nice oily hair,
And full of hot air,
I'm an expert at shooting the bull-eo.

I'll find me a fair senorita
Not thin and yet not too much meat-a.
I'll woo her a while
In my Argentine style
And sweep her right off of her feet-a.

I'll tell her I'm of the nobilio
And live in a great big castillio.
I must have a miss
Who will long for a kiss
And not say "Oh don't be so silly-io.

It was at a gay cabaretta
While wining and dining I met her.
We had one or two
As other folks do.
The night was wet but we got wetter.

She was a dancer and singer
At me she kept pointing her finger,
And saying to me
"Si, Senor, Si Si"
But I couldn't see a durn thing-er.

She told me her name was Estrella.
She said, "Stick around me, young fella,
For mosquitos they bite
And they're awful tonight
And you smell just like citronella".

She told me that she was so lonely
So I climbed upon her balcony.
While under her spell
I heard someone yell
"Get away from here you big baloney".

I swore I would win this senorita
I wooed her on the sofita.
Then her husband walked in
What he did was a sin.
I can still hear the birds sing "Tweet tweet-a".

Oh, I am a sad caballero
Returning from Rio Janeiro,
Minus my hair,
With a bruise here and there,
And her husband he bit off my ear-o.

Hamish Robertson Junior remembers a childhood version which had an endearing chorus sung after each and every verse.
The chorus went thus:

There once was a gay Caballero
An exceedingly gay Caballero
Who cut off his el
His el tel morel
His el tel morel tel merino.

A slightly racier version goes as follows:

A GAY CABALLERO

I am a gay caballero
I come from Rio de Janeiro.
I carry with me my wee trembeli
And both of my latra baleros.

I met a gay young senorita
Who gave me a dose of clapita,
Right on the end of my wee trembeli
And both of my latra baleros.

I went to a wise surgeano
He said, "I prescribe purgeano,"
He cut off the end of my wee trembeli
And both of my latra baleros.

And now I'm a sad caballero
Returning to Rio de Janeiro.
But not as you see with my wee trembeli.
And both of my latra baleros.

At night as I lie on my pillow
Seeking to finger my willow.
All I find there is a handful of hair
And one dried up latra balero.

Another version, which is described as being in limerick form with a repeating line at the end of each rhyme, builds to the final pun at the end. This was probably sung on a ship, like a Johnny Cash song with a slow beat:

There once was a bold caballero
who hailed from Rio de Janeiro.
And his lum bum ba dee
hung down to his knee
with one of his lum bum dieros.

He met a pretty senorita
oh, what a pretty senorita.
And he said won't you see
My lum bum ba dee
and one of my lum bum dieros?

She said I think I had naughta
You see my father's a preacha.
But, for a quarter I'll see
Your lum bum ba dee
and one of your lum bum dieros.

He whipped out a bright shiny quarter
Oh, what a bright shiny quarter.
And she stripped to her knees
Grabbed his lum bum ba dee
and one of his lum bum dieros.

The next day he went to the medico
They said that he had the Patigo,
and it festered the end
of his lum bum ba dee
and one of his lum bum dieros.

So he took out a nice sharp stiletto
Oh, what a nice sharp stiletto,
and he lopped off the end
of his lum bum ba dee
and one of his lum bum dieros.

[Sung slowwllyyy for effect]
Now each night as he lay on his pillow
and he reaches down to play with his willow.
Now all that is there
Is a handful of hair
And one of his lum bum dieros.

Whichever the version, however it's sung, it has given and still gives the Stotters real belly-laughs and a chance to remember a very special man.

APPENDIX 4 – THE STOTTERS' HISTORY SONG

This delightful version of One Direction's "History" was composed by Amanda, Eilidh, Tara and Julia, and sung – to the One Direction tune – by a choir of Stotters' children – and the odd adult or two – at the 2016 Clubhouse Concert.

We can't believe it's
Been 50 years
The thought of us all together moves us all to tears
We are still going strong
We are still holding on
Aren't we?

The first week in August
It's set in stone
Tain and Portmahomack become our second home
We are still going strong
We are still holding on
Aren't we?

Chorus:
You and me got a whole lot of history (woah-oh)
We could be the greatest team
That the world has ever seen
You and me got a whole lot of history (woah-oh)
So don't let it go
We can make some more
We can live forever.

All of the meetings
All of the fights
But we always find a way to make it out alive
We are still going strong
We are still holding on
Aren't we?

Chorus:
You and me got a whole lot of history (woah-oh)
We could be the greatest team
That the world has ever seen
You and me got a whole lot of history (woah-oh)
So don't let it go
We can make some more
We can live forever.

Rusty nails, epic fails
Holes in one – we've had none
Playing Tain in the pouring rain
But we don't need anything
The truth is out we realise that without Golf Week life is incomplete
This is not the end
This is not the end
We can make it – you know it, you know.

Chorus:
You and me got a whole lot of history (woah-oh)
We could be the greatest team
That the world has ever seen
You and me got a whole lot of history (woah-oh)
So don't let it go
We can make some more
We can live forever.

APPENDIX 5 – FORBIE URQUHART – SEASONS IN THE SUN

Forbie Urquhart had an enormous influence on both the Stotters and Tain Golf Club, and his loss to Margaret and family is profound.

On the 12th of March 2017, his old friend Frank Cougan told fellow Stotters: "It is with sadness and grief that I inform you that our old pal Forbie Urquhart passed away on Saturday, 11th March.

With fond memories of a very good friend".

Magi in Tain said: "It is with great sadness that I write to inform you of the passing of our President Forbie Urquhart.

Forbie was such a huge part of this club for so many years and a friend to everyone. He was so full of fun and always had a great story to tell.

He will be greatly missed and our thoughts go to Margaret and all his family".

Appended is the aide memoire from the Humanist Service held in his honour at Inverness Crematorium. There was a fine turnout of over 120 people.

Margaret and family (Forbie's sister from Australia, and his son and daughter) greeted everyone as they came in.

The Stotters were represented by Donald (and Morag), Malcolm, Andrew (and Tina) and Hamish (and Shirley) and the service was intimate and touching, covering as it did several of the other dimensions of Forbie's life beyond golf – his double bass playing as a youngster, love of classical and jazz music, and his time working in Canada.

Amongst the many tributes paid by fellow Stotters and families were the following:

Chris Rafferty: "I didn't know Forbie as well as many of you, but from day one it was obvious to me he was a real gentleman. A pillar of the club and the Stotters. Many thanks Forbie, rest well".

Hugh Walkington: "A giant of TGC and a legend of the Stotters. A complete privilege to have known him – he has given us all unforgettable memories.

Another link to the past gone".

Ken Ross: "We were both very saddened to hear about Forbie.

I first met him in 1958 and remember him well for his sense of fun, and the twinkle in his eye which stayed with him for all of his life.

He always had the Stotters' interests at heart and did much work for us, for which we should always be grateful.

RIP Forbie".

Geraldine Houston: "Total Stotters legend".

Anne Fraser (Houston): "Such fond memories of 4B over the years – an absolute legend".

Tina Urquhart: "Forbie was such a star in every way. Everyone loved him. As with the rest of the Stotters we will miss him. I've just had a large brandy and having lots of memories of those whose names are on the Stotters' bench. I might even have another".

Bon Voyage, Forbie.

INVERNESS CREMATORIUM

Ceremony Led By: Wendy Armstrong
Date of Ceremony: Tuesday 21st March 2017

A CEREMONY
IN LOVING REMEMBRANCE
of

WILLIAM FORBES URQUHART
"FORBIE"

(Passed away on 11th March 2017 aged 89 years)

Seasons in the Sun

Goodbye my love, 'twas hard to see you die
When all the birds were singing in the sky
Now that Spring is in the air
With the flowers everywhere
I wish we both could still be there;

We had joy, we had fun
We had seasons in the sun
But the wine and the song
Like the seasons are all gone;
Yet the memories go on and on.

~~~~~

The Family would like to thank you for your attendance here today and for your many kind thoughts received over the past few days. Thanks are also expressed for your kind donations to Tain and District Medical Practice and The Tain Community Nurses.

You are warmly invited to join with The Family at Tain Golf Club, following this service.

APPENDIX 6 – HIC-CUP ROLL OF HONOUR

The Hic-cup, donated by Wilson Kemp, was originally awarded for the best pairing in an annual match, initially played for in a Team Trials/Spring Meeting usually held at Kilmacolm, and later at Portmahomack.

1979 JL MacPherson & W Kerr
1980 S Ferguson & G Raeside
1981 S Ferguson & Dr J Houston
1982 T Young & T Irvine
1983 T Young & W Kerr
1984 J Campbell & G Raeside
1985 W Kerr & S Ferguson
1986 G Raeside & T Young
1987 W Kerr & JL MacPherson
1988 T Young & D Wilson
1989 T Young & K Greig
1990 W Kerr & F Cougan
1991 K Greig & S Ferguson
1992 W Kemp & F Cougan
1993 W Kemp & S Ferguson
1994 A Wilson & W Kemp
1995 No engraving
1996 F Urquhart & W Kemp
1997 F Cougan (engraved as Kougan) & K Ross
1998 S Houston & K Ross
1999 S Houston & G Ross
2000 H MacIntyre & D Sutherland
2001 K Ross & S Houston

In 1982, T Irvine appears on the Trophy – he was a Kilmacolm member who made up the numbers that year.

From 2002 onwards, the Hic-cup was awarded to the Stotters' pairing achieving the biggest margin of victory over their Tain counterparts in the Annual Sunday Match.

2002 J Houston & S Ross
2003 K Ross & R Robertson
2004 K Ross & H Robertson
2005 H Robertson & S Houston
2006 M Lloyd & S Houston
2007 G Toal & C Rafferty
2008 F Cougan & K Ross
2009 C Fraser & C Rafferty
2010 M Lloyd & H MacIntyre
2011 F Cougan & K Ross
2012 C Fraser & A Gordon
2013 C Fraser & K Ross
2014 J Houston & H MacIntyre
2015 H MacIntyre & K Ross
2016 H Walkington & C Rafferty

The Hic-Cup

APPENDIX 7 – GILBERT'S GOBLET ROLL OF HONOUR

Gilbert's Goblet is presented to the Stotter with the lowest net score in the first qualifying round of the Four Day Tournament.

Forbie remembers: "It became the practice, for a few years, that we had everyone connected with the Stotters to our house in Queen Street, for drinks and nibbles on Monday nights before dinner at the Royal (only 2 mins walk away) or wherever, and this was combined with the Presentation of Gilbert's Goblet.

These proved enjoyable occasions but it was fortunate that they usually coincided with a lovely evening enabling proceedings to spill out onto the patio and into the garden as the public rooms in our house were not very big and every year saw numbers swell.

As usual with Stotter gatherings, there was much hilarity and unusual happenings. There was the time Frank divested himself of his trousers on the patio – something to do with showing off an injured knee!"

Gilbert's Goblet has been presented, usually on Monday evenings, in many places, including the Castle Hotel in Portmahomack, and in several of the houses rented by Stotters during Golf Week – and always accompanied by some food and the never absent drink or two.

1979	J Campbell
1980	J Campbell
1981	W Kemp
1982	J Campbell
1983	J Houston
1984	W Kemp
1985	F Urquhart
1986	F Urquhart
1987	F Urquhart
1988	F Urquhart
1989	W Kerr

1990	F Urquhart
1991	F Cougan
1992	W Kemp
1993	HC Robertson
1994	GW Ross
1995	K Greig
1996	HC Robertson
1997	H MacIntyre
1998	SRA Ross
1999	SRA Ross
2000	JC Houston
2001	JC Houston
2002	F Cougan
2003	L Hughes
2004	JC Houston
2005	S Houston
2006	C Rafferty
2007	JC Houston
2008	JC Houston
2009	G Toal
2010	JC Houston
2011	T Lloyd
2012	M Lloyd
2013	KR Ross
2014	JC Houston
2015	A Gordon
2016	JC Houston

Gary Toal proudly displays Gilbert's Goblet.

The Dr. John Trophy – with Ken Ross and Mike Lloyd.

APPENDIX 8 – DR. JOHN'S ROLL OF HONOUR

Dr. John's Silver Salver is awarded for the best net aggregate score from Golf Week's Monday and Tuesday Qualifying Rounds.

1991	F Cougan
1992	W Kemp
1993	HC Robertson
1994	GW Ross
1995	GW Ross
1996	KR Ross
1997	KR Ross
1998	KR Ross
1999	MT Lloyd
2000	GW Ross
2001	GW Ross
2002	J Houston
2003	L Hughes
2004	No winner
2005	Mike Lloyd
2006	Simon Houston
2007	J Houston
2008	S Houston
2009	C Rafferty
2010	L Hughes
2011	G Toal
2012	J Houston
2013	L Hughes
2014	J Houston
2015	J Houston
2016	J Houston

APPENDIX 9 – A BRIEF HISTORY OF STOTTERS' TIME

1966: A number of visiting golfers, many with Tain connections, agree with Tain Golf Club to play a match against the Club. The Stotters are born and Dr John Houston is elected as the first Captain with Roddy Mackenzie as his Vice-Captain.

1967: Dr John Houston captains The Stotters in the very first match, with Roddy Mackenzie as Vice-Captain. The match is won by the Tain Golf Club Captain's Select, captained by Robin Graham.

1968: Roddy Mackenzie takes over Captaincy and Ian McColl is Vice-Captain. Tain win again, captained by Hugh Munro.

Ian MacPherson provides ties for the Stotters to wear "at all times they meet". Alan Robertson MPS is elected as Hon Pharmaceutical Advisor.

1969: Ian McColl becomes Captain with Ian MacPherson as Vice-Captain, and the Stotters win for the first time.

1970: Ian MacPherson is Captain and Raeburn Robertson his Vice-Captain. The Stotters win the match again.

Willie Mackenzie passes away and the Stotters agree to provide a seat for the course in Willie's memory. Walter Kerr becomes the first Stotters' Secretary. Frank Cougan is elected as Hon Shirt Maker.

1971: Raeburn Robertson takes over as Captain and his young brother Hamish (J.G.) becomes Vice-Captain. Bob Beveridge takes the trophy on behalf of Tain. The seat in Willie's honour, is positioned at the eleventh tee. Frank Cougan provides shirts and pullovers for the Stotters, and is elected as a Stotter. Wilson Kemp is elected an Associate Stotter.

Ann Chalk/Rutherford dies.

1972: Hamish Robertson is Captain with Tommy Young as Vice-Captain and Tain win the trophy again – Ian Anderson accepting it.

Tommy Young presents badges, designed and made up by his daughter Tina for the Stotters to wear on their blazers. Ian Walkington designs a Stotters' Flag which Tain Golf Club agree to fly at each years' annual match.

1973: Tommy Young becomes Captain and Walter Kerr Vice-Captain (in addition to his secretarial role). Ian Anderson again lifts the trophy for Tain.

Raeburn Robertson dies and his name will join Willie Mackenzie's on the bench at The Alps. Wilson Kemp is elected as a Stotter, and Tommy Armstrong an Associate Stotter.

1974: Walter Kerr is Captain and Hamilton Mitchell Vice-Captain. Walter lifts the trophy for the Stotters. Doug Torrance and Forbie Urquhart are elected as Associate Stotters.

Alan Robertson dies later in the year.

1975: Hamilton Mitchell captains the Stotters to victory with Gilbert Tocher as his Vice-Captain. Miss Christina Young accepts the Cup from Roy Mackenzie, Captain of Tain on behalf of Hamilton Mitchell.

It is agreed that David Robertson MPS (Alan's son and now the owner of Ross the Chemist's shop) be approached to take up the position of Hon. Pharmaceutical Advisor.

1976: Gilbert Tocher assumes Captaincy with Ian Walkington as Vice-Captain. Frank Cougan stands in as Acting Vice-Captain in Ian's absence. The Stotters win the trophy for the 3rd year in a row. Ian McColl withdraws from The Stotters and Tommy Armstrong is elected as a Stotter.

1977: Frank Cougan is Captain with Ian Walkington as his Vice-Captain. In Ian's absence again, Wilson Kemp acts as Vice-Captain. The Stotters make it four in a row. Scott Ferguson is elected as an Associate Stotter.

1978: Wilson Kemp is Captain with Tommy Armstrong as Vice-Captain. Five in a row for the Stotters. Dr Roy Mackenzie has restored the Stotters' seat to its former glory.

1979: Tommy Armstrong is Captain and Ian Walkington Vice-Captain. The Stotters win again. Gilbert Tocher dies. Scott Ferguson and John Campbell are elected as Stotters.

Mary, Gilbert's widow, donates a delightful thistle-shaped cup – Gilbert's Goblet, and it is agreed that this would be awarded to the lowest scorer on Monday's tournament round. Tommy Armstrong resigns.

Earlier in the year, the Hic-Cup, courtesy of Wilson Kemp, was played for and won for the first time by Ian MacPherson and Walter Kerr at a Western Gailes team trial.

1980: Tain Golf Club decide that because of the huge entry for the Sunday One Day Open it is impossible to continue the match against the Stotters.

The game continues however over Invergordon Golf Club for the next five years.

Dr. John Houston becomes Captain, but there is no apparent election of Vice-Captain. The Stotters win the trophy again.

There are no Minutes and no record of Office Bearers for the gap years, but George Raeside appears now to have become a Stotter.

1981: Tain win, breaking a run of seven consecutive Stotters' victories.

1982: Tain win.

1983: Tain win.

1984: Stotters win.

1985: George Raeside is Captain and Wilson Kemp his Vice-Captain. Walter Kerr refuses to take the Minutes any more and Wilson Kemp is forced into that duty. The Stotters win the trophy.

1986: Wilson Kemp becomes Captain and Forbie Urquhart his Vice-Captain, Forbie also being elected as the Stotters' local representative. Tain win the trophy. Wilson Kemp is demoted to the position of Permanent Secretary.

1987: Forbie Urquhart is now Captain and George Raeside his Vice-Captain. The Stotters win.

Dr Ken Greig and Robert Towart are elected as Stotters, and John Houston (Junior) is elected an Associate Stotter.

Tommy Armstrong dies.

1988: Forbie Urquhart remains as Captain with Frank Cougan Vice-Captain. Tain win the trophy.

Ian McColl passes away.

1989: Frank Cougan is Captain and J.G. (Hamish Senior) is Vice-Captain. The Stotters win the match.

Simon Houston is appointed an Associate Stotter.

1990: Hamish Robertson (Senior) is Captain with Dr Ken Greig his Vice-Captain. Tain win the match.

The Stotters present a crystal goblet with the Stotters' emblem to Tain GC on the occasion of their Centenary.

Ken Ross is elected an Associate Stotter.

1991: Ken Greig is now Captain with Scott Ferguson as Vice-Captain. Tain win the trophy in the year of the Stotters' silver anniversary. Ken Ross is elected as an Associate Stotter for the second year in a row (!) and is joined by two of Hamish (Senior's) sons, Hamish (Junior) and Roddy.

John Campbell and Dr John Houston die.

1992: Scott Ferguson is Captain and Robert Towart his Vice-Captain. The Stotters win the trophy.

The Houston family donate the Dr. John trophy to be awarded to the player with the net best score over the two qualifying rounds during Golf Week.

1993: Robert Towart is now Captain with John Houston (Junior) as Vice-Captain. The Stotters win the match.

Walter Kerr and Scott Ferguson die during the year.

1994: With John Houston as Captain, brother Simon Houston is Vice-Captain. The Stotters win again. History is made as Morag Sutherland becomes the first female to play in the match – for Tain.

Ian Ferguson, George Ross and Andrew Urquhart are elected as Associate Stotters.

It is agreed that the Stotters' bench have a plaque attached, saying: 'The Stotters – formed 1966', and further, that those Stotters who have passed before be recognised with plaques showing their year of inception to the Stotters and the year of their death.

During the year, Ian MacPherson and Tommy Young die.

1995: Simon Houston is Captain with Ken Ross as Vice-Captain. The Stotters win for the fourth year in a row. Ian Ferguson is elected as a Stotter.

1996: Ken Ross is now Captain with Hamish Robertson (Junior) Vice-Captain. The Stotters win the trophy for the fifth year in a row. Hector MacIntyre is elected as an Associate Stotter.

1997: The Stotters win again. Hamish Robertson becomes Captain with Ian Walkington as Vice-Captain. Hamish is unable to come to Tain so Sport captains the team.

Roddy Mackenzie dies. George Raeside is struck off for non-attendance.

It is agreed that the Stotters present Tain Golf Club with a new Trophy Cabinet.

1998: The Stotters win yet again. Hamish Robertson is elected as Vice-Captain to Sport's Captaincy.

Wilson Kemp steps down as Secretary after 12 years and Simon Houston is elected in his place.

Simon Ross is elected an Associate Stotter and Donald Sutherland an Honorary Stotter.

1999: The Stotters win again – a record-breaking eight in a row. George Ross is Vice-Captain to Hamish's Captaincy. Simon Houston is elected as Secretary.

Hammie Mitchell and Ken Grieg die.

Mike Lloyd is elected as an Associate.

Hamish Robertson Senior who is now a non-playing Stotter, becomes the second Honorary President of the Stotters, the first being Anne Chalk.

2000: Tain win! George Ross is Captain with Forbie Urquhart as Vice-Captain.

2001: Tain win again. Forbie is Captain with Hector MacIntyre as Vice-Captain. Tom Lloyd is elected as an Associate.

2002: The Stotters win. Hector is now Captain with Frank Cougan as Vice-Captain.

2003: Tain win. Frank Cougan is Captain with John Houston Junior as Vice-Captain. Liam Hughes is elected as an Associate.

2004: The Stotters win. John Houston is Captain with Mike Lloyd as Vice-Captain.

Hamish Senior dies, and Roddy Robertson and Tom Lloyd become full Stotters. Ken Ross is elected as Special Envoy with a questionable brief.

2005: Tain win. Mike Lloyd is Captain with Simon Ross as Vice-Captain. Chris Rafferty is elected an Associate.

Ian Walkington is elected President.

2006: The Stotters win. Simon Ross is Captain with Ken Ross as Vice-Captain.

The 40th Anniversary Dinner Dance in the Royal Hotel is a great success, complete with a display of photos of The Stotters v Tain through the years, organised by Forbie and Margaret Urquhart, and Donald Sutherland.

The Special Envoy organises a successful match in Eastbourne in which the Stotters defeat an East Sussex National team by 2½ matches to 1½.

Wilson Kemp and Frank Cougan are elected as joint Vice-Presidents.

Liam Hughes becomes a full Stotter.

Bob Beveridge and Johnny Urquhart are given Honorary Stotter Status.

Malcolm Fraser, Gary Toal and Chris Fraser are elected as Associates.

Roddy dies and a silver salver inscribed "Roddy's Round" is presented by Alice and family and makes its debut on the first tee at 7.30am filled with whisky glasses.

2007: Tain win. Ken Ross is Captain with Simon Houston as Vice-Captain.

2008: Tain win. Simon Ross is Captain with Hamish Robertson as Vice-Captain. Chris Rafferty becomes a full Stotter.

2009: Tain win. Hamish Robertson is Captain with Tom Lloyd as Vice-Captain. Hugh Walkington is elected as Honorary Stotter.

2010: Tain win. Tom Lloyd is Captain with Liam Hughes as Vice-Captain. Wilson Kemp and Pat Houston die.

2011: The Stotters win. Liam is Captain with Frank Cougan as Vice-Captain. A Sub-Committee is set up to plan 2016, the 50th year of the Stotters.

2012: The Stotters win. Frank is Captain for a record fourth time, with Hector MacIntyre as Vice-Captain.

Sport and Johnny Urquhart die. Chris Fraser and Gary Toal become full Stotters and Alan Gordon an Associate Stotter.

2013: Tain win. Hector is Captain with Chris Rafferty as Vice-Captain.

The Stotters win again in East Sussex.

2014: Tain win. Chris is Captain with George Ross as Vice-Captain. Hugh Walkington is elected as the first official Treasurer.

Bob Beveridge dies.

2015: Tain win. George is Captain with Johnny Houston as Vice-Captain. Simon Houston demits office as Secretary after a record-breaking 17 years and is succeeded by Hugh Walkington who now has two roles to play.

2016: The Stotters win. Johnny is Captain for the third time, with Hamish Robertson as Vice-Captain in the semicentennial or quinquagenary year of the Stotters.

There are great celebrations!

APPENDIX 10 – THE STOTTERS' CAPTAINS AND OFFICE HOLDERS

CAPTAINS

1967	John Houston Senior
1968	Roddy Mackenzie
1969	Ian McColl
1970	Ian MacPherson
1971	Raeburn Robertson
1972	Hamish Robertson Senior
1973	Tommy Young
1974	Walter Kerr
1975	Hamilton Mitchell
1976	Gilbert Tocher
1977	Frank Cougan
1978	Wilson Kemp
1979	Tommy Armstrong
1980	John Houston Senior
1981	Unrecorded
1982	Unrecorded
1983	Unrecorded
1984	Unrecorded
1985	George Raeside
1986	Wilson Kemp
1987	Forbie Urquhart
1988	Forbie Urquhart
1989	Frank Cougan
1990	Hamish Robertson Senior
1991	Ken Greig

1992	Scott Ferguson
1993	Robert Towart
1994	John Houston Junior
1995	Simon Houston
1996	Ken Ross
1997	Ian Walkington
1998	Ian Walkington
1999	Hamish Robertson Junior
2000	George Ross
2001	Forbie Urquhart
2002	Hector MacIntyre
2003	Frank Cougan
2004	John Houston Junior
2005	Mike Lloyd
2006	Simon Ross
2007	Ken Ross
2008	Simon Houston
2009	Hamish Robertson Junior
2010	Tom Lloyd
2011	Liam Hughes
2012	Frank Cougan
2013	Hector MacIntyre
2014	Chris Rafferty
2015	George Ross
2016	John Houston Junior
2017	Hamish Robertson Junior

SECRETARIES

1970 1984	Walter Kerr
1985 – 1997	Wilson Kemp
1998 – 2015	Simon Houston
2016 –	Hugh Walkington

TREASURERS

2014 –   Hugh Walkington

PRESIDENTS

1966 – 1971 Mrs Ann Chalk
1999 – 2004 Hamish Robertson Senior
2005 – 2012 Ian Walkington
2012 –   Frank Cougan

VICE-PRESIDENTS

2006 – 2010 Wilson Kemp
2006 – 2012 Frank Cougan

APPENDIX 11 – THE STOTTERS' MEMBERS

Listed in order of the year they became Stotters.

The Original 12

John Houston Senior 1966
Walter Kerr 1966
Roddy Mackenzie 1966
Willie Mackenzie 1966
Hamilton Mitchell 1966
Ian MacPherson 1966
Ian McColl 1966
Hamish Robertson Senior 1966
Raeburn Robertson 1966
Gilbert Tocher 1966
Ian Walkington 1966
Tommy Young 1966
Mrs Ann Chalk 1966

Alan Robertson 1968 *
Frank Cougan 1971
Wilson Kemp 1971
Tommy Armstrong 1973
Doug Torrance 1974
Forbie Urquhart 1974
David Robertson 1975 *

Scott Ferguson 1977
John Campbell 1979
George Raeside 1980
Ken Greig 1987
Robert Towart 1987
John Houston Junior 1987
Simon Houston 1989
Ken Ross 1990
Hamish Robertson Junior 1991
Roddy Robertson 1991
Ian Ferguson 1994
Andrew Urquhart 1994
George Ross 1994
Hector MacIntyre 1996
Simon Ross 1998
Donald Sutherland 1998
Mike Lloyd 1999
Tom Lloyd 2001
Liam Hughes 2003
Chris Rafferty 2005
Bob Beveridge 2006
Chris Fraser 2006
Malcolm Fraser 2006
Gary Toal 2006
Johnny Urquhart 2006
Hugh Walkington 2009
Alan Gordon 2012

Hon. Pharmaceutical Advisor

APPENDIX 12 – HUGH's FIRST AGM MINUTES

At the 2017 AGM, which reflected on the events of 2016, it was agreed that the publication of the Stotters' Story presented too good an opportunity to miss publishing Hugh Walkington's first ever Minutes, which are cleverly worded, brilliantly funny, and mark a stunning debut for the Stotters' fourth Secretary.

MINUTES OF THE FIFTY-FIRST ANNUAL GENERAL MEETING – SUNDAY 31ˢᵀ JULY, 2016

Held at the Royal Hotel, Tain.

The fiftieth annual match of Tain versus the Stotters – the Stotters won the match.

Captain John Houston in the chair.

APOLOGIES

Apologies were received from Donald Sutherland – to a member of the public who found him wandering in a confused state in Chapel Street, not entirely aware of where he was, who he was, or of the extent of the calamitous defeat that his team had just suffered. The annual sweepstake to see how many minutes would elapse before Sutherland fell asleep was therefore declared null and void.

Simon Ross snored his apologies from the chaise longue. Apologies were also received later from the President, Frank Cougan, who like a Jon Pertwee-era Dalek, was completely defeated by a flight of stairs. Probably wisely, he refused the enthusiastic offers of a fireman's lift.

CAPTAIN'S REMARKS

The Captain cleared his throat, and the golfing world held its collective breath. What followed was a tirade of unrepeatable obscenity – until Mike

Lloyd was sufficiently reassured that a kitty had been taken and that drinks were indeed on their way.

Clearing his throat once more, Captain Houston surveyed his team with a look of quiet satisfaction. He declared that the fiftieth anniversary weekend had been a resounding success, which was met with general approbation.

He thanked Hamish Robertson for his outstanding work in organising everything and everyone, commenting that if he never received another e-mail from Hamish it would be a good deal too soon.

He thanked Chris Rafferty, Treasurer Walkington, Geraldine Houston, Claire Cougan, and Bridget Ross for their varied and invaluable contributions.

He thanked Ken Ross for his after-dinner speaking (or through-the-night speaking as Ken prefers to call it). He reassured Ken not to believe the vicious rumour circulating that (twenty minutes into Ken's beautifully-turned oratory) various members of the catering staff had been seen drawing lots as to who could stick their heads in the gas oven first.

Turning to the match itself, the Captain admitted that he and Vice-Captain Robertson had buckled under the onslaught from the Tain pairing.

He paid particular tribute to Frankie Sutherland, following his retirement after the third green, having taken nine fresh-air shots. There was a vote of appreciation for the epic performance of Morag Sutherland, stepping into Frankie's breach and playing with his club for the remainder of the match.

With a tear in his eye (or it might have been sweat), the Captain reflected on the dark days of Stotters' exile at Invergordon, and on how wonderful it was for the Stotters to be once again firmly ensconced in the welcoming bosom of Tain Golf Club.

The overall match score now stands at 26 – 24 in favour of The Stotters.

Captain Houston also paid tribute to Anne and Geraldine Houston and everyone associated with setting up what he was sure would be a fantastic concert night on the Monday.

Fifteen jaws, and approximately thirty four chins dropped, as Hector MacIntyre re-entered the board room carrying a tray laden with drinks ... until everyone remembered the drinks kitty.

MINUTES OF THE PREVIOUS MEETING

These were read by Simon Houston. Mike Lloyd proposed that they be adopted as correct. This was seconded by Chris Fraser.

MATTERS ARISING FROM MINUTES

Mike Lloyd observed that Simon Houston would be a huge ass, sorry huge act, to follow as Secretary – just as well that the new Secretary is a huge act. The new Secretary observed that his predecessor's finely turned prose had entertained and enthralled Stotters over many seconds, and that he fully intended to try and emulate the guiding principle of any Sun journalist: to never let the facts get in the way of a good story.

Freed from his secretarial shackles, Simon Houston took advantage of the presence of a flipchart and some multi-coloured pens to give his uninterested colleagues the benefit of an unwanted and unwarranted golf lesson. He sketched out an unusual design of golf hole, the details of which were to remain an un-minuted secret, but which caused vast merriment to those still awake.

There was an emotional reunion between Alan Gordon and Hamish Robertson, which was frankly slightly nauseating. Cries of "Get a room!" and "No tongues" echoed round the Board room as they metaphorically embraced.

Captain Houston reflected on the Sodom & Gomorrah of the previous year's meeting – your correspondent has no idea what this related to, but it is perhaps better left to the imagination.

President Cougan joined the meeting at this point through the magic of technology. No, not a hoverboard, but a conference-call via Simon Houston's phone. Simon Houston felt this the perfect moment to declare a break, permanently cutting off the President and conveniently forgetting to reconnect him.

ELECTION OF OFFICE BEARERS

Captain Houston proposed Vice-Captain Hamish Robertson as captain for 2017. This was seconded by Simon Houston.

There then followed an interminable discussion as to the wherefores and whys of how the Stotters elect Vice-Captains, which was about as comprehensible as it was memorable. In the course of the general ramblings, Hamish Robertson suggested approaching Tain Golf Club to see if they could put out 16 players every year. Ken Ross pointed out that 12 is the number limited by Tain. There was general agreement that it was important to encourage the juniors.

Hugh Walkington, Alan Gordon and Malcolm Fraser all made clear that they were not pushing to play – they were honoured to represent the Stotters when picked, but not agitating when there were no places.

Hugh Walkington indicated his willingness to take on the onerous duty of being Stotters' Secretary, but pointed out that his time was getting increasingly stretched by also having to valet Ken Ross's car.

He was nominated to continue by Captain Houston, and this was seconded by Chris Rafferty. The Treasurer expressed his delight at the appointment of the new Secretary, congratulating him and remarking how brilliant it was finally to have two office-holders who had at least a vague Scooby's of what the hell was going on!

In the general discussion that followed, Alan Gordon proposed that the £10 monthly subscription that had been established to pay for the 50th anniversary celebrations continue. Treasurer Walkington emphatically supported this suggestion. He pointed out that having enjoyed a new car, house extension and two-week holiday to Egypt during the previous 18 months, he was looking into real estate in Monaco, and wasn't the price of super yachts shocking?

On a more serious note, continuing the subs would generate funds that would allow the Stotters to support projects of real substance at Tain Golf Club, without seriously hurting members' pockets. The proposal was seconded by Hamish Robertson and carried with unanimous approval.

Gary Toal proposed that funds should be set aside on an annual basis to provide dancing girls.

ANY OTHER COMPETENT BUSINESS

Hector MacIntyre said that he very much hoped to return to Eastbourne to play golf in the very near future. Mike Lloyd responded that Hector would be extremely welcome to come and play at Eastbourne whenever he wanted – but that since Mike and Ken Ross were members at East Sussex National, they wouldn't be able to offer much in the way of practical assistance to Hector in his personal golfing quest.

Ken Ross and Tom Lloyd both made surprisingly outrageous proposals which again failed to translate into the virgin Secretary's scrap paper, but given that Tom somewhat unwisely admitted to the Secretary a month after the meeting that he had a very hazy memory of what had happened, now is probably the right time to record his proposal to buy everyone a round. This was enthusiastically seconded by Mike Lloyd.

Mike Lloyd asked if the Stotters still had an overseas envoy. Ken Ross announced that he had done an enormous amount of research which he was prepared to share with everyone. He reluctantly agreed to deny his fellow Stotters the benefit of his findings after the threat of physical violence. He did say that he might be prepared to invite Stotters to his private golf course in South Africa, all expenses paid. I may just have imagined the last three words of that sentence.

Captain Houston then asked yet another entirely inappropriate question about what might or might not happen on South African golf courses, on which Ken Ross was – most unusually – reluctant to comment.

Gary Toal suggested that a percentage of Stotters' subscriptions should be put on a bet each month with a view to boosting the total amount of money in the kitty. It was agreed that this was not entirely fiscally prudent as a financial strategy, but he was thanked for his suggestion.

As Simon Ross's snores echoed round the board room, the AGM Titanic struck the iceberg of finality around 4.27pm, prompting the first known use by the Royal Hotel manager of the cry for help of "S.O.S" ... or, "Sod Off Stotters".

The future of the AGM Minutes is clearly in safe hands.

The Future's Bright – the 2017 Line-Up – Hamish Robertson (2017 Captain), Lynn Houston, Simon Houston (2017 Vice-Captain), Shirley Robertson, Graeme Ross (Tain's 2017 Captain), Eilidh Mackenzie, Gus Gurney (Tain's 2017 Vice-Captain).

ACKNOWLEDGMENTS

Writing the Stotters' story has been an incredible mixture of nostalgia and joy, memories and discoveries.

Those who unknowingly started writing the Stotters' story are no longer able to read the still unfolding tale, but I like to think they would have a good few chuckles and perhaps shed a tear or two in seeing how this wonderful fellowship has developed and matured over 50 years.

It has been a labour of love for me, as so many family and friendship memories are embedded in these chapters.

I couldn't have written the book without an enormous degree of support, input and encouragement from the Stotters, as a body, and as individuals; from many of their relatives and friends; and from the Tain players and Golf Club staff, especially the unflagging Magi whose support has been invaluable.

I'd particularly like to single out the input from the late Forbie Urquhart and his wife Margaret – the detailed memories and memorabilia fed in by Forbie have been a solid foundation for the story.

Frank Cougan and daughter Claire have given much atmosphere to the early years of the Stotters, as has David Rutherford, and I was particularly glad to have captured some of Bob Beveridge's memories before he sadly passed away.

The book would not have existed without the incredible AGM Minutes which form its backbone, and whilst Walter Kerr and Wilson Kemp are no longer with us, I'd guess they would have many a laugh at the brilliant Minutes continued by Simon Houston.

A huge thank you to Bridget Ross who painstakingly typed all the hand-written Minutes in a format which I could use as my own base line.

Hugh Walkington was kind enough to support this enterprise right from the start and has acted as an unofficial editor, reading everything and commenting and critiquing expertly as the book took shape; and Donald Sutherland – our "man in Tain" – has run an objective eye over the total content, and made some practical amendments and comments.

Colin Cumming kindly undertook the onerous task of proof-reading and commenting on the book, and his detailed input and excellent insights and overviews, as a non-Stotter, have really enriched the finished article – thank you Colin.

Thanks also to Simon Ross and Geraldine Houston who put together all the photos from over the years from which the photos for the book have been chosen.

And Simon Ross also deserves a Stotter-like round of applause for volunteering to design and produce the brilliantly evocative cover which graces the book.

I would add a big tribute to Stephen Baker, from *ebooksbydesign*, for his diligent and detailed skills in converting my text to the formats enabling the printed and e-books to be published.

There will no doubt be errors and omissions in the book, and for any which are spotted I offer apologies – nothing has been deliberately misrepresented, and I've painstakingly checked facts and historical details, and am as satisfied as I can be that they are accurate, but sometimes my attention to detail may have slipped.

I would like to pay tribute to The Tain Golf Club website which I have unashamedly plagiarised, and also thanks to Tony Watson, whose wonderful Tain Golfing History of People, Places and Past Times I have drawn from, as I have from the Golf Club Centenary booklet written by Ian McGregor.

And to all those who gave me their own stories, memories, anecdotes and who shared their emotions with me – my heartfelt thanks.

I hope you like the outcome.

Finally, to my amazing wife, Shirley, an enormous tribute for your unstinting love and support, patience and encouragement as the book was born, took shape and matured. Thank you too for the book's inspirational title.

You truly worked with me to make it come together – thank you.

Hamish C. Robertson

September 2017